Changing labour markets in Europe

Changing labour markets in Europe

The role of institutions and policies

Edited by
Peter Auer

INTERNATIONAL LABOUR OFFICE • GENEVA

Auer, P. (ed.)
Changing labour markets in Europe: The role of institutions and policies
Geneva, International Labour Office, 2001

Labour market, hours of work, labour relations, equal employment opportunity, economic development, tripartism, employment policy, Austria, Denmark, Ireland, Netherlands, OECD country. 13.01.2

ISBN 92-2-111385-X

ILO Cataloguing in Publication Data

ILO publications can be obtained through major booksellers or ILO local offices in many countries, or direct from ILO Publications, International Labour Office, CH-1211 Geneva 22, Switzerland. Catalogues or lists of new publications are available free of charge from the above address.

Printed in the United Kingdom ALD

FOREWORD

"*The primary goal of the ILO today is to promote opportunities for women and men to obtain decent and productive work, in conditions of freedom, equity, security and human dignity.*" This ambitious goal, proclaimed in the Director-General's Report to the 87th Session of the International Labour Conference, 1999,[1] requires an understanding of the functioning of labour markets and of the conditions that improve employment opportunities in both quantitative and qualitative terms.

Labour markets are complex entities, and the many determinants of supply and demand, in particular the way they are filtered through institutions, are difficult to analyse in their entirety. The majority of jobs in both the developed and developing worlds are created by private enterprises, and often by small businesses, which constitute most enterprises in all countries. However, enterprises do not operate in a vacuum, but in an environment of institutions which shapes the longer-term rules, and therefore the behaviour of actors in employment and labour markets. The institutional environment varies between countries, and the interplay between enterprises and institutions, and the market and regulatory frameworks, takes many different forms. This interplay is efficient if it succeeds in reconciling "decent work" objectives with those of productivity and competitiveness.

Policies and institutions – whether publicly organized or administered by the social partners – while they might need reform, can play an important role in creating the conditions for the economy to develop. This is especially true of policies and institutions which affect the labour market. Pursuing a "decent work" agenda requires institutions to support the economy in its adjustment process, while also giving security to workers. For example, in the absence of labour market policies, such as unemployment insurance or training measures, structural adjustment and even business-cycle downturns could leave those workers who are negatively affected in long-term unemployment and poverty.

[1] ILO: *Decent work*, Report of the Director-General, International Labour Conference, 87th Session, 1999 (Geneva, 1999), p. 3.

This is not only a theoretical possibility, as was demonstrated by the Asian financial crisis in 1997–98, which clearly showed that the absence of even basic institutions of social protection may result in massive social disruption. It also holds true for the transition economies, which continue to experience social turmoil and poverty, and are eagerly striving to build up their labour market institutions. The developed world has in general managed to mitigate the negative effects of major adjustments. A major reason is the coexistence in a market economy of competitive enterprises and labour market institutions which provide for both adjustment flexibility and workers' security. This does not refer to ad hoc safety nets, but to longer-term policies, that is, institutions which shape the behaviour of enterprises and workers, and are a precondition of efficiently functioning labour markets.

However, institutions may become obsolete and even pose obstacles to adjustment. Therefore, institutional change is required in interaction with changes in labour markets. Women's increasing labour force participation is particularly telling in this respect. Institutions which protected the "sole breadwinner" are ineffective in supporting women with more heterogeneous career patterns. To meet this challenge, institutions such as retirement systems may have to be reformed. Change is under way, and this book shows how it affects industrial relations, and policies on macroeconomics, working time and gender, with particular reference to four smaller European countries (Austria, Denmark, Ireland and the Netherlands).

Göran Hultin
Executive Director
Employment Sector

CONTENTS

List of tables

List of figures

List of boxes

ACKNOWLEDGEMENTS

This book is first of all the work of the four authors, who invested much time in preparing several drafts of their papers to reach a final version. In addition, publication was possible only because of a collective effort on the part of various people who all contributed in one way or another to shaping this volume. I would particularly like to mention the authors of the country reports (Karl Pichelmann and Helmut Hofer, Per K. Madsen, Philip O'Connell and Joop Hartog). The so-called "gate-keepers" in the Ministries of Labour of the four countries were of tremendous help in providing material, assistance, comments and support during the course of the longer-term study from which this volume profited: for Austria, Stefan Potmesil; for Denmark, Lone Adler; for Ireland, Frank Doheny; and for the Netherlands, Arthur van de Meerendonk.

I am indebted for comments to the members of the ILO advisory group, set up for the project: Anne Trebilcock, Muneto Ozaki, Michael Henriques, Björn Grunewald, Heribert Scharrenbroich, Kim Eling, Riswanul Islam (represented by Steve Miller and Eric de Vries) and Bob Kyloh.

Werner Sengenberger, Director of the Employment Strategy Department, was very supportive throughout. Several colleagues, in particular Muhammed Muqtada, Rolph van der Hoeven, Sandrine Cazes-Chaigne, Peter Richards, and at the beginning of the research Sylvia Walter, Anita Guelfi and Arne Klau, provided useful inputs.

I am very much indebted to Ghazwa Yousif-Dandashi, helped at times by Lynda Pond, Margaret Roberts and Anne Drougard, for typing and formating the manuscript. My thanks extend also to the editor of the volume, Geraldeen Fitzgerald, and to the staff of the ILO Publications Bureau, May Ballerio-Hofman, Rosemary Beattie, Lilian Neil and Ksenija Radojevic Bovet, who made publication possible. The index was compiled by Paul Johnson.

Peter Auer
Editor

LIST OF ABBREVIATIONS

ArbVG	Arbeitsvertragsgesetz (Austrian law on collective agreements)
AWVN	Algemene Werkgeversvereniging Nederland (General Employers' Association)
AC	Confederation of Professional Associations
BAK	Bundesarbeiterkammer (Chamber of Labour)
BLSA	Bureau of Labour Statistics
CEC	Commission of the European Communities
CEPR	Country Employment Policy Review
CERC	Centre d'études du revenu et des coûts
CNV	Christelijk-Nationall Vakverbond (Christian-National Union Federation)
DA	Dansk Arbejdsgiverforening (Danish Employers' Confederation)
DI	Dansk Industri (Confederation of Danish Industry)
DIW	Deutsches Institut für Wirtschaftsforschung
EC	European Commission
ECB	European Central Bank
ECLM	European Commission Labour Markets
ECU	European Currency Unit
EMS	European Monetary System
EMU	European Monetary Union
ETUI	European Trade Union Institute
EU	European Union
EWC	European Works Councils
EWERC	European Work and Employment Research Centre
FIE	Federation of Irish Employers
FNV	Federatie nederlandse Vakbeweging (Netherlands Trade Union Confederation)
FTF	Confederation of Salaried Employees

FUE	Federated Union of Employers
GDP	Gross domestic product
GNP	Gross national product
HK	Handels- of Kontorfunktionærernes Forbund (Danish general union, trade sector)
IAT	Institut Arbeit und Technik
IBEC	Irish Business and Employers' Confederation
ICTU	Irish Congress of Trade Unions
IFO	Institut für Oekonomische Forschung (Institute for Economic Research)
ILO	International Labour Organization
IMF	International Monetary Fund
IMPACT	Irish Municipal, Public and Civil Trade
INOU	Irish National Organisation of the Unemployed
ITGWU	Irish Transport and General Workers' Union
JA	Jernets Arbejdsgivere
KAD	Kvindeligt Arbejderforbundet (Danish unskilled female workers' union)
LFS	Labour Force Survey
LO	Landesorganisation (Swedish Trade Union Confederation)
LO-DK	Danish Confederation of Trade Unions
LTO-Nederland	Land- en Tuinbouw Organisatie Nederland (Dutch agricultural employers' federation)
MKB-Nederland	Midden- en Kleinbedrijf-Nederland (Dutch SME employers' federation)
MHP	Federation of Staff and Managerial Personnel
MNE	Multinational enterprise
NAIRU	Non-accelerating-inflation rate of unemployment, "equilibrium" rate of unemployment
NESC	National Economic and Social Council
NESF	National Economic and Social Forum
NWA	National Wage Agreement
OBI	Organization of Business Interests
OECD	Organisation for Economic Co-operation and Development
ÖGB	Österreichischer Gewerkschaftsbund (Austrian Federation of Trade Unions)
PCW	Programme for Competitiveness and Work
PESP	Programme for Economic and Social Progress
PK	Paritätische Kommission (Parity Commission)
PNR	Programme for National Recovery
SALA	Danish agricultural employers' organization
SER	Sociaal-Economische Raad (Social-Economic Council)
SiD	Specialarbejderforbundet (Danish unskilled workers' union)

SIPTU	Services, Industrial, Professional and Technical Union
SME	Small and medium-sized enterprise
SNA	System of National Accounts
SOEP	Socio-economic Panel
STAR	Stichting van de Arbeid (Foundation of Labour)
SZW	(Ministerie van) Sociale Zaken en Werkgelegenheid (Ministry of Social Affairs and Security)
UMIST	Manchester School of Management Research Centre
UNICE	Union des confédérations de l'industrie et des employeurs de l'Europe (European Employers' Federation)
UTET	Unione Tipografico-Editrice Torinese
VHP	Federation of White-Collar and Senior Staff
VNO-NCW	Vereniging Nederlandse Ondernemers – Nederlands Christelijk Werkgeversverbond (Dutch peak employers' organization)
VÖI	Vereinigung der Österreichischen Industriellen (Association of Austrian Industrialists)
WKÖ	Wirtschaftskammer Österreichs (Austrian Economic Chamber)

Note: Names in brackets in lower case denote institutions that exist only in language of origin. They have been translated for clarity.

INTRODUCTION 1

Peter Auer[*]

1.1 INSTITUTIONS DO MATTER

The labour markets of industrialized countries currently face many challenges, such as the globalization of trade and production, technological and organizational change, and changes in family structures and social values. All these trends lead to continuous structural changes in national economies and affect both labour supply and labour demand. This, in turn, requires specific policy responses in a variety of areas.

Some of these areas and their responses are examined in this volume. One general lesson can be drawn from all four of the following analyses: institutions do matter and are a stabilizing force in the face of continuous structural change. In an era in which policy thinking is dominated by deregulation, privatization and the strengthening of the entrepreneurial spirit, it is easily forgotten that institutions – whether established by the State or by collective agreement – and their policies, while they might be in need of reform, still play an important role in creating the conditions in which private firms operate and can develop.

This is especially true of policies and institutions that affect the labour market.[1] For example, in the absence of labour market policy, each business cycle downturn – not to mention extended periods of structural adjustment – would result in uncontrolled and "uncushioned" labour shedding, leading to mass unemployment and widespread poverty. That this is not only a theoretical possibility, but actually happens in the real world, has been shown during the Asian financial crisis, which clearly indicated that institutions "in between" firms (and not only worker protection within firms) are required to prevent massive social disruptions. We are not talking here, however, about ad hoc safety nets, swiftly strung together in response to a crisis, but rather about longer-term policies, that is, institutions which shape the behaviour of firms

* Head, Labour Market Policy Unit, Employment Strategy Department, Employment Sector, International Labour Office, Geneva.

and workers and are a precondition if labour markets – notoriously imperfect – are to function efficiently.

Seen from the institutional angle, modern industrialized economies require institutions that exist alongside firms, supporting them in their adjustment process, while also constraining their behaviour and protecting jobs and workers. For example, negotiated adjustment within the institutions of collective bargaining, employment security (e.g. dismissal regulation) and labour market policy can provide firms in the developed world with a mix of flexibility and security conducive to the creation of decent work and, ultimately, to corporate profitability.

However, institutions may become obsolete and even degenerate into obstacles to adjustment. Therefore, institutional change is required in interaction with changes in the labour market.

Women's increasing employment participation is particularly telling in that regard. Institutions which protected the "sole breadwinner" (usually the man) quite efficiently are frequently ineffective in protecting women with a more heterogeneous career pattern. In such cases institutional reform – of retirement systems, for example – is required. And as the four chapters that make up this volume show, institutional change is under way in each of the policy areas treated.

Chapters 2, 3, 4 and 5 were originally drafted as background articles for the ILO's Country Employment Policy Reviews of smaller European countries. However, they discuss problems and challenges which reach beyond those smaller countries and are relevant to industrialized countries in general, and enable conclusions of a more general nature on the determinants of employment and unemployment in OECD countries to be drawn.[2]

Four policy areas have been chosen: macroeconomic policy, working-time policies, equality of opportunity and industrial relations. This selection was based on the conviction that:

- macroeconomic policy – and macroeconomic conditions in general – provide a necessary framework for any labour market and, together with the microeconomic decisions taken by individuals and firms in a given national institutional context, do much to determine overall employment and unemployment outcomes;
- working time is one of the sources of labour market flexibility, from both a supply and a demand point of view. In addition, reductions in working hours are still widely seen as a potential source of employment creation;
- equality of opportunity in the labour market, and especially a sound gender balance, is important for achieving high employment participation rates, a crucial indicator of genuine full employment;
- labour market governance systems matter for employment success, and those based on a social dialogue between workers' and employers' organizations

and the government have been found particularly conducive to labour market success, at least in the four countries under study.

The choice of these four areas implies, of course, the exclusion of other policy areas that are doubtless also important in determining employment and unemployment levels, such as education and training, or labour market policy. Our choice reflects not least the fact that the training dimension has recently been dealt with in the ILO's *World Employment Report 1998–99: Employability in the global economy. How training matters*, while labour market policy issues have been addressed thoroughly in another publication related to this project (*Employment revival in Europe: Labour market success in Austria, Denmark, Ireland and the Netherlands*, Auer, 2000).

1.2 INSTITUTIONS AND LABOUR MARKET FORCES

Many studies of labour markets in the European Union argue that the main cause of high European unemployment lies in the continent's rigid, over-regulated labour markets. Accordingly, deregulation of European labour markets and their institutions has been seen as the principal condition for an employment recovery and lower unemployment (see various IMF, OECD and World Bank reports). Yet deregulation, as a policy recommendation, giving more room to market forces and the free interplay of supply and demand, raises the question of the functions and effects of the regulations and labour market institutions that currently exist in European countries.

In general terms, "labour institutions are those which affect the structure and functioning of the labour market, from within or without, which determine who supplies what sort of labour where, who has access to what sort of employment and income opportunities, what sort of jobs are on offer and the conditions under which they are carried out, and how labour is represented and organized" (Rodgers, 1994, p. 9).

As such, the four policy areas selected for this volume all comprise labour institutions, whereby such institutions are usually defined in relation to markets. Whereas in standard theory it is assumed that in markets the exchange between supply and demand occurs in abstraction of any power relation or regulations, the term "institutions" implies a socio-economic regulation of the "unbridled" working of the markets. For example, the institutions of wage bargaining in industrialized countries are such that market power is exercised by two major agents (unions and employer organizations), which set wages according to certain principles in repeated rounds of bargaining. The third agent, the government, often has a stake in wage setting, manifested by indirect or direct intervention in wage bargaining.

While most economists agree that some form of regulation of the market is needed, mainstream neoclassical economists argue that the market should be the rule – and regulation the exception. Regulation can address market failures, but otherwise disturbs the functioning of markets and leads to suboptimal results, as the market is more intelligent than any plan devised by humans can ever be. This view culminates in Lucas' argument that any form of intervention in the market leads to distortions, which require further interventions to repair the perverse effects of the first attempt, ultimately resulting in a permanent vicious circle of regulation.

By contrast, the view expressed in this book is that in empirical terms the free operation of market forces is the exception – and regulation is the rule. Access to labour markets, career patterns in internal company labour markets and also exit from labour markets are all filtered through institutions. For example, access to the labour markets for each age cohort depends, among other things, on education and training institutions and on (collectively bargained) entry wage levels; career progress depends on, among other things, wage classification and seniority rules; exits from the labour market on dismissal and retirement regulations and/or social plans. While public administrations might be seen as extreme cases of regulated labour markets, large companies also have rules to structure their internal labour markets, and even small firms rely (and have to rely) on some form of regulation. That is not to say that the law of supply and demand is irrelevant, but it is filtered – at least in the formal labour market – by regulations and institutions, and thus by (power) relations between the agents involved, which are usually enshrined in more or less formal rules.

The underlying view here is that both institutions (or regulation[3]) and markets matter: what counts is the regulating effect of institutions on "spontaneous" market forces. Perfect markets are an illusion (the nirvana fallacy) as there are always some "interferences" from regulation. However, institutions, too, vary in terms of their efficiency with respect to their specific goal(s). Therefore institutional change is required. Moreover, changes in regulations/institutions usually lead to collateral changes. For example, the reduction of working time is frequently associated with greater working-time flexibility.

The difficult task for policy makers, whether in government or working on behalf of the social partners or other actors, is to construct or modify labour market institutions in such a way that labour markets function efficiently, maximizing employment opportunities and contributing to social welfare.

Accordingly, the four policy areas (macroeconomic policy, working time, equality of opportunity and industrial relations) are analysed from an institutional angle, in terms of the way that, for example, monetary and fiscal policies, wage formation processes, working-time regulations and equality of opportunity policies all influence both the supply and the demand side of the labour market.

1.3 MACROECONOMIC POLICY

Macroeconomic policy might not always qualify for the term "labour market institution", but some of its central elements (fiscal and monetary policies) clearly serve to influence the behaviour of labour market agents. However, the macroeconomic environment also includes exogenously given conditions to which countries have to respond (not least by using their filtering institutions), such as the state of the world economy, the phases of the business cycle and economic growth, which to some extent is exogenous to policy intervention.

In Chapter 2, Ronald Schettkat analyses macroeconomic policy and its effects on the labour market of small countries, in comparison with two of the larger European countries (France and Germany). He shows that some of the hypotheses frequently put forward in the economic literature are not easily squared with the facts: for example, the argument that globalization undermines any demand-side policy – because the effects of such a policy are not confined to the national level but are immediately dissipated throughout the global economy – is only very partially confirmed, and it still makes sense to use fiscal policy levers in a careful manner. The alleged negative displacement effects of trade on low-skilled labour are also in doubt, because the countries selected have reduced unemployment for the low-skilled, despite being among the most open economies of the world. Another of the economic stereotypes discussed is the "crowding out" of private by public investment and activity.

Again, the evidence does not support the standard argument: private and public spending and investment seem to grow and contract in parallel, whereas crowding out would imply a negative relation, that is, that shrinking government spending is accompanied by growing private spending on investments and consumption. While the countries considered have all pursued fiscal consolidation (not least because of the Maastricht convergence criteria and the Stability and Growth Pact), some of them (Austria and Denmark) have also temporarily used public budgets to stimulate demand, but without triggering an inflationary spiral, as another widely held theoretical assumption would predict.

At the same time, the freedom to manoeuvre of national macroeconomic policy has clearly been reduced, in particular that of monetary policy, which is now under the auspices of the independent European Central Bank. Yet European Union Member States also face strict limits with regard to fiscal policy under the conditions of the Maastricht convergence criteria and the Stability and Growth Pact. And, indeed, macroeconomic policy has been increasingly stability-oriented, resulting in (or contributing to) low inflation rates, "sound" growth rates and an increasing employment intensity of economic growth.

Indeed, another finding is that while there might be sectors of jobless growth (economic growth without employment growth), for instance in industry, the European economies generally exhibit an increasing employment intensity of economic growth. This is partly due to the shift towards a service economy where labour intensity is comparatively high.

And, there is more good news: the positive impact of economic growth on unemployment – a relationship known as Okun's law – also increased between

1982 and 1998 in all six countries investigated. Both results together – if they are sustained – would mean that by stimulating economic growth, more employment problems could, in principle, be solved than before. From an institutional perspective this also means that filters have become more efficient in translating economic growth into employment. This, in turn, could stem from – besides the sectoral shift already mentioned – more flexible employment contracts (e.g. more part-time work), better job matches and more active labour market policies. However, economic growth alone will not be able to tackle all Europe's employment problems. Thorny issues remain to be solved: inefficient school-to-work transition, skill mismatches, age discrimination in dismissals and hiring, and insufficient work incentives for some benefit recipients.

Wage setting is on the borderline between macroeconomic policy and industrial relations: macroeconomic policy, especially a stability-oriented approach that tightly restricts the room to manoeuvre for both monetary and fiscal policies, needs to be underpinned to a moderate "wage policy" by collective-wage bargainers, if overall stability is to be achieved. Clearly, wage restraint geared to supporting macroeconomic stability has been one of the outcomes of the social dialogue and a significant element of success in some countries. The question is, How far can wage moderation go? In the face of a rapid rise in profit margins, workers will be less easily convinced of the benefits of such a policy, especially if the trade-offs given (such as working-time reductions and tax cuts) are no longer forthcoming.

1.4 WORKING TIME: FROM REDISTRIBUTION TO MODERNIZATION

In Chapter 3, Gerhard Bosch shows that working-time reduction can take several forms: for example, by shortening weekly hours of work, or by extending various sorts of annual leave. A decline in average working hours in an economy can also be the consequence of an increase in part-time employment relations. In most countries, all these forms have been used, albeit to different degrees. Usually a trade-off occurred for a reduction in working time, consisting of an extension of labour deployment flexibility and/or wage moderation. The result has been a more heterogeneous pattern of individual and household working times. This differentiation reflects a changing structure of labour supply (e.g. more married women are looking for work) combined with different working-time preferences and, on the demand side, the need for more flexible employment in the service sector and changes in work organization.

Differences both within and between countries are also explained by differences in wage levels: Bosch notes that short hours are a "luxury good" and the option for leisure is more readily taken if it can be afforded. However, many other factors intervene, such as tax and contribution systems. Childcare provisions also influence supply behaviour: a lack of such provisions might induce women to work only part time or not at all.

As some countries, notably France, have embarked on a policy of reducing working time to a 35-hour week (in the wake of a similar reduction in important sectors of the German economy), it is worth identifying the possible employment effects of such reductions. This chapter provides some indications based on a variety of sources: while the employment effects of (collective) working-time reductions are hard to measure because of the difficulties of isolating working-time effects from other influences, such as output and productivity growth, most authors point to a positive employment impact, the extent of which depends on the conditions under which the reduction is implemented. For example, in order to maximize the employment effects, the wage-cost increases resulting from the reduced hours can be offset by lower hourly wage rises, while increases in overtime can be partially avoided by adequate skills provision. The adaptation of work organization – for example, through an extension of plant operating times/opening hours, despite a reduction in individual working time – will increase the flexibility of working time and may also enhance the employment effect of working-time reductions.

Working time has a gender dimension that can clearly be seen in part-time work. Part-time work is overwhelmingly a form of female labour force participation, a fact linked to a supply behaviour that is dependent on family structures and labour market and social institutions, such as parental leave and childcare facilities.

1.5 EQUALITY OF OPPORTUNITY

In Chapter 4, Jill Rubery extends this equality of opportunity perspective to an analysis of entire employment systems. Equality of opportunity issues are an important element in industrial relations, education and training, labour market flexibility and welfare regimes in general. The evidence collated here offers a powerful illustration of the need for gender mainstreaming. For example, raising employment rates, as prescribed by the present European Employment Strategy, implies, in particular, raising the employment participation rate of women (along with that of older workers, both female and male). However, a policy of increasing employment rates requires changes in (or favourable) labour market institutions, such as education and training programmes, or social protection, including childcare provisions, all geared to the needs of working women.

The analysis of gender equality highlights the existence of gender differences in employment. Differentiation can take the form of occupational segregation, which means that women are concentrated in certain occupations or hierarchies, usually with lower pay and lower grades. Or it is based on less segmentation and a more equal distribution of women over the employment system, but even then pay and hierarchical grades are usually also strongly gender differentiated, with women usually earning less than men for the same type of work.

Extending the analysis of labour force participation from the individual to the household level reveals country and gender differences with respect to single-earner or double-earner participation, and national labour markets prove even more highly differentiated if working time is also considered: one finds double-earner households in which both men and women work full time, and households in which men work full time and women part time.

The once-dominant single (male) earner household, with dependent wife and children (breadwinner model), is declining in importance, while both the double-earner household and lone-parent families in which (usually) a woman is the head of household are on the rise.

A concern is the rise in the number of households with no one at work. These shifts have implications for the social welfare regime and seem to indicate the need to change the basis of social protection from derived rights (i.e. usually derived from the working male) towards a system based on individual rights. As the shifts in labour force participation patterns have so many implications for labour market institutions, future trends in these labour supply patterns are of crucial importance for the adaptation of institutions to ensure an effective labour market. For example, participation patterns such as in the Netherlands, in which men now typically work full time and women part time, might not prove permanent, as more women demand full-time jobs and adequate child-care facilities. As has been seen in Scandinavian countries, part-time work for women might cross a threshold above which women increasingly demand full-time jobs. On the other hand, this might be offset by men increasingly looking for part-time work.

1.6 INDUSTRIAL RELATIONS AND SOCIAL DIALOGUE

In Chapter 5, Jelle Visser underlines that social dialogue, as part of national systems of industrial relations (IR), has been one of the major factors explaining labour market success in several European countries. Despite persisting diversity in national IR systems, there are also common features. The most important of these is that in the four small successful countries (Austria, Denmark, Ireland and the Netherlands), systems of governance have developed in which the three actors (government, unions and employers' associations) play a determining role in the labour market. Different names have been given to these systems of tripartite governance, such as social partnership, concertation or "neo-corporatism". The latter is defined as an institutionalized system of interest representation between the social partners and government with a large degree of cooperation between the partners. Three of the successful countries have such institutionalized systems, and the fourth (Ireland) is developing structures along similar lines.

Neocorporatism is not *per se* a superior form of governance of labour market and social policy issues: its efficiency is dependent on certain conditions. For example, Dutch neocorporatism went through difficult times in the 1970s and early 1980s. An institutional setting that produces positive results in certain circumstances can be an empty shell, if the will to reach consensus is lacking. Indeed, if confrontational attitudes predominate, a system with such strong "partners" might even exacerbate problems. The common will to tackle problems in a cooperative manner is a precondition for success; its absence is often a main reason for failure. It seems that a common consciousness of the existence of a crisis helps to trigger such a spirit of cooperation. Certainly, once a cooperative mood is fostered, there have to be exchange relations of a give-and-take kind which nurture trust.

What exactly can social dialogue – under favourable conditions – achieve? Wage moderation is the core result, but labour market and social security reforms have also been carried out with the help of social partner cooperation, mostly in an atmosphere of industrial peace. Although government has offered something in return for wage moderation and social security reforms, for example tax cuts and active labour market policies, the reforms have nevertheless sometimes cut deep into vested interests. That this was done in an atmosphere of industrial peace is all the more remarkable. And industrial peace is important in stabilizing expectations and creating a favourable climate for economic activity.

According to neoliberal economists, market regulation through collective bargaining will produce suboptimal results on the labour market. This view is not corroborated by empirical facts in the successful countries. Rather, some of the larger European countries with high unemployment rates seem to be experiencing problems with their tripartite social dialogue. For example, in France, because of fragmentation on the union side and the fact that all the "partners" are rather conflict oriented and there is no basic mutual acceptance, the State is forced to intervene as a "macro-agent". However, in doing so it often has to overrule one or both of the partners. The recent working-time law is an example of how labour market regulations are sometimes introduced against the will of one party, in this case the employers. By contrast, there were fewer conflicts in the four successful countries over working time, which was one of the important issues in collective bargaining during the 1980s and 1990s.

1.7 CONCLUSIONS

One of the ILO's main objectives is to "promote opportunities for women and men to obtain decent and productive work" (ILO,1999), which is seen as the basis for social progress. This ambitious goal requires, as a basic precondition, an understanding of the functioning of labour markets and of the conditions that maximize employment opportunities in both quantitative and qualitative terms. It is here that the present volume seeks to make a contribution.

Labour markets are complex entities, and the many determinants of supply and demand, in particular the way they are filtered through institutions, are difficult to analyse in their entirety. The policies scrutinized here affect labour demand and labour supply in various ways. Macroeconomic policy can have a direct effect on labour demand by expanding/reducing the level of government consumption and investment or by affecting the structure of spending; more important, however, are its indirect effects on labour demand through its impact on inflation, interest rates, and taxes and social security contributions. The institutions of industrial relations also have an impact on the demand for labour via their effects on wage bargaining, as is shown by the apparent success of wage moderation. The other two policy areas discussed in this volume, working-time policies and equality of opportunity, also impinge on the demand side of the labour market. Private companies and public agencies may well offer more part-time jobs if working-time regulations provide appropriate incentives for triggering organizational change, for example; while working-time reduction – in all its different forms – has undoubtedly stimulated additional demand for labour, although to a greater or lesser extent according to circumstances. Equal opportunity policies impact on labour demand in a variety of ways, ranging from imposed quotas to voluntary activities.

At the same time, all these policies also impact on the supply side: changes in taxes and contributions (fiscal policies) may stimulate supply (for example, by making low-paid work an attractive alternative to benefit receipt), and wage bargaining outcomes clearly also influence labour supply decisions. Equality of opportunity policies may stimulate supply (via the creation of childcare facilities), as may working-time policies (for example, those that realize in practice the principle of equality of treatment of full- and part-time work).

In providing empirical and theoretical insights into these four central policy areas, this volume aims to increase the body of knowledge on the challenges facing developed countries and possible responses to these challenges. The principal lessons here are: a sound macroeconomic environment based on price stability, low interest rates and fiscal prudence is a precondition for labour market recovery. However, within narrower margins, demand-side policies are still feasible and beneficial to the economies implementing them. Working-time policies have contributed to employment creation and are an important tool of labour market flexibility. High rates of labour market participation are only possible if gender equality is enhanced. If all these policies – along with effectively designed and implemented labour market policies in the narrower sense – are coordinated, even loosely so, through social dialogue, we have clear evidence that European welfare States can indeed recover from the main disease afflicting their societies – the inadequacy of employment growth and persistent high unemployment that constrain the opportunities of women and men to find decent and productive work.

Notes

[1] Very generally, institutions are social constructs, which influence behaviour of individuals (or social actors such as firms) not only in the short term but in the longer term. They shape expectations and are the filter through which decisions are channelled. Major institutions in the labour market

include the wage-setting institutions, labour market policies (unemployment benefit systems and active policies such as support for retraining), dismissal protection legislation, and other legislation affecting working conditions. In opposition to orthodox economics, institutional economics does not assume autonomous behaviour by individuals, but sees the behaviour of individuals in their institutional context. And, again in opposition to many neoclassical economists, institutions are seen as having not only constraining but also enabling qualities (see for example Schmid, 1994; Rodgers, 1994).

[2] The present volume has been prepared as part of the ILO's work on the follow-up to the World Summit on Social Development held in Copenhagen in 1995. In pursuit of its task of monitoring Commitment Three of the Summit (freely chosen, productive full employment as a precondition for social progress), the ILO has conducted a series of Country Employment Policy Reviews (CEPRs) of, among others, four smaller European countries which have recently experienced relative labour market success. Several publications have reported on the results of these CEPRs in addition to the present volume: a first publication summarized the whole project (Peter Auer: *Employment revival in Europe: Labour market success in Austria, Denmark, Ireland and the Netherlands*, ILO, 2000); the four individual country reports have been published in the ILO/POLEMP discussion paper series (Hartog, Kongshoj Madsen, O'Connell, Pichelmann and Hofer, all 1999).

[3] Institutions and regulations are mostly used here as synonyms. One could argue that for a regulation to acquire the character of an institution it must have a certain longevity.

Bibliography

Auer, P. 2000. *Employment revival in Europe: Labour market success in Austria, Denmark, Ireland and the Netherlands* (Geneva, ILO).

Hartog, J. 1999. *So what's so special about the Dutch model?*, Employment and Training Paper No. 54 (Geneva, ILO).

International Labour Office (ILO). 1998. *World Employment Report 1998–99: Employment in the global economy. How training matters* (Geneva).

——. 1999. *Decent Work*, Report of the Director-General to the 87th Session of the International Labour Conference (Geneva).

Kongshoj Madsen, P. 1999. *Denmark: Labour market recovery through labour market policy*, Employment and Training Paper No. 53 (Geneva, ILO).

O'Connell, P. 1999. *Ireland: Astonishing success – Economic growth and the labour market in Ireland*, Employment and Training Paper No. 44 (Geneva, ILO).

Pichelmann, K. (with Hofer, H.). 1999. *Austria: Long-term success through social partnership*, Employment and Training Paper No. 52 (Geneva, ILO).

Rodgers, G. 1994. *Workers, institutions and economic growth in Asia* (Geneva, International Institute for Labour Studies).

Schmid, G. 1994. *Labour market institutions in Europe* (London, M.E. Sharpe).

SMALL-ECONOMY MACROECONOMICS 2

*Ronald Schettkat**

2.1 INTRODUCTION

Relative economic performance and some institutional characteristics

Europe used to be written off as representing an old-fashioned model of over-generous welfare States, over-regulated labour markets and demotivating tax rates. The European economies were seen as unable to adjust to new requirements and to be losing out in competition with the dynamic, newly industrializing Asian economies and the United States. More recently, however, the Asian economies have been in the news for quite different reasons, and the new "tigers"[1] are European. Four small European economies – Austria, Denmark, Ireland and the Netherlands – have increasingly been portrayed as shining examples of successful employment policies, attracting wide interest in the business press, in academia, and among politicians. While the rest of Europe is suffering from low or zero employment growth and persistently high unemployment, these four countries are being celebrated as holding the keys to the solution of the European job crisis.

All four have achieved employment expansion or a consistently high level of employment, accompanied by low and even declining rates of inflation, justifying the current interest in the economic policies of these success stories. Yet in the business press the star of a country can rise if it has success in a single economic policy dimension, and conclusions on causal links are quickly drawn. In fact, economic success is not one-dimensional but multidimensional, and causes and effects are usually not easily disentangled. Closer analysis of the various dimensions of macroeconomic policy in the four European economies may put long-held views in a different perspective, or at least shake extreme beliefs. The four cannot be claimed as belonging to any one particular school, but are probably better seen as examples of a pragmatic policy mix

*Department of Socio and Institutional Economics, University of Utrecht, Utrecht.

rather than a "clean policy". The economic success of Austria, Denmark, Ireland and the Netherlands poses a challenge to the views expressed by many observers.

Those who blame Europe's current economic malaise on globalization are faced with the success of truly open and global economies. It is sometimes argued that globalization – the increasing integration of national economies into the world economy – has "destroyed" or at least severely reduced the scope for national economic policy. Global capital markets force national economies to adjust their interest rates to world levels (with some variation for expected exchange rate movements), while demand-side policies are made impossible because the rest of the world, rather than the national economy, stands to benefit. Countries running a government deficit will suffer a loss of reputation and come under pressure to devalue their currencies. Low-wage competition from the "South", so another argument runs, will reduce the wages of less skilled workers or destroy their jobs in the "North".[2] Given these arguments, it is more than surprising that four small economies have become the stars of economic policy debates in the 1990s. By any standard, these economies are truly global. If we use as a measure for globalization the ratio of imports and exports to GDP, small economies almost inevitably top the rankings. The ratio is around 40 per cent in Denmark, 60 per cent in the Netherlands and over 70 per cent in Ireland, compared with just 15 per cent in the United States. Despite this wide variation, the ratio has increased in every industrialized economy. If globalization is harming the industrialized world so much, why are four small open economies doing so well? These are the most "global" economies and the ones that might be expected to be suffering most.

"Excessive" welfare States and "over-regulation" of labour markets are commonly put forward as explanations for Europe's employment problems. But three of the four – and in some cases all four – successful European economies have well-developed welfare States with generous unemployment benefits (see table 2.1), high trade union density and corporatist wage-setting structures. These are hardly the preconditions for bringing down unemployment recommended by neoliberal economists and their political supporters.

"Jobless growth" is another, less theoretically sound but certainly popular, explanation for stagnating employment. According to this view, economic growth does not lead to further employment growth because productivity growth is too high. But productivity growth has actually slowed down since the early 1970s, and today more employment is created by every 1 per cent of additional economic growth than in the 1960s. Another popular "supply-side hypothesis" emphasizes demographic and labour supply factors as an explanation for persistently high unemployment. The puzzle which proponents of this hypothesis have to solve, however, is that increases in unemployment have been small in countries with a tremendous growth in employment-to-population ratios.

Table 2.1 Some structural and policy characteristics of Austria, Denmark, Ireland and the Netherlands

	Austria	Denmark	Ireland	Netherlands
Globalization				
Exports as a share of GDP (%)	43	39	77	61
Welfare State				
Average tax rates (1993)	43.8	51.7	45.0	48.9
Total tax wedge (%)	43.0	39.0	35.0	45.0
Taxes and social security contributions as % of GDP (1995)	42.4	51.3	33.8	44.0
Unemployment replacement rate (%)				
Net (1995)	n.a.	81.0	37.0	69.0
Gross (1994–95)	26.0	71.0	26.0	46.0
Employment protection legislation (high values = difficult to dismiss)	11.0	5.0	6.0	8.0
Wage bargaining system	Corporatist	Corporatist	Decentralized with coordination elements since 1987	Corporatist
Monetary policy and budget consolidation				
Exchange rates	Fixed to DM[a]	EMS[b]	EMS	Fixed to DM
Fiscal policy	Budgetary consolidation	Budgetary consolidation	Budgetary consolidation	Budgetary consolidation
Inequality				
Proportion of labour force below 2/3 of the median wage (%)	13	n.a.	24	12
Decile 9:1 (1994, Denmark 1990)	3.7	2.2	.9	2.6
Active labour market policy				
Expenditure on active labour market policy (% of GDP)	0.4	2.3	1.8	1.1

n.a. = not available. [a] Deutschmark. [b] European Monetary System.
Sources: OECD: *Employment Outlook*, various years; ILO country reports (Hartog, 1998; Kongshoj Madsen, 1998; Pichelmann/Hofer, 1998; O'Connell, 1998); Walter, 1998; see also Visser in Ch. 5 of this book.

Those who blame Europe's employment stagnation on tight monetary policy in general, and the Bundesbank in particular, must also be puzzled by the employment success of Austria, Denmark, Ireland and the Netherlands: all four countries have pursued a tight monetary policy and two of them (Austria and the Netherlands) have actually pegged their currencies to the Deutschmark (DM) and thus tied their monetary policy hands to Bundesbank policy. The other two countries participate in the European Monetary System (EMS) and have therefore been at least indirectly linked to the policy pursued by the Bundesbank. Those who believe that public sector activity crowds out private economic activity will find their view confirmed to the extent that all four economies have pursued a policy of budgetary consolidation, and in the Netherlands fiscal consolidation was implemented before economic recovery.

However, all of them exhibit average tax rates well above the 40 per cent level and – with the exception of Ireland – social security contributions and taxes that represent well above 40 per cent of GDP (table 2.1 and Walter, 1998).

Nor does rising unemployment seem to be a precondition for a moderate wage policy. Rising employment and falling unemployment went hand in hand with moderate wage increases despite, or probably due to, the fact that these countries have corporatist wage-setting systems (Teulings/Hartog, 1998; Appelbaum/Schettkat, 1996; see also Visser in Chapter 5 of this volume). There is also another important dimension in which Austria, Ireland, Denmark and the Netherlands are a puzzle for conventional analysis. High wage inequality is often thought of as the key to employment expansion, and the American "job miracle" is frequently adduced in support of this. However, wage dispersion is far lower in the four successful European economies than in the United States, and the former are by no means a homogeneous group in this respect (see table 2.1). Nor does active labour market policy seem to be a necessary precondition for employment success. Denmark spends about 2.4 per cent of its GDP on active labour market policies but Austria only 0.4 per cent. The summary statistics in table 2.1 appear to demolish any belief in monocausal economic policy hypotheses. This is reason enough to investigate the performance of the four economies with greater analytical rigour.

Figures 2.1 and 2.2 illustrate the employment and economic performance of the four European success stories relative to that of France and Germany. Figure 2.1 shows their unemployment rates and employment-to-population ratios, compared with the unweighted French/German average. Ireland's unemployment levels have fallen substantially; they now approximate those of the reference countries (France and Germany) and are, moreover, still on a declining rather than a rising trend. Levels in Denmark and the Netherlands initially fluctuated around those of their neighbours, but have been lower since the mid-1990s and mid-1980s respectively; only Austria has achieved unemployment rates consistently below the French/German average. In the case of employment-to-population ratios, Austria has been consistently slightly above France and Germany, but Denmark – with some variation – has been consistently substantially above them. Employment-to-population ratios have risen in the Netherlands and in Ireland but only reached the reference level in the late 1990s.

Figure 2.2 clearly shows the pronounced narrowing of inflation rates, particularly in the 1990s. Again Ireland's rates were off the map in the 1970s, but within the general European range in the 1990s. These trends can be explained by the impact of the EMS. Growth rates of per capita GDP (population aged 15–65 years) show fluctuations around the reference level and, except for Ireland in the 1990s, nothing like increasing divergence. They have been higher than the reference since the early 1990s, however (except for Austria).

Thus the development of the indicators over time has been heterogeneous. Starting at a very diverse unemployment situation, unemployment rates in all

Figure 2.1 The labour market performance of Austria, Denmark, Ireland and the Netherlands (relative to France/Germany)

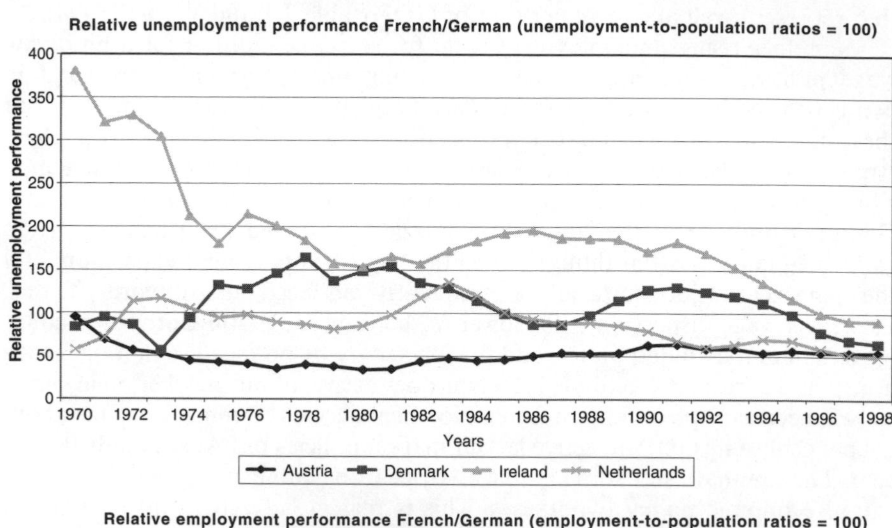

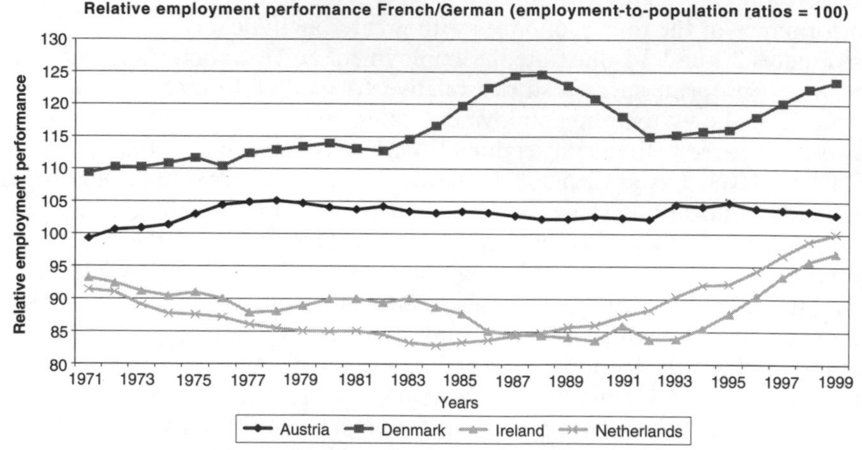

four countries fell to below the French/German average by the mid-1990s, in some cases substantially. Inflation rates have converged and are now close to the French/German average, but the relative performance in terms of per capita income growth has been very uneven.

Macroeconomic policy options in small open economies

The positions held by economic policy advisers may be described in terms of the two extremes. At one end of the spectrum are those who assume aggregate

Figure 2.2 The inflation and income performance of Austria, Denmark, Ireland and the Netherlands (relative to France/Germany)

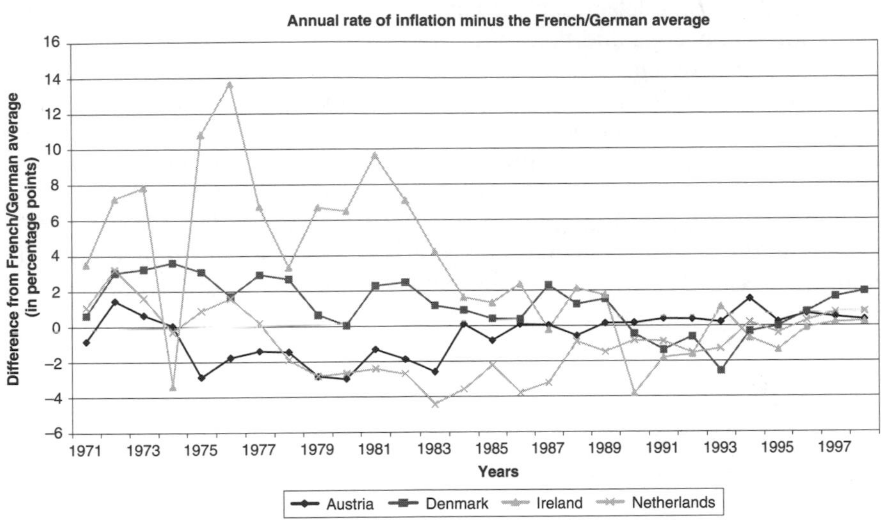

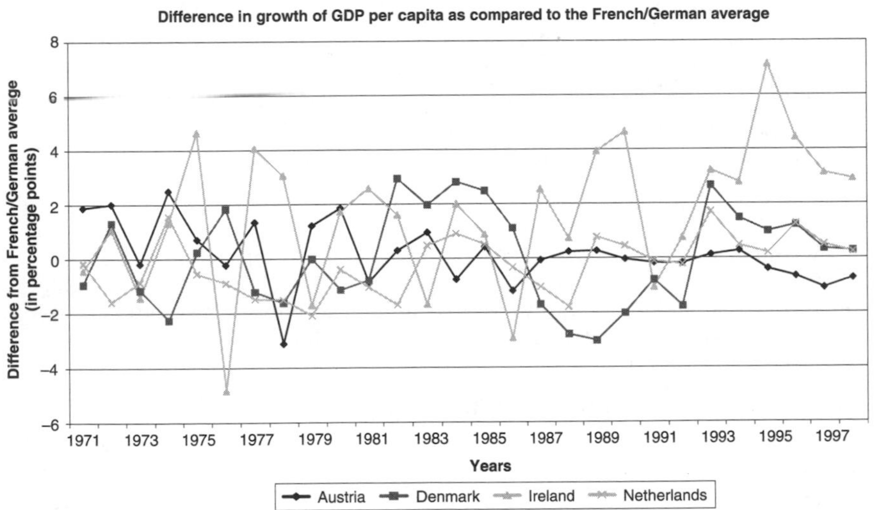

demand to be exogenous, and thus believe that supply will adjust once demand expansion takes place (e.g. Eatwell, 1997). This position constituted the mainstream view in the 1960s and early 1970s but has become a minority position since then. At the other extreme are those who assume demand to be endogenous, and therefore think that one has to "get the supply-side variables right" (e.g. Siebert, 1997); demand will then adjust.[3] At the risk of oversimplification, it may be said that the central difference between the extremes lies in the choice of the variable that is assumed to be exogenous. It is clear both that models which exchange the endogenous and exogenous variables cannot converge, and that for actual policy formulation the real world is somewhere in-between.

Monetary and fiscal policies are the two conventional tools of macroeconomic policy. Several arguments have been put forward against the effectiveness of demand-side policies, ranging from the theoretical arguments of new-classical economics to more pragmatic arguments that the openness of modern economies makes demand policies impossible. The Lucas critique (Lucas, 1976)[4] and its emphasis on rational expectations posited that the Phillips curve – the alleged trade-off between inflation and unemployment – was vertical not only in the long run but also in the short run (Lucas/Sargent, 1978): Keynesian demand-side policies, it is argued, will fail to increase employment and will simply result in higher inflation.[5] Unemployment is at its natural level.[6] To change that level requires changes in the institutional frameworks but not demand stimulation. The economy is in equilibrium, so demand stimulation can only cause inflation and no real effects (for a summary discussion see Schettkat, 1992).

This theoretical position dominated macroeconomics in the 1970s and 1980s, despite the fact that it was based on extreme assumptions on the functioning of markets. It required, among other things, markets to be in equilibrium and prices to respond quickly to external shocks. Within this theoretical framework government activity can only crowd out private economic activity, but cannot stimulate overall economic activity. This was a return to the classical position (hence "new-classical macroeconomics"):

> Before Keynes, it was commonplace that government spending and taxation were powerless to affect the aggregate level of spending and employment in the economy: they could only redirect resources from the private to the public sector. This, of course, is an immediate corollary of Say's law. "In a full-employment context, each dollar of additional government spending can only 'crowd out' exactly one dollar of private spending; it cannot alter the overall level of aggregate spending." (Blinder/Solow, 1973).

More generally, in imperfect markets economic relationships in general, and policy effectiveness in particular, are not as clear as in the perfect market world, and most economists agree that the relations summarized in the following overview are a good approximation to reality, at least in the short run (see box 2.1).

In an open economy, the effectiveness of fiscal and monetary policy depends on whether exchange rates are fixed or floating. With fixed exchange rates, fiscal policy is effective but with floating exchange rates monetary policy is to be preferred. The "crowding-out" argument is relevant to a closed economy (see Chapter 1) but less so to an open economy, where capital can move freely. In this case, a public deficit will not affect the interest rate because

Box 2.1 Effects of expansionary policies in different macroeconomic contexts

Monetary policy	Fiscal policy
Closed economy	
Increasing money supply leads to a fall in the interest rate, stimulating investment and, through the multiplier effect, production and private consumption.	Public deficit will lead to a higher interest rate, which will crowd out some private investment, but less than the impact of the budget deficit. Production and private consumption increase.
Aggregate demand, production and employment will be higher.	**Aggregate demand, production and employment will be higher.**
If the economy was in equilibrium before the monetary expansion, prices will rise, causing the real money supply to fall and the interest rate to return to its initial level.	If the economy was in equilibrium before the fiscal expansion, prices will rise, reducing real money supply and pushing up the interest rate. This effect may offset the expansionary effect.
Open economy – Fixed exchange rates	
The falling interest rates will lead to a capital outflow, reducing money supply and thus neutralizing the expansionary effect of the initial expansion.	The public deficit will leave the interest rate unchanged if capital markets are perfect (capital inflow); there will be no crowding out of private investment.
Aggregate demand, production and employment will be unchanged.	**Aggregate demand, production and employment will be higher.**
Open economy – Floating exchange rates	
The falling interest rate will lead to a capital outflow and a depreciation of the currency. The latter will lead to a rise in net exports, production and employment.	The public deficit will lead to a capital inflow (leaving the interest rate unchanged), which will appreciate the currency. Net exports will decline, reducing production and employment.
Aggregate demand, production and employment will be higher.	**Aggregate demand, production and employment will be unchanged.**

capital will flow into the economy. It is therefore with fixed exchange rates that fiscal policy is most powerful. However, this does not mean that economies – especially small economies – can run deficits for long. Long-run deficits may sooner or later bring the economy under pressure to devalue as the maintenance of the fixed exchange rate would require higher interest rates. However, expansionary fiscal policy is a powerful short-term response to recessions.[7]

Work on the micro-foundations of macroeconomics, which has examined more closely how markets really work, new-institutional economics and new-Keynesian economics all focus on the existence of imperfect markets, a hypothesis that is increasingly gaining acceptance. In imperfect markets, institutions are important and there may once again be a role for policy. However, the thrust of the Lucas critique (that people learn and that economic action is future-oriented and therefore driven by expectations) is also widely accepted in modern macroeconomics. The credibility of policy became a major issue and institutions, especially central banks, are certainly concerned about this. Once expectations enter the scene, macroeconomics becomes less mechanical and more of a social science (Blanchard, 1997).

Given the importance of expectations, even a policy of budget consolidation – which "old Keynesians" would surely classify as contractionary – may show "perverse effects" (Giavazzi/Pagano, 1990) that is, it may be expansionary. Given a situation in which public budget deficits become structural rather than fluctuating over the business cycle, economic agents may fear future tax increases and thus become reluctant to consume and invest. Consolidating public budgets can therefore be expansionary if the expectations of economic agents are positively affected, that is, if they believe in the success of the policy. Aside from expectations, there are also fears that public spending (whether financed by debt or by taxes makes no difference according to the Ricardian equivalence) will crowd out private investment and consumption (the German position according to Giavazzi and Pagano). This may be the case, and the fears on this point make it worthwhile to investigate the relation between public and private spending. However, this turns out to be negative, rather than positive.

Crowding out private investors in credit markets requires investment to be interest elastic, meaning that higher interest rates substantially reduce private investment.[8] There are doubts that private investment depends strongly on the interest rate. Fazzari (1994) found, in a study based on company data, that the main determinant for investment decisions was expected sales rather than the interest rate. This is not good news for "crowding-out" theorists, but it also causes problems for "demand-side" economists, who believe that lower interest rates can stimulate investment substantially. However, capital markets are imperfect and firms may be capital constrained. This may explain the observed positive correlation between profits and investment (Blanchard, 1997), which should not be found in perfect capital markets, where the price of loans would be the only relevant variable.

Globalization, it is argued, has destroyed – all other theoretical arguments aside – the ability of national governments to pursue demand-side policies. Flexible exchange rates would immediately compensate for the expansionary effect of such policies (assuming that exchange rates react to changes in the real economy). But even with fixed exchange rates – the regime most suitable for fiscal policy – the openness of economies will make expansionary policies too costly. It is the cornerstone of Keynesian theory that autonomous demand growth has an income effect on the domestic economy which, depending on the marginal rate of consumption, may be a multiple of the initial impulse (the multiplier). In open economies, however, a proportion of the increase in consumption is spent on imports and therefore reduces the multiplier (at least for the domestic economy). A back-of-an-envelope calculation for the consumption multiplier in a small open economy – where imports amount to about 50 per cent of GDP – and for marginal consumption is approximated by the average consumption rate (about 60 per cent, which is surely a conservative estimate, shifting the odds in favour of a high multiplier); this would suggest a multiplier of about 1.1. In other words, in small open economies a demand impulse would be limited to little more than its initial value. This is bad news for expansionary fiscal policy but good news for a policy directed towards budget consolidation. Just as the expansionary effects spread to the rest of the world, so do the contractionary effects.

It may well be the case that small open economies can consolidate their budgets without themselves experiencing the contractionary effects in full. If nominal exchange rates are fixed at the same time, budget consolidation may stimulate optimistic views of the future and help to restrain wage increases, real exchange rates may depreciate and exports may consequently be boosted. This, however, brings another crucial variable into the picture: wage setting.

Among economists, an imperfect competition model of the labour market developed by Layard/Nickell (1987), Carlin/Soskice (1990), and Franz (1999) has gained wide acceptance. In this model, unions set (real) wages[9] in accordance with their market power, which is a negative function of unemployment (the bargained real wage (BRW) in figure 2.3, also known as the "targeted real wage"). Employers also operate in imperfect markets and set prices with a mark-up over (wage) costs (the price-determined real wage (PRW) in figure 2.3, also known as the "feasible real wage"). The price-setting function is either horizontal (constant mark-up) or negative sloping (varying mark-ups).

Both functions are strongly influenced by the institutional frameworks of the economy in question. Openness, for example, reduces the market power of firms and lowers their mark-ups (shifting PRW up to a higher real wage). Openness may also affect the BRW. If unions fear foreign competitors, they are likely to be more cautious in their wage demands, and this will shift the BRW curve downwards. Both will result in higher employment.

The organizational structure of the unions is also important within the framework outlined here. Institutions, especially wage bargaining institutions, have increasingly been integrated into macroeconomics. Traditionally, economists have favoured the decentralized model of wage bargaining, because it is best suited to produce efficient allocation in perfect markets. But this may not be the case in imperfect markets, where asymmetric information, transaction costs, uncertainty and interdependence of actions exist and where both

Figure 2.3 Wage setting in the imperfect competition model

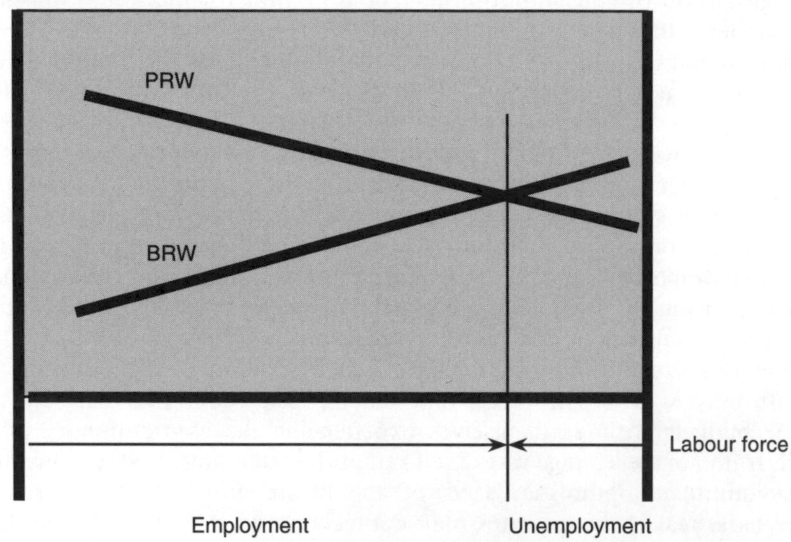

employers and unions have market power. Bruno/Sachs (1985) and others have argued that countries with "corporatist" wage-setting institutions may be better equipped to adjust to aggregate shocks. Shocks such as the oil price increases in the 1970s increase costs and thus shift the PRW downwards, meaning that profits will capture a higher share of value added. With an unchanged BRW, unemployment will rise. In response to negative shocks, however, the BRW curve in figure 2.3 may shift downward in "corporatist" wage-setting systems, and thus allow for price (wage) rather than quantity (employment) reactions. Real-wage flexibility may be higher in "corporatist" wage-setting systems. Such a reaction may require organized labour institutions, which take macroeconomic considerations into account. Thus, the role which organized labour plays in wage setting is more complex than the reduction of unions to monopolies would suggest.

Organized labour may actually be a force for good in this model, rather than a force for evil. The argument is that more comprehensive unions will be more responsive to unemployment: they will internalize the negative effects of their actions and these should shift the BRW curve downwards (see Layard/Nickell/Jackman, 1991; Appelbaum/Schettkat, 1996). Thus wage-setting systems may be very important in a context of imperfect labour markets and, indeed, three of the four countries (Austria, Denmark, the Netherlands) can be classified as "corporatist", while Ireland has also recently implemented a long-term wage agreement reached at central level.

Although the Danish krone and the Irish pound have been allowed to fluctuate within the band of the European Exchange Rate Mechanism, all four economies may be regarded for the sake of simplicity as economies with fixed exchange rates. In other words, monetary policy has more or less had to adjust to that pursued by the Bundesbank. In theory, if exchange rates are fixed, there is a potential for active fiscal policy. However, these four small economies have been unable to pursue expansionary fiscal policies for two reasons: first, they are all very open economies, so expansionary fiscal policies would be expensive relative to the domestic benefits (inefficient); second, expansionary fiscal policies would have created inflationary pressure and thus speculation on currency devaluation, which would have required increased interest rates (as was in fact necessary for a while; see below). This would have had a negative effect on economic activity. Not surprisingly, all four governments opted for a policy of budgetary consolidation as part of their low inflation policy. As long as the exchange rate to the DM was fixed, they relied on wage restraint to keep inflationary pressure low.

Section 2.2 discusses the monetary and fiscal policies pursued by the four countries and analyses their impact on rates of inflation, interest and exchange (nominal and real). Section 2.3 then examines trends in overall economic growth and in its components, and section 2.4 investigates labour market trends. The dimensions of labour market performance discussed are unemployment and employment trends, especially in relation to economic growth.

2.2 MONETARY AND FISCAL POLICIES: AIMING FOR STABILITY

Monetary and fiscal policies in all four European economies under study have been directed towards price stability. To some observers, this fact may make it even more surprising that these economies have become examples of successful employment policies. Obviously the relationship between price stability, budgetary consolidation, and economic growth and employment is more complex than is commonly believed.

Monetary and fiscal policy

During the 1980s and 1990s, most central banks quietly moved away from targeting the money supply as their prime monetary policy guideline, since the central tenet of the monetarist theory on which such a policy had been based – the close link between changes in the money supply and nominal GDP – had turned out to be untenable. "In a word, no sturdy long-run statistical relationship exists between nominal GDP and *any* of the Federal Reserve's three official definitions of the money supply for *any* sample that includes the 1990s" (Blinder, 1998, p. 29). This is as much a problem for monetarism as the alleged instability of the Phillips curve had been for Keynesianism in the

1970s. Nowadays central banks focus instead on the interest rate. However, their direct influence is restricted to short-term nominal interest rates, whereas investment decisions are based on long-term real interest rates, which are dependent on the expectations of economic agents. It is only if central banks (and/or governments) are credible that their policies are able to influence expectations concerning long-run interest rates. Therefore national institutional frameworks are extremely important, and the independence of central banks from government may be a necessary element in establishing a credible institutional framework (Alesina/Summers, 1993). However, a credible institutional framework may require more than just the central bank independence: it may, for example, also call for coordinated wage setting.

All four economies have tried to give credibility to their stability-oriented policies by pegging their currencies directly (Austria and the Netherlands) or indirectly via the EMS (Denmark and Ireland) to the DM, and so effectively delegating their monetary policies to the Bundesbank.[10]

However, if the policy outlined here was successful, this should have led to the convergence not only of short-term interest rates but also of long-term interest rates. To assess whether these goals were actually achieved by monetary policy, the ratios between national short-term interest rates and the German rate are presented in the upper panel of table 2.2. The ratios (columns 2, 4, 6, 8) clearly show the process of monetary integration within the European Union (EU), and especially between Austria, the Netherlands and Germany. Short-term interest rates actually remained slightly below the German rate in Austria and the Netherlands, a sign that their commitment to stability was regarded as even more credible than that of the Bundesbank. Denmark and Ireland, less closely linked to the DM, have had to maintain short-term interest rates above the German rate. This is especially true of Ireland, but here too the gap narrowed substantially.

To determine whether central bank policy (or national policy in general) affected expectations in the way central bankers and other policy makers hoped, the ten-year yield is presented in the lower panel of table 2.2. If policy was credible in its commitment to stability, that is, low rates of inflation and budgetary consolidation, the yield – representing expectations of future inflation rates – should also have narrowed against the German yields. The long-term yield shows a convergence similar to that of the short-term interest rate. Austria and the Netherlands had yields roughly equal to those in Germany for the entire period, while Denmark and Ireland experienced a substantial relative decline in their yields. This demonstrates the successful integration of financial markets in the EU, culminating in the decision to introduce the euro in 1999.

Public budget deficits became a major problem in all four economies in the late 1970s and early 1980s, and governments subscribed to a policy of budget consolidation. As a result, except in Austria, public debt was lower in the mid-1990s in relation to GDP than in the early 1980s. Net public borrowing in the

Table 2.2 Short-term interest rates and long-term yields

Year	Austria		Denmark		Ireland		Netherlands		Germany
	Interest rate (1)	Ratio 1/9 (2)	Interest rate (3)	Ratio 3/9 (4)	Interest rate (5)	Ratio 5/9 (6)	Interest rate (7)	Ratio 7/9 (8)	Interest rate (9)
Short-term interest rate									
1980	10.3	107.9	17.6	184.5	15.2	159.0	10.7	112.2	9.5
1985	6.2	113.2	10.2	188.0	11.9	218.9	6.3	116.3	5.4
1986	5.3	114.2	9.1	197.1	12.5	270.1	5.7	122.6	4.6
1987	4.3	107.5	10.1	250.7	10.8	268.7	5.4	132.9	4.0
1988	4.6	105.3	8.5	195.7	8.0	185.8	4.8	111.2	4.3
1989	7.5	105.2	9.8	137.6	10.0	141.0	7.4	103.8	7.1
1990	8.5	100.7	10.8	127.2	11.3	133.2	8.7	102.3	8.5
1991	9.1	98.4	9.7	105.2	10.4	112.8	9.3	100.4	9.2
1992	9.3	97.9	11.5	121.3	14.3	150.4	9.4	98.3	9.5
1993	7.2	98.6	10.3	141.0	9.1	125.0	6.9	94.0	7.3
1994	5.0	93.4	6.2	115.1	5.9	110.5	5.2	96.5	5.4
1995	4.3	95.9	6.0	133.0	6.2	137.9	4.4	96.5	4.5
1996	3.3	98.3	3.9	117.1	5.4	164.0	3.0	90.8	3.3
1997	3.1	99.4	3.5	109.5	5.5	174.0	3.2	100.0	3.2
1998	3.2	100.0	3.6	112.5	4.9	152.0	3.2	100.0	3.2
Yield (10 years)									
1980	9.32	111.0			15.35	182.7			8.4
1985	7.77	111.0			12.64	180.6	7.34	104.86	7.0
1986	7.33	118.2			11.06	178.4	6.35	102.42	6.2
1987	6.94	111.9	11.34	182.9	11.27	181.8	6.38	102.90	6.2
1988	6.67	102.6	9.60	147.7	9.49	146	6.29	96.77	6.5
1989	7.14	102.0	9.78	139.7	8.95	127.9	7.21	103.00	7.0
1990	8.74	99.32	10.58	120.2	10.08	114.6	8.93	101.48	8.8
1991	8.62	101.4	9.25	108.8	9.17	107.9	8.74	102.82	8.5
1992	8.27	104.7	8.91	112.8	9.11	115.3	8.10	102.53	7.9
1993	6.64	102.2	7.19	110.6	7.72	118.8	6.69	102.92	6.5
1994	6.69	96.96	7.94	115.1	8.19	118.7	7.20	104.35	6.9
1995	6.47	95.15	8.28	121.8	8.29	121.9	7.20	105.88	6.8
1996	5.30	86.89	7.13	116.9	7.48	122.6	6.49	106.39	6.1

Source: Calculations based on OECD: *Statistical Compendium, Economic Outlook*, various years.

Netherlands reached double-digits in the late 1970s and early 1980s (one reason for the commitment to a consolidation policy of the first Lubbers Government and the subsequent Wassenaar agreement; cf. Schettkat/Reijnders, 1998). Although Denmark has generally pursued a policy of budgetary consolidation, it nevertheless increased government net borrowing in 1993–94 (table 2.3), and this is seen as one reason for Denmark's successful employment record (Kongshoj Madsen, 1998; OECD, 1997). Also Austria pursued an anti-cyclical fiscal policy (an important element in the approach dubbed "austro-keynesianism",

Table 2.3 Fiscal policy

	Government net borrowing (% of GDP)				Government debt (% of GDP)			
Year	Austria	Denmark	Ireland	Netherlands	Austria	Denmark	Ireland	Netherlands
1970	0.2	0.9	−1.4	0.0	19.4	n.a.	n.a.	51.5
1971	−0.2	0.6	−1.1	0.0	18.2	n.a.	n.a.	49.1
1972	−0.5	0.6	−0.5	0.0	17.5	n.a.	n.a.	46.0
1973	1.2	0.6	0.8	0.0	17.5	n.a.	n.a.	42.8
1974	−1.3	0.3	0.0	0.0	17.6	n.a.	56.5	40.8
1975	−5.6	−2.4	−2.2	0.0	23.9	n.a.	62.4	41.8
1976	−3.4	−0.7	−2.0	0.0	27.4	n.a.	66.9	41.4
1977	−2.4	−0.8	−0.8	−7.3	30.1	n.a.	63.9	40.8
1978	−2.4	−2.1	−2.3	−9.4	33.9	n.a.	65.9	42.1
1979	−2.6	−0.8	−3.0	−11.1	36.0	n.a.	71.2	44.1
1980	−2.9	0.0	−4.2	−12.3	37.3	44.7	72.7	46.9
1981	−3.7	−1.9	−5.4	−13.0	39.3	54.9	77.4	50.9
1982	−3.3	−2.8	−6.6	−13.4	41.8	67.0	83.3	56.5
1983	−2.6	−3.2	−5.8	−11.4	46.5	77.8	97.3	62.7
1984	−1.9	−2.8	−5.5	−9.5	48.6	79.3	101.6	67.0
1985	−1.2	−2.9	−3.6	−10.9	50.5	76.6	104.6	71.7
1986	−1.3	−2.7	−5.1	−10.7	54.9	73.4	116.3	73.5
1987	−1.9	−1.9	−5.9	−8.6	58.7	70.2	117.6	76.2
1988	−2.2	−1.7	−4.6	−4.5	59.5	68.2	113.6	79.2
1989	0.1	−1.2	−4.7	−1.8	58.9	66.9	103.7	79.1
1990	−2.1	−1.6	−5.1	−2.3	58.3	68.0	96.3	78.8
1991	−3.3	−2.0	−2.9	−2.4	58.7	69.1	96.6	78.8
1992	−2.8	−3.8	−3.9	−2.5	58.3	73.2	94.0	79.6
1993	−3.5	−5.6	−3.2	−2.5	62.8	82.6	97.1	80.6
1994	−2.4	−5.6	−3.4	−1.8	65.1	80.5	91.0	77.3
1995	−3.6	−5.0	−4.1	−2.1	69.3	76.9	84.9	79.5
1996	−3.8	−4.2	−2.4	−0.9	69.8	74.8	76.5	78.5
1997	−3.2	−3.2	−2.3	−1.2	71.3	71.5	72.0	74.5
1998	−2.7	−3.0	−1.7	−1.0	72.6	66.5	67.3	72.6

n.a. = not available.
Source: Calculations based on OECD statistics, *Economic Outlook*, OECD CD-ROM.

see Pichelmann/Hofer, 1998; Nowotny, 1999), but public deficits remained at fairly low levels (table 2.3). Thus, while there seems to be room for short-term deficit spending, such a policy clearly cannot be sustained.

However, the critical question for economic policy is whether budget consolidation is contractionary, or whether it may show "perverse effects" and even be expansionary. The effect of budget consolidation will depend not only on expectations concerning future economic developments but also on the wealth effect, which lower expected interest rates may have (Giavazzi/Pagano, 1990). Expectations in macroeconomics are usually linked to the Lucas critique (Lucas, 1976) which posits that, since people learn from experience, future policy effects cannot be predicted on the basis of past trends. Lucas closed his model with the concept of "rational expectations", which allowed him to work in a neoclassical macroeconomic framework. The essence of the Lucas critique is generally accepted (see Blinder, 1989) but the concept of rational expectations is not easily accepted (e.g. Arrow, 1987) because it requires strong assumptions regarding human behaviour.

Inflation and exchange rates

As discussed above, the DM has been used as an "anchor currency" to stabilize price trends in all four economies. With government policy committed to pegging the Austrian schilling and the Dutch guilder against the DM, the nominal exchange rates should have been stable. This is clearly shown in figure 2.4 by the horizontal line for the schilling (over the entire period displayed) and the guilder (from 1983).[11] By contrast, the Irish pound and the Danish krone experienced a substantial nominal devaluation against the DM over the period as a whole (i.e. the ratio of the national currency to the DM increased as 1 DM could buy more national currency). Their nominal exchange rates were quite stable in the late 1980s and 1990s, however, thanks to monetary integration within the EMS; an exception was the turmoil within the system in 1992.

Real exchange rates take into account the purchasing power of currencies.[12] Denmark, for example, experienced a nominal depreciation of its currency against the DM, while inflation was higher in Denmark than in Germany (see table 2.4). One DM could buy an increasing amount of Danish kroner but these represented a decreasing amount of goods. In 1998 1 DM bought roughly 4 kroner as compared to only 2 kroner in 1970s, but the 1998 price level in Denmark was about 5.2 times as high as in 1970. Over the same period, prices in Germany approximately tripled. Thus the devaluation of the krone was roughly offset by price changes, resulting in a very stable real exchange rate of the krone against the DM (see figure 2.4). A similar reasoning holds for the Irish pound, which depreciated in nominal terms against DM but has exhibited quite a stable real exchange relation.

By contrast, the two countries with stable nominal exchange rates, Austria and the Netherlands, experienced a real appreciation in the first case and depreciation in the second, meaning that 1 DM could buy fewer products in Austria, but more in the Netherlands. Products from Austria became more expensive and products from the Netherlands became cheaper from the German perspective. Since most of the foreign trade of all four countries is within the EU – accounting for between 60 and 70 per cent of exports – the real depreciation of the Dutch guilder against the DM, reflecting fixed nominal exchange rates together with lower rates of inflation that made real depreciation possible, thus stimulated foreign demand in the Netherlands and resulted in trade surpluses.[13] In employment terms it is important to note, however, that the increase in net Dutch exports has been concentrated in manufacturing

Figure 2.4 Nominal and real exchange rates against the Deutschmark

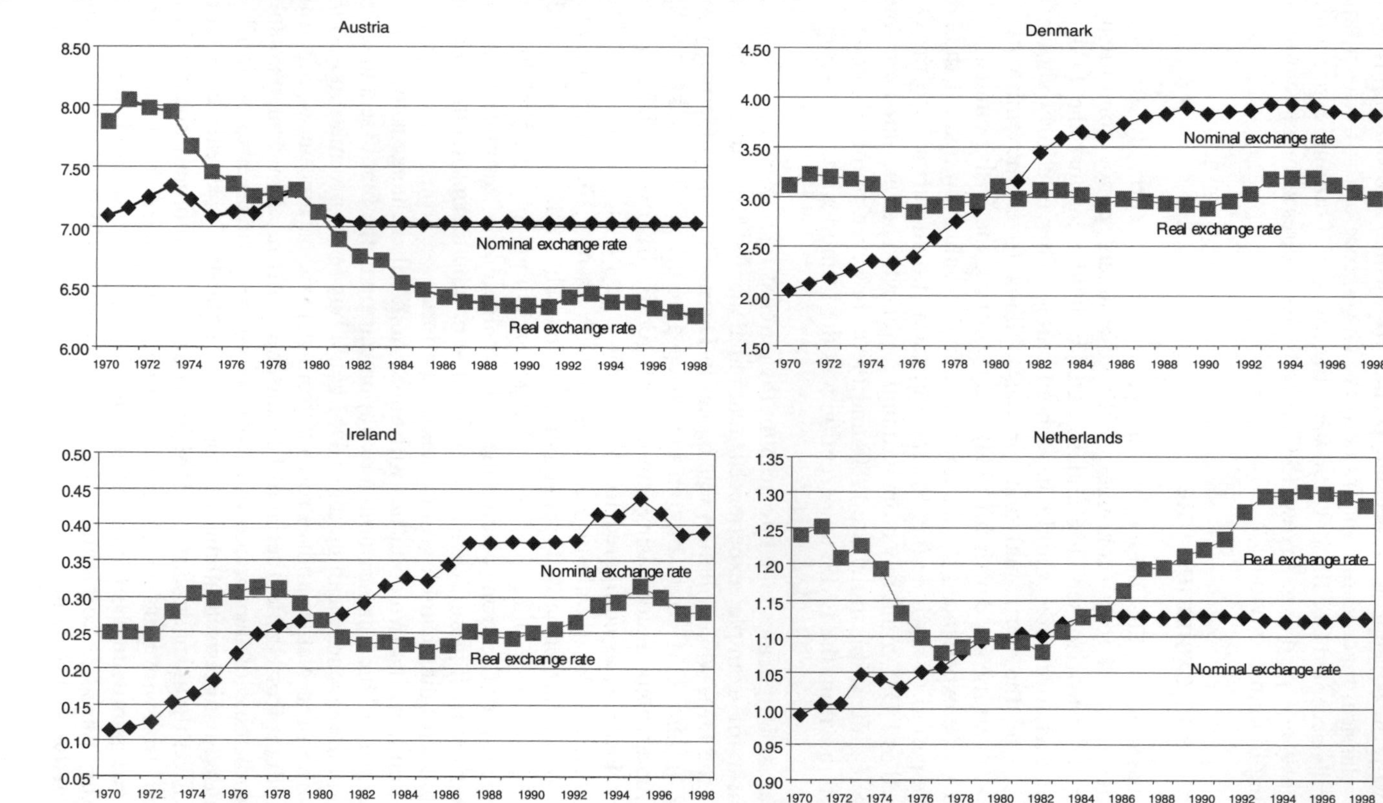

Source: Computations based on OECD: *Employment Outlook*, CD-ROM. Real exchange rates are computed with GDP price deflator.

Table 2.4 Annual rates of inflation, consumer prices

Year	Austria	Denmark	Ireland	Netherlands	Germany	France
1971	5.0	8.3	9.4	7.9	5.1	6.0
1975	7.9	9.9	18.0	10.1	6.0	11.8
1980	6.4	10.7	18.6	6.8	5.8	13.3
1981	7.6	12.0	19.6	6.4	6.2	13.0
1982	6.0	10.2	14.9	5.0	5.1	11.5
1983	3.4	6.8	9.2	2.9	3.2	9.7
1984	5.6	6.4	7.3	1.9	2.5	7.7
1985	3.3	4.3	5.0	2.4	1.8	5.8
1986	1.9	2.9	4.6	0.3	−0.6	2.7
1987	1.0	4.6	2.4	0.2	0.5	3.2
1988	1.4	4.0	5.4	0.5	1.3	2.7
1989	2.7	4.3	2.5	1.2	2.9	3.4
1990	3.3	2.7	2.1	2.2	2.7	2.8
1991	3.4	2.4	2.9	3.2	3.7	3.2
1992	3.9	2.0	2.5	3.1	4.7	2.4
1993	3.4	0.4	1.9	2.1	4.0	2.2
1994	3.0	1.8	2.6	2.7	2.9	2.1
1995	2.3	2.1	2.0	0.9	1.9	1.6
1996	1.9	2.1	1.8	1.8	1.9	1.8
1997	2.0	2.2	2.0	1.8	1.7	1.6
1998	1.9	2.7	2.7	1.9	1.8	1.4

Source: OECD: *Economic Outlook*, OECD CD-ROM.

industries (Schettkat/Reijnders, 1998), whereas the main employment gains have occurred in service industries.

2.3 ECONOMIC GROWTH

If the measure of success is economic growth, only one of the four economies can be labelled a "tiger". Ireland achieved very high rates of GDP growth, especially in the 1990s. Its rapid growth was, however, from a comparatively low initial level of per capita income; high foreign direct investment and EU subsidies have been important growth components. Austria, Denmark and the Netherlands achieved growth rates above those of Germany (western) and France in the 1990s, but they are at similar levels as those achieved in the 1980s. There has been no such thing as a "take-off" in economic growth to explain the employment success of the three economies (see also section 2.4). This clearly suggests that the success in employment growth at least partly depends on the employment intensity of economic growth, and not merely on economic growth itself, a conclusion further supported by the fact that economic growth in the United States has not been dramatically higher than in many European countries (see also Freeman, 1988; Schettkat, 1992; Boltho/Glyn,1995).

If economic growth itself gives no clear indication of the source of the success of the four economies, the composition of GDP growth might be considered relevant. But even in the case of government spending – frequently considered an important explanatory factor – there is no clearly distinguishable common pattern. In the 1990s, government consumption grew less than the economy as a whole in Denmark, Ireland and the Netherlands, but not in Austria (table 2.5). Figure 2.5 shows the generally positive relations between government spending and private consumption, investment and total domestic spending (all variables measured as deviations of the growth rates of these variables from the growth rate of potential output) in the four economies concerned, but also in Germany, France and the United States. The correlation is positive and comparatively high between government spending (government consumption) and total domestic expenditures ($r = 0.61$) and private consumption ($r = 0.46$), but low for growth in investment ($r = 0.20$) for all countries and across the entire period (figure 2.5). The correlation is generally closer if the sample is restricted to the four economies: the coefficients are 0.77 (total domestic demand), 0.56 (private consumption) and 0.61 (investment). Leaving out the 1970s strengthens the correlations further to 0.88, 0.72 and 0.87 respectively. The positive correlation between government spending and the variables mentioned above means that if government consumption grows more than potential output, the other GDP components also tend to grow more rapidly than potential output and vice versa. This is certainly not the pattern one might expect from theories that blame every economic malaise on public sector growth. On the other hand, a correlation is not a causal relation. Moreover, the share of government consumption varies substantially between the economies (table 2.5, lower panel). All the economies have reduced the share of government consumption in GDP since 1980, but so has Germany.

Other straightforward explanations likewise fail to match the observed patterns. For example, it would be difficult to argue that economic development in the four economies was investment driven. Gross fixed capital formation grew less than GDP (except in Austria, table 2.5, top panel) and even declined as a share of GDP (table 2.5, lower panel). The picture with respect to private final consumption is equally mixed. In some countries it grew roughly in line with GDP, while in others it lagged behind somewhat. As a share of GDP, private consumption declined in two of the economies (Denmark and Ireland) but remained roughly stable – although at lower rates – in Austria and the Netherlands.

With respect to overall domestic demand, again two broad patterns appear. In Austria, domestic demand evolved roughly in line with GDP, remaining around the 100 per cent level (table 2.5, lower panel). By contrast, in Denmark and the Netherlands total domestic demand declined to a ratio of about 90 per cent, and in Ireland to just 80 per cent. According to accounting rules, a decline in the share of domestic demand is compensated by an expansion of foreign demand. Indeed, Ireland achieved spectacular growth rates in exports

Figure 2.5 Changes in government spending and total domestic demand, private consumption and investment (deviation of growth rates in the variables from the growth rate of potential output)

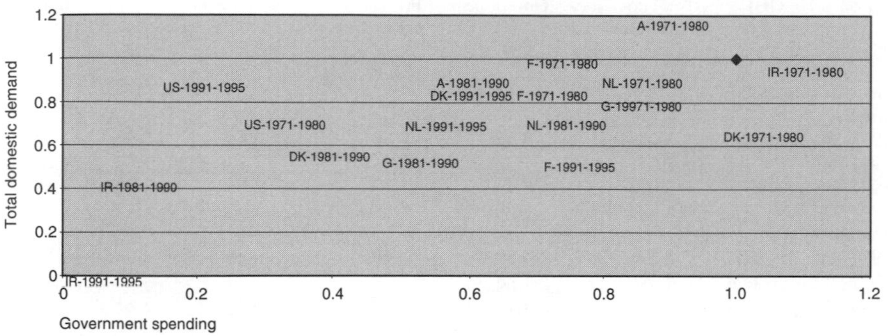

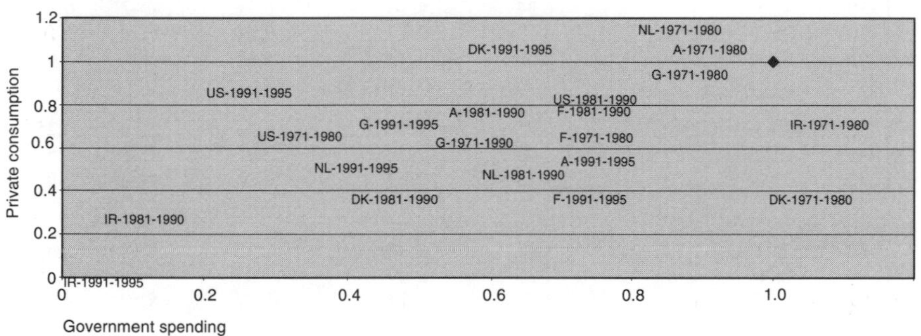

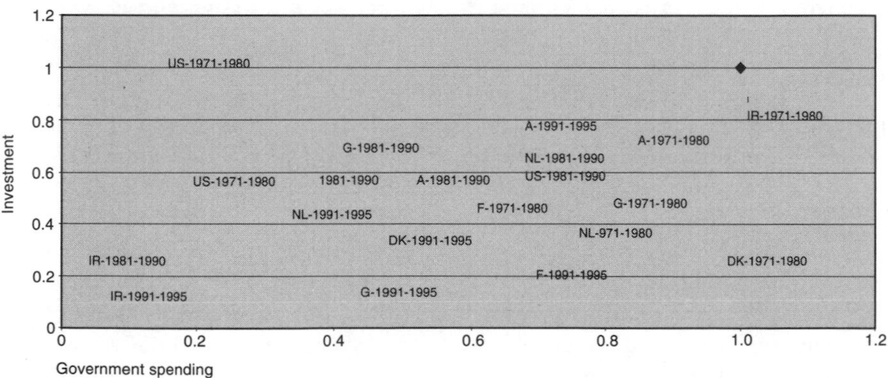

Key: A = Austria, DK = Denmark, F = France, G = Germany, IR = Ireland, NL = Netherlands, US = United States.

Source: Computations based on OECD National Accounts Statistics and OECD: *Economic Outlook*, OECD CD-ROM.

Table 2.5 Components of economic growth: Average annual growth rates and GDP shares, 1990 prices

Period	GDP	Total domestic expenditure	Government	Private consumption	Investment	Exports	Imports
Growth rates							
Austria							
1971–80	3.66	3.75	3.65	3.88	3.66	6.98	7.18
1981–90	2.16	2.01	1.33	2.41	2.17	5.12	4.68
1991–95	2.02	2.69	2.43	2.17	3.09	3.20	4.59
Denmark							
1971–80	2.27	1.59	4.39	1.40	−0.38	4.36	1.88
1981–90	2.04	1.34	1.06	1.29	2.11	4.80	2.93
1991–95	2.04	2.12	1.11	2.87	−0.27	3.81	4.30
Ireland							
1971–80	4.75	4.70	6.34	4.16	6.31	7.42	6.93
1981–90	3.67	1.76	0.13	2.17	0.64	8.58	5.16
1991–95	5.78	2.59	2.59	3.79	1.17	11.81	7.85
Netherlands							
1971–80	2.93	2.48	2.85	3.40	0.33	5.32	4.25
1981–90	2.20	1.70	2.05	1.54	2.01	4.36	3.51
1991–95	2.12	1.53	1.12	2.19	1.26	4.53	3.66
Germany (West)							
1971–80	2.74	2.74	3.48	3.35	1.33	5.34	5.34
1981–90	2.26	1.82	1.25	2.09	1.67	5.25	3.75
1991–94	1.77	1.34	1.43	2.14	−1.17	5.59	4.94
France							
1971–80	3.21	3.06	3.35	3.27	2.31	7.53	6.77
1981–90	2.19	2.35	2.24	2.31	2.35	3.99	4.82
1991–95	1.07	0.72	2.27	1.11	−1.24	3.97	2.55
United States							
1971–80	2.72	2.57	0.96	3.02	3.08	6.87	4.77
1981–90	2.72	2.92	2.67	3.01	2.54	5.22	7.08
1991–95	2.31	2.55	−0.32	2.42	6.00	7.56	9.09
Shares							
Austria							
1970	100.0	99.6	19.2	53.0	25.0	22.4	22.5
1980	100.0	100.3	19.3	54.1	24.7	30.5	30.9
1990	100.0	98.7	17.8	55.4	24.6	40.4	39.1
1995	100.0	102.0	18.1	55.8	25.8	42.8	44.2
Denmark							
1970	100.0	109.1	22.7	61.2	24.6	22.3	29.3
1980	100.0	101.7	27.9	56.0	18.2	27.2	27.7
1990	100.0	94.6	25.3	51.9	17.4	35.5	30.1
1995	100.0	94.8	24.2	54.1	15.4	38.6	33.3

Table 2.5 (continued)

Period	GDP	Total domestic expenditure	Government	Private consumption	Investment	Exports	Imports
Shares							
Ireland							
1970	100.0	114.9	18.0	72.7	22.2	29.0	38.9
1980	100.0	113.5	20.9	68.5	24.7	37.1	45.9
1990	100.0	94.1	14.8	59.1	17.9	58.6	52.7
1995	100.0	80.7	12.7	53.8	14.2	77.2	57.9
Netherlands							
1970	100.0	105.0	14.8	59.8	28.0	35.4	38.9
1980	100.0	100.3	14.7	62.6	21.5	44.0	43.8
1990	100.0	95.4	14.5	58.7	20.9	54.2	49.5
1995	100.0	92.6	13.8	58.9	20.0	60.8	53.2
Germany (West)							
1970	100.0	98.5	18.8	52.2	25.9	19.1	17.8
1980	100.0	98.4	20.2	55.4	22.4	24.2	22.9
1990	100.0	94.1	18.3	54.4	20.9	32.1	26.3
1995	100.0	92.5	18.1	55.2	18.5	37.0	29.5
France							
1970	100.0	100.1	17.6	58.6	23.3	12.7	12.9
1980	100.0	98.6	17.9	58.9	21.2	19.1	17.6
1990	100.0	100.0	18.0	59.6	21.4	22.6	22.6
1995	100.0	98.3	19.1	59.7	19.0	25.9	24.2
United States							
1970	100.0	101.1	21.3	62.7	17.3	5.5	6.5
1980	100.0	99.6	17.9	64.6	17.4	8	7.7
1990	100.0	101.4	17.8	66.4	16.9	10	11.4
1995	100.0	102.6	15.7	66.8	20.1	12.8	15.7

Source: OECD, National Accounts, OECD CD-ROM.

in the 1990s, while growth in exports was also stronger than import growth in Denmark (in the 1980s) and the Netherlands.

To summarize: there is no clear and easily identifiable pattern in the composition of GDP on the expenditure side. In the 1990s in all four economies (and also in Germany), the growth of government consumption was lower than that of potential output (though in the Netherlands growth rates were equal), but other domestic demand categories (private consumption and investment) also grew less than potential output. In other words, all the countries were in the south-west quadrant of the graphs in figure 2.5. If government consumption simply crowded out investment or private consumption, we would expect a negative correlation, that is, the points would have been either in the north-west or in the south-east quadrant. There may be complicated time lags in the relation between government consumption and investment, and expectations may play an important role, but the available data do not provide confirmation for any single explanation of labour market success, suggesting rather that there are diverse routes to success.

2.4 UNEMPLOYMENT

General unemployment performance

Figure 2.6 shows that the most remarkable achievement of three of the four European economies is the decline in unemployment rates in the 1990s. The exception is Austria, where the unemployment rate was comparatively low over the whole period. This decline marks a change in the trend since the mid-1970s, and stands in sharp contrast to developments in France, Germany and many other Western European countries. It is this relative performance of the four European economies that has made front-page news, rather than the actual levels of unemployment achieved. Although the United States had lower unemployment rates than the European countries in the 1990s, its unemployment performance has not been spectacular when judged over the full period. The strength of the United States has been its employment generation rather than its unemployment performance, which was worse than that of most European countries in the 1970s and 1980s (Schettkat, 1992).

Figure 2.6 Unemployment rates in 1970, 1980, 1990 and 1998 (percentages)

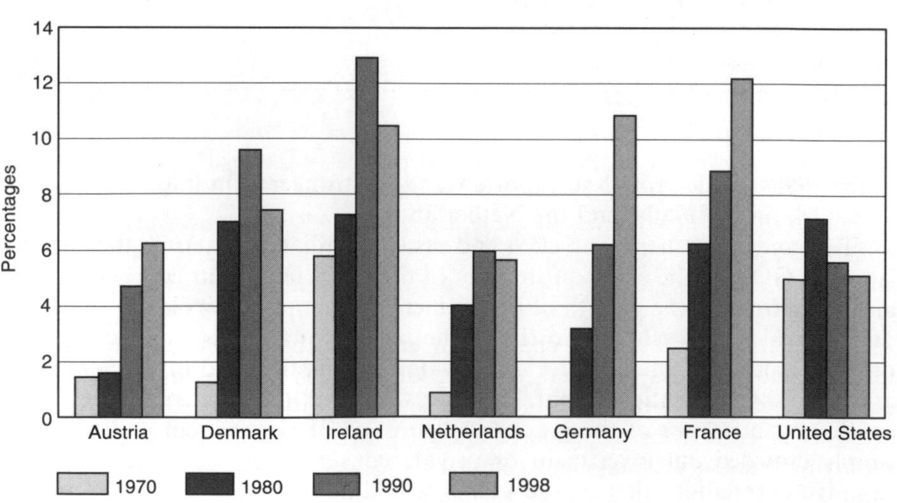

Table 2.6 Long-term unemployment (12 months and over) as a share of overall unemployment

Year	Austria	Denmark	Ireland	Netherlands	Germany	France	United States
1980	n.a.	33	36.9	50.5	39.3	42.2	13.3
1990	n.a.	29.9	66	49.3	46.8	38.0	5.5
1997	28.7	27.2	57	49.1	47.8	41.2	8.7

n.a. = not available.
Source: OECD: *Employment Outlook*, various years. Data are not strictly comparable between countries and over time.

As can be seen from table 2.6, one of the main causes of concern about European unemployment is the particularly and apparently persistently high share of unemployed persons out of work for more than 12 months (long-term unemployment). Even in the four economies, the long-term unemployment share fell only slightly, if at all. Austria and Denmark have done better than Europe generally in this respect, but still far worse than the United States. Long-term unemployment has often been related to low-skilled labour, and it has been suggested that wage flexibility in the United States creates jobs for those workers who are unemployed under the high reservation wages typical of Europe (for a qualification, see Freeman/Schettkat, 1998 and 2000). Nickell and Bell (1995) have shown, however, that there is no systematic correlation between low-skill unemployment rates and wage flexibility across countries. This leaves one other possible candidate for the explanation of long-term unemployment: the unemployment insurance system, which is generally more generous in Europe than in the United States. Various analyses have found a correlation between the generosity of unemployment benefits and the duration of unemployment (Layard/Nickell/Jackman, 1991; Nickell, 1998), but it is difficult to establish this relation within countries over time (Nickell, 1998; Schettkat, 1996). In contradiction to what is commonly believed, recent analysis has shown that it is not the level of benefits – the basis for opportunity cost explanations of unemployment – but rather their duration that influences the length of unemployment (Steiner, 1997; Hunt, 1996). However, there are other paths out of unemployment, besides employment. Early retirement is particularly relevant in Europe, and work inactivity in the United States (Schettkat, 1992).

The relationship between changes in employment and unemployment is shown in table 2.7. As expected, the relation between changes in employment and the unemployment rate is negative and generally quite strong. Austria seems to diverge from the general pattern, with a low correlation between employment and unemployment rates. This means that labour supply in that country must be very responsive to employment variations, thus smoothing out unemployment variations (Pichelmann/Hofer, 1998).

Table 2.7 Coefficients of correlation between changes in employment and changes in unemployment rates

Period	Austria	Denmark	Ireland	Netherlands	Germany	France	United States
1971–98	−0.53	−0.8	−0.81	−0.87	−0.85	−0.86	−0.87
1971–82	−0.84	−0.85	−0.85	−0.9	−0.83	−0.83	−0.98
1982–98	−0.46	−0.82	−0.8	−0.89	−0.86	−0.94	−0.95
1990–98	0.07	−0.91	−0.92	−0.95	−0.88	−0.96	−0.91

Source: Computations are based on OECD Labour Force Statistics, OECD CD-ROM.

Investigating Okun's law

The impact of economic growth (here measured by GDP growth rates) on unemployment rates is usually called Okun's law. Arthur Okun related changes in the deviations of GDP growth from the average growth rate (or from the "normal rate of growth") to changes in the unemployment rate. In general we expect the relationship between economic growth and the unemployment rate to be negative, meaning that higher rates of economic growth reduce the unemployment rate and vice versa. Indeed, this proves true for every country in all periods (see table 2.8, top panel). GDP growth of 1 per cent generally reduces the unemployment rate by 0.3 to 0.4 percentage points. However, there are variations in the coefficients over time and between countries. In accordance with the above discussion on the relation between employment and unemployment, Austria had the lowest "Okun coefficient" in the 1990s; that is, economic growth has affected unemployment rates in Austria only weakly because the country's labour supply reacts strongly to changes in employment opportunities (Pichelmann/Hofer, 1998).

The other economies exhibit higher "Okun coefficients" in the 1990s (and in the Netherlands in the 1980s) than in earlier periods. There may be various reasons for this, including unemployment becoming a more usual mode of entry into the labour market, exhaustion of other labour reserves (hidden unemployment), or a stronger impact of economic growth on job creation (the latter will be investigated in more depth in the next subsection). In welfare States with generous unemployment benefit systems, once employment starts growing the link between economic growth and unemployment will free substantial resources otherwise used for transfers. Just as rising unemployment creates additional labour costs, which may further harm employment, so declining unemployment lowers these costs and may support employment growth; the stronger the growth-to-unemployment link, the greater is this effect. Okun's law is often associated with so-called "normal growth rates". These are the GDP growth rates necessary to keep employment and unemployment constant. In other words, GDP must grow in line with the sum of productivity and labour

Table 2.8 Investigating Okun's law

Period	Austria	Denmark	Ireland	Netherlands	Germany[a]	France	United States
Okun's law[b] coefficients (the impact of GDP growth on unemployment rates)							
1971–98	–.13	–.37	–.35	–.37	–.30	–.22	–.39
1971–82	–.13	–.34	–.18	–.30	–.31	–.21	–.39
1982–98	–.19	–.37	–.41	–.62	–.32	–.35	–.41
1990–98	–.17	–.52	–.50	–.38	–.24	–.39	–.37
Normal growth rates							
1971–98	0.027	0.024	0.047	0.027	0.030	0.027	0.027
1971–82	0.032	0.028	0.048	0.029	0.027	0.035	0.030
1982–98	0.024	0.022	0.046	0.024	0.032	0.023	0.024
1990–98	0.023	0.019	0.053	0.024	0.038	0.020	0.020
Components of normal growth rates							
Productivity growth							
1971–98	0.021	0.017	0.036	0.016	0.017	0.021	0.009
1971–82	0.026	0.017	0.035	0.023	0.021	0.026	0.006
1982–98	0.019	0.018	0.035	0.011	0.013	0.018	0.010
1990–98	0.016	0.020	0.033	0.008	0.009	0.015	0.010
Labour force growth							
1971–98	0.006	0.006	0.012	0.011	0.013	0.007	0.018
1971–82	0.006	0.010	0.012	0.007	0.005	0.009	0.024
1982–98	0.005	0.004	0.012	0.013	0.018	0.005	0.014
1990–98	0.007	–0.001	0.02	0.016	0.028	0.005	0.012

[a] Due to reunification the German data presented here are distorted.
[b] Okun's law was estimated as: $(uer_t - uer_{t-1}) = \beta(gdp_t - \text{average}(gdp))$.
Source: Computations based on OECD Labour Force and National Accounts statistics and OECD: *Economic Outlook*, OECD CD-ROM.

force growth in order to achieve a constant unemployment rate. The normal growth rate and its components are shown in the lower panel of table 2.8.

The decomposition of the "normal growth rates" into productivity growth and growth of the labour force reveals the major difference between economic developments in Europe and the United States. "Normal growth" in Europe is dominated by productivity growth, whereas labour force growth predominates in the United States. It may come as a surprise that the successful European economies have not achieved their unemployment reduction through low productivity growth rates, but are in fact around the European average in this respect, and in some cases substantially above it (Ireland). Only the Netherlands may arguably have achieved employment success through low productivity growth.

Employment elasticity of economic growth

The fact that in many European countries employment has stagnated at a time when their GDP growth was positive has been interpreted by some commentators as "jobless growth". As a description of the situation this term seems appropriate, but it is mistaken if interpreted as implying a causal relationship between economic growth and productivity growth. As a causal relationship, "jobless growth" would require that productivity growth be endogenous to economic growth with a coefficient of at least unity. Under this condition, economic growth would raise productivity proportionally or to an even greater extent, and employment would indeed stagnate or shrink despite rising GDP growth rates. However, this scarcely fits the situation in highly industrialized countries. Productivity growth has slowed since the early 1970s and has not risen as one would expect under "jobless growth" scenarios. Furthermore, the relation between economic growth and productivity growth – the so-called Kaldor-Verdoorn relation – has become weaker rather than stronger.

An entirely different question is, however, whether GDP growth rates are high enough to increase employment – so-called employment thresholds or normal growth rates, which are essentially the rates of productivity growth – and whether such growth rates can be achieved given the relatively high rates of productivity growth in most European countries (see below). As table 2.8 shows, productivity growth is declining everywhere but at very different rates: it is substantially lower in the United States than in the European countries, although figures for the Netherlands are remarkably close to those of the United States.

The four European economies have achieved high or increasing employment-to-population ratios with GDP growth rates which are not too different from those of the rest of Europe. Has the employment elasticity of economic growth risen, and if so, what explains this? It is well known that the "employment miracle" in the United States is largely based on a high employment elasticity of economic growth, rather than on high rates of economic growth itself (Schettkat, 1992; Freeman, 1988; Buttler et al., 1996).[14] Therefore, it is important to analyse the relation between employment growth and economic growth in the four economies and investigate whether higher employment elasticities distinguish them from the rest of Europe.

- What factors may cause the employment elasticity of economic growth to vary? As mentioned above, a weaker impact of economic growth on productivity growth would increase the employment elasticity. This may happen because service industries come to outweigh manufacturing industries in which economic growth may have induced more investment and thus endogenous productivity growth (Kaldor's engine of growth), rather than employment growth.
- If labour markets become more flexible, that is, if labour input can be adjusted more easily to match demand variations, the relationship between employment and economic growth will strengthen.
- A decline in average hours worked may have contrary effects on the employment elasticity of economic growth, depending on the circumstances. With

rising employment and positive GDP growth rates, the employment elasticity of GDP will rise, assuming that shorter working hours require more persons to be employed. However, with falling employment, a reduction in hours worked will – again assuming a positive effect of such a reduction on employed persons – reduce the employment elasticity of GDP growth. An evaluation of the impact of working hours on employment elasticity will therefore need to include a check for potential asymmetries.

This section contains an analysis of differences in employment elasticities over time and between countries. The coefficients in regressions of changes in employment on GDP growth may differ depending on the definition of employment used: different results may be obtained if employment is measured in overall hours worked (working volume) rather than in persons employed. The real world, however, places many constraints on researchers: information on hours worked is not regarded as very reliable (see the warnings on hours worked in table E of *Employment Outlook*, 1998, p. 206), and is available for only a few countries. Nevertheless, the following analysis uses both persons employed and working volume, in order to gain an impression of the effects that variations in hours may have had on employment.

Trends in average working hours vary remarkably between countries, although their impact on persons employed is not obvious at all. Table 2.9 shows the enormous decline in average hours worked in the Netherlands, but the employment-to-population ratio of the Netherlands is 14 percentage points below that in the United States, where average hours worked have remained roughly constant. Nevertheless, the Netherlands has increased its employment-to-population ratio substantially. The reduction in average hours worked is mainly an effect of part-time working; the Netherlands is the only "part-time economy in the world" (Freeman, 1998; see also table 2.9 and Hartog, 1998). Working volume per head of population (15–65 years) has declined in the European economies, in stark contrast to the United States, where it has grown.

These trends seem to support the scepticism of many economists of the view that "working less" can bring more people into production. Few would contest that shorter working hours – given a set GDP growth rate – will increase employment, but that GDP is endogenous and not exogenous. The positive employment effect of shorter working hours may be compensated or even over-compensated by counter-effects such as higher wage costs, increasing non-wage costs, productivity growth (through higher capital intensity), reductions in flexibility and rising labour supply. To analyse these effects in depth requires a complex econometric model, which is not available for the present chapter.

Figure 2.7 gives an overview of the trends in GDP growth and employment variations. In general, GDP growth rates are positive but their relation to employment growth rates seems to vary substantially between countries and

Table 2.9 Comparison of different employment measures

Year	Austria	Denmark	Ireland	Netherlands	Germany	France	United States
Employment population ratios (%)							
1970	66.9	73.7	62.8	61.6	68.8	66.0	61.9
1980	67.5	73.6	58.6	55.4	66.1	64.1	65.9
1990	64.2	74.1	53.9	54.8	64.8	60.6	72.2
1998	61.9	74.3	58.4	60.2	61.1	59.2	74.1
Actual working hours (per employee per year)							
1970	n.a.	n.a.	n.a.	1 916.0	1 949.1	1 962.5	1 913.9
1980	n.a.	n.a.	n.a.	1 611.0	1 748.5	1 809.8	1 883.4
1990	n.a.	n.a.	n.a.	1 433.0	1 616.0	1 668.1	1 942.6
1996	n.a.	n.a.	n.a.	1 372.0	1 553.0	1 630.8[a]	1 951.0
Working volume (1970 = 100)							
1970	n.a.	n.a.	n.a.	100.0	100.0	100.0	100.0
1980	n.a.	n.a.	n.a.	86.8	91.1	97.3	124.2
1990	n.a.	n.a.	n.a.	84.0	88.9	92.3	153.3
1998	n.a.	n.a.	n.a.	88.1	83.3	89.4	164.2
Working volume per head of population aged 15–65 and standardized working time of 1,950 hours							
1970	n.a.	n.a.	n.a.	60.5	68.8	66.4	60.8
1980	n.a.	n.a.	n.a.	45.8	59.3	59.5	63.6
1990	n.a.	n.a.	n.a.	40.2	53.7	51.8	71.9
1998	n.a.	n.a.	n.a.	41.0	49.6	49.4	73.1
Part-time work as a share of total employment[b]							
1983	n.a.	n.a.	n.a.	n.a.	n.a.	n.a.	n.a.
1990	n.a.	19.9	10.7	27.3	13.2	12.6	13.8
1996	10.8	17.0	15.7	29.4	15.0	14.8	13.2
Women's share of part-time employment[b]							
1983	n.a.	n.a.	n.a.	n.a.	n.a.	n.a.	n.a.
1990	n.a.	72.4	74.1	69.4	91.7	79.6	68.2
1996	89.9	66.7	74.9	78.5	87.6	78.8	69.8

n.a. = not available. [a] France 1995. [b] Part-time usually means less than 30 hours per week; break in the series after 1990 (see OECD: *Employment Outlook* 1998, table E, page 206).
Source: OECD, Labour Force Statistics, *Employment Outlook*, OECD CD-ROM.

over time. A brief look at the graph for the Netherlands suggests that the recent employment success cannot be just an "hours artefact", since growth rates for working volume have been positive since the early 1980s. This distinguishes the Netherlands from those other European economies for which data on total hours worked are available (i.e. Germany and France), where the growth rates for working volume are around zero and often actually negative (see also table 2.9).

Table 2.10 shows estimates of employment elasticities. The figures in the upper panels give coefficients for employment elasticities where the dependent variable is the deviation of employment growth from the mean, and the

Figure 2.7 GDP growth rates, employment growth rates, and growth rates of working volume (difference of natural logs)

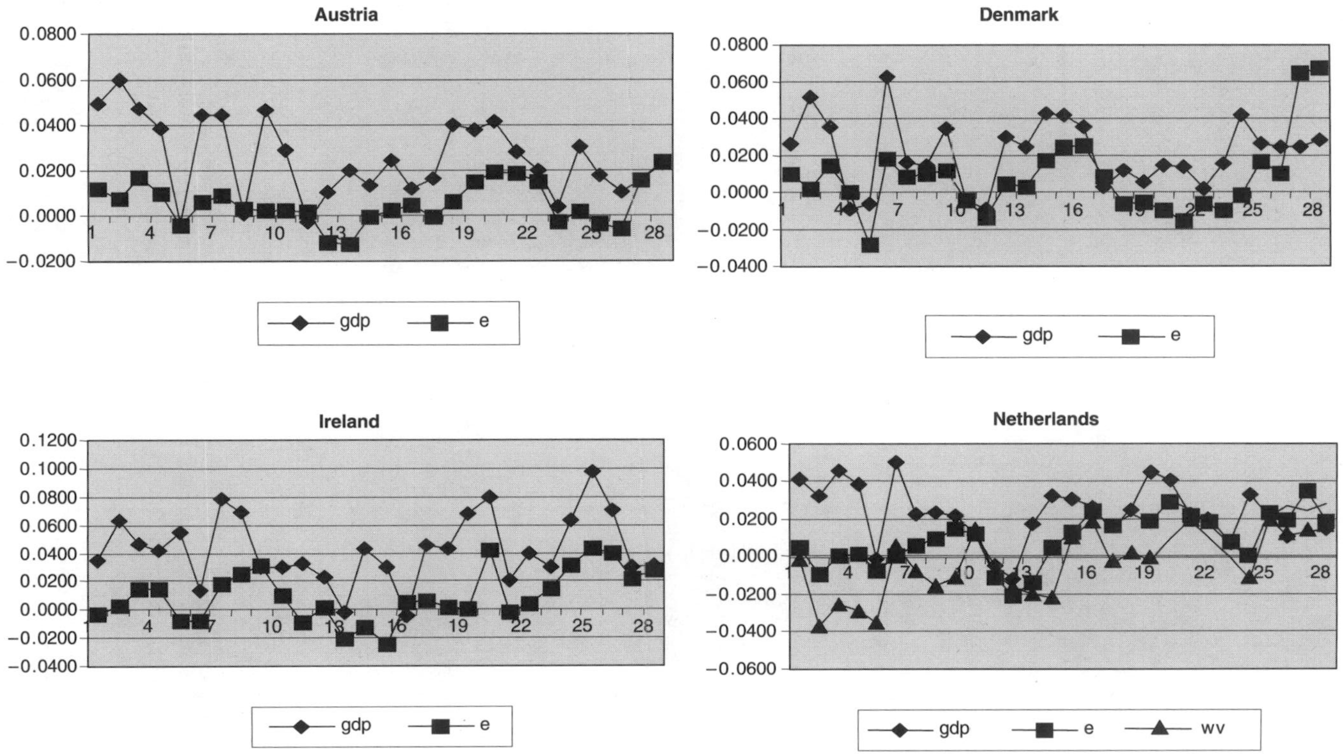

Figure 2.7 (continued)

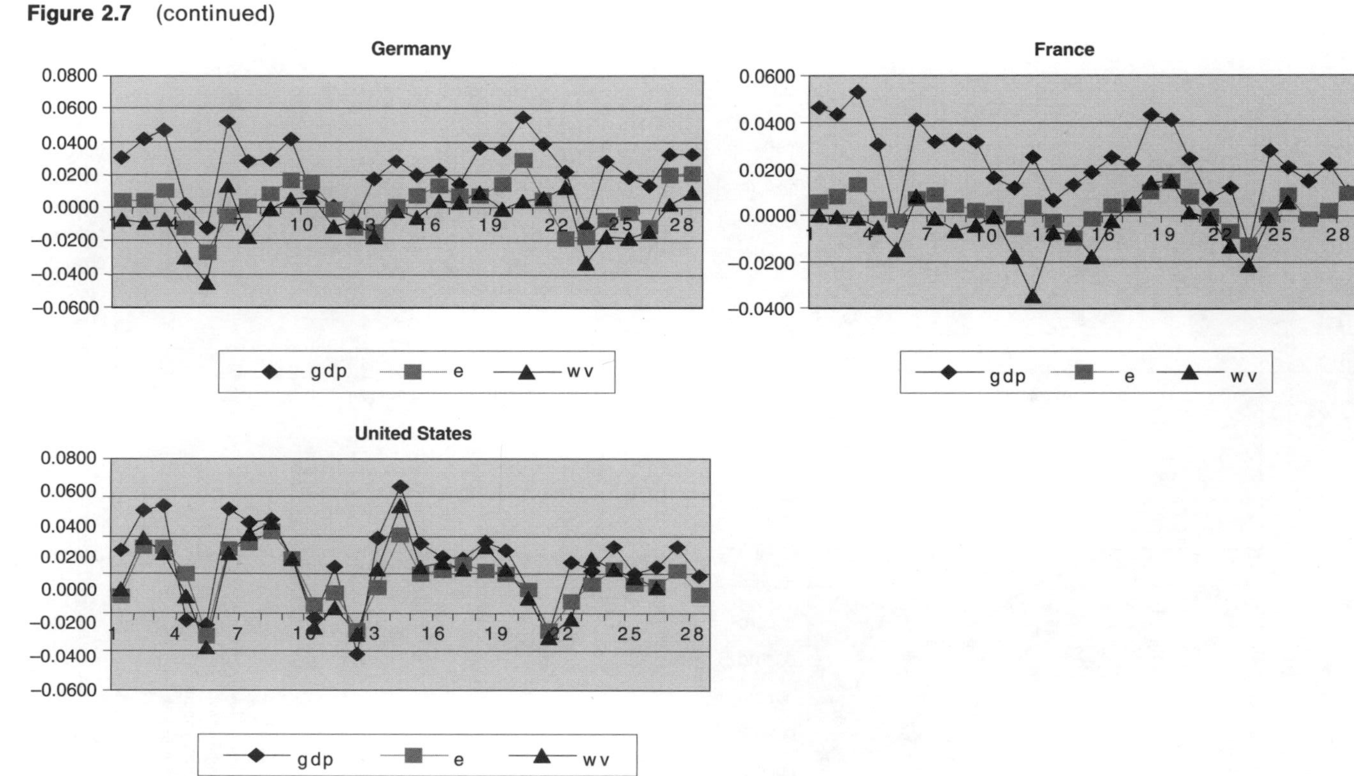

Key: gdp: gross domestic product e: employment wv: volume of working hours

Note: Numbers 1–28 correspond to annual observations for the years 1970–97.

Source: Calculations based on OECD: *Employment Outlook*, OECD CD-ROM. Working volume is estimated by multiplying average hours worked (according to *Employment Outlook*) by number of people in employment.

Table 2.10 Employment elasticities and intensities of economic growth

Period	Austria	Denmark	Ireland	Netherlands	Germany[a]	France	United States
Coefficients (employed persons)							
1972–98	.46	.78	.72	.59	.55	.45	.77
1972–82	.29	.71	.65	.00	.62	.34	.81
1982–90	.53	.84	.00	.70	.57	.67	.64
1990–98	.80	.78	.62	.76	.40	.67	.90
Working volume (hours)[b]							
1972–98				.00	.50	.38	.98
1972–82				.67	.57	.34	.98
1982–90				.74	.00	.00	.72
1990–98				.70	.47	.56	.98
Means of variables							
*Mean employment growth rate (log difference *100)*							
1972–98	.39	.40	.98	.88	−.05	.30	1.82
1972–82	.58	.26	.77	.19	.13	.44	2.22
1982–90	.02	.90	−.57	.82	.32	.32	1.95
1990–98	.49	.11	2.62	1.79	−.59	.10	1.22
*Mean working volume growth rate (log difference *100)*							
1972–98				−.48	−.70	−.45	1.91
1972–82				−1.37	−.94	−.41	1.99
1982–90				−.41	−.23	−.46	2.50
1990–98				.80	−.85	−.51	1.10
*Mean GDP growth rate (log difference *100)*							
1972–98	2.56	2.14	4.55	2.49	2.33	2.43	2.74
1972–82	3.23	1.93	4.50	2.57	2.45	3.06	3.02
1982–90	2.17	2.44	3.05	2.26	2.07	2.46	3.11
1990–98	2.12	2.11	5.93	2.58	2.40	1.62	2.06
Employment intensities (employment growth/GDP growth *100)							
Employed persons							
1972–98	15.2	18.7	21.5	35.3	−2.1	12.3	66.4
1972–82	18.0	13.5	17.1	7.4	5.3	14.4	73.5
1982–90	0.9	36.9	−18.7	36.3	15.5	13.0	62.7
1990–98	23.1	5.2	44.2	69.4	−24.6	6.2	59.2
Working volume							
1972–98				−19.3	−30	−18.5	69.7
1972–82				−53.3	−38.4	−13.4	65.9
1982–90				−18.1	−11.1	−18.7	80.4
1990–98				31	−35.4	−31.5	53.4

[a] Due to reunification the German data are distorted. [b] Working volume equals average hours worked times employment (*Employment Outlook*, various years).

The reported employment elasticities are based on the model:
$(\Delta \ln E_t - \text{mean}(\Delta \ln E)) = \alpha + \beta_1(\Delta \ln Y_t - \text{mean}(\Delta \ln Y)) + \beta 2(\Delta \ln Y_{t-1} - \text{mean}(\Delta \ln Y))$, reported coefficients are $\beta_1 + \beta_2$.

$\Delta \ln$ = first difference in logs, E = total employment, Y = GDP.

Source: Regressions based on OECD data (*Economic Outlook*, various years); figures for 1998 are estimates.

independent variable is the deviation of GDP growth from the mean. Employment is measured in persons employed (top panel) and in overall hours worked (second panel from the top). The regression analysis clearly shows that there is no such thing as jobless growth in a causal sense: above-average GDP growth leads to higher employment growth and vice versa.

Very high coefficients (not only for persons in employment but also for working volume) are recorded for the United States. One explanation may be easier hiring and firing procedures and therefore a closer match between labour input and economic output. This would appear to be confirmed by the high coefficients in Denmark, where constraints on dismissals are relatively low (Kongshoj Madsen, 1999), which seem to have an impact on labour turnover (Schettkat 1996). Another interpretation for the high American coefficients could be that employment elasticity is high when employment is growing, especially if it is growing over long periods; the United States experienced only three years in which employment declined during the 28 years covered by the analysis. Due to lack of data, this hypothesis cannot be tested here.

To summarize, higher GDP growth positively affects employment, whether measured in persons or in working hours. In the United States this relationship is strong, but it also became quite strong in the successful European economies in the 1980s and 1990s. However, a major difference between the United States and the successful European economies (for which data are available), on the one hand, and the other Western European countries, on the other, is the strong growth in working volume in the former, compared with a decline in Germany and France. The Netherlands initially experienced the same negative trend in working volume, but working volume started to grow once more in the 1990s. Thus the Netherlands' employment success is not simply an "artefact" of part-time work. The employment creation potential can also be evaluated using so-called employment intensities, that is, the employment growth divided by GDP growth. These can be misleading, however, because shrinking employment will produce a negative intensity (compare the lower panel of table 2.10), which should not be interpreted as a causal relationship. As discussed previously, the United States is an exception with respect to the employment intensity of economic growth. But there are two sides to this coin: high employment growth at given rates of GDP growth is accompanied by low productivity and wage growth, whereas the most favourable situation is certainly high employment growth accompanied by high income growth.

Employment rates and sectoral trends

Employment trends are presented in terms of ratios of employment to population, i.e. standardized with respect to the population of working age (15–65 years). There are substantial differences between Denmark and the rest of Europe, where employment-to-population ratios are substantially lower. Denmark's ratio actually exceeds that of the United States and has remained

Table 2.11 Employment-to-population ratios by sector (civilian employment/population, aged 15–65)

Year	Austria	Denmark	Ireland	Netherlands	Germany	United States
Agriculture						
1970	9.7	8.4	16.6	3.5	5.9	2.8
1980	6.7	5.3	10.4	2.6	3.4	2.3
1990	5.2	4.2	7.8	2.8	2.3	2.1
1996	5.0	2.9	6.0	2.6	2.1	2.1
Manufacturing						
1970	27.5	27.6	18.3	22.3	33.4	21.3
1980	25.5	24.1	18.5	16.7	28.4	20.1
1990	24.2	21.0	14.9	16.0	25.3	18.9
1996	22.9	19.8	15.2	14.8	24.1	17.4
Services						
1970	29.2	36.9	26.5	31.5	28.5	37.9
1980	31.2	44.6	28.0	33.8	33.1	43.4
1990	36.2	51.0	29.3	42.0	36.1	51.2
1996	41.2	50.5	34.8	48.7	38.0	53.4

Source: Calculations based on OECD Labour Force Statistics, OECD CD-ROM.

constant at a level of about 74 per cent since the 1970s. By contrast, the United States only reached this level in the 1990s: its 1970s ratio was well below that of many European countries (see Freeman/Schettkat, 1998, for a discussion). Measured in terms of employment-to-population ratios, Denmark is clearly the champion. Austria's employment-to-population ratio comes close to the 70 per cent mark, and soon the Netherlands may also attain this level. However, the most remarkable achievement of the Netherlands has been the reversal of the downward trend in the 1980s. Ireland, which still had an agricultural employment-to-population ratio of 17 per cent in the 1970s, still has a substantially lower employment-to-population ratio than the rest of Europe. It is also the only country where manufacturing employment has increased rather than declined. All other economies have faced a shrinking manufacturing sector (as measured by employment-to-population ratios).

Employment gains have been concentrated in the service industries and at first glance this seems to explain the differences in employment levels (table 2.11). Countries differ remarkably in their service employment-to-population ratios, although a rising trend can be observed everywhere. Yet Germany, for example, had the same service employment-to-population ratio at the end of the 1990s as Denmark and the United States in the early 1970s. The level in Ireland is even lower than that in Germany, while levels in the other countries fall between these extremes. The employment potential obviously lies mainly in service industries (Appelbaum/Schettkat, 1996). Austria and the Netherlands have increased their employment-to-population ratios in the service industries by 10 and 14 percentage points respectively, and Denmark – already at a remarkably high level in 1980 – has actually increased its employment-to-population ratio by more than Germany, which started from a much lower level.

Service demand and service employment are often explained with reference to income levels. The higher the income, the more services are consumed as a proportion of income, because services are regarded as satisfying higher needs (for a discussion, see Appelbaum/Schettkat, 1996). Income differences may help to explain the United States/Europe dichotomy (Freeman/Schettkat, 1998), but they can hardly serve as an explanation for differences within the leading Western European countries, where per capita income differentials are relatively small.

It is true that the United States has a high share of service employment and high wage differentials. However, in Denmark – a typical Scandinavian country with comparatively low wage dispersion (see table 2.1) – service employment is almost as high in relative terms as in the United States. If anything, the relation between service sector employment and wage differentials is U-shaped rather than linear (Appelbaum/Schettkat, 1996).

Wage trends

Wage growth (as measured by hourly wages in manufacturing) in the Netherlands has been substantially below that in Germany and France (table 2.12). The growth of real wages has been substantially below 1 per cent in most years since 1983 (the Wassenaar Agreement was concluded in the winter of 1982; see Hartog, 1998, for details). This is the basis for the graph on wage trends in the Netherlands that has appeared in almost all newspapers, suggesting that wage restraint was the basis of employment expansion in that country. Wage restraint also seems to have played a role in the other three economies, although it has certainly been less pronounced there than in the Netherlands. The trend in the United States is similar to that in the Netherlands, but includes periods of real-wage decline.

Wage trend differentials emerge very clearly in table 2.13, which summarizes developments on the basis of indices. In the United States, real hourly earnings were in 1990 about 7.5 per cent below the 1980 value, and even in 1998 (after a long expansionary period in the American economy) about 4 per cent below the 1980 level. By contrast, all the European countries increased their real-wage levels in comparison with the level in 1980, although the Netherlands did so only very modestly. Wages rose quite substantially in Austria, Denmark and Ireland, and wage growth in Austria and Ireland actually exceeded that in France. Again, the story appears to be less simple than the common view suggests.

Wages rose substantially less than productivity in the four economies (lower panel of table 2.13), but productivity growth was quite uneven. In Ireland, it had

Table 2.12 Nominal and real hourly wage growth

Year	Nominal hourly wage growth (manufacturing)							Real hourly wage growth (manufacturing)						
	Austria	Denmark	Ireland	Netherlands	Germany	France	United States	Austria	Denmark	Ireland	Netherlands	Germany	France	United States
Annual growth rates														
1971	15.10	n.a.	16.08	12.07	13.57	12.85	6.46	10.11		6.64	4.17	8.46	6.87	1.95
1972	13.11	12.29	14.85	13.23	10.77	10.28	7.00	6.63	4.13	5.20	4.97	5.18	3.95	3.49
1973	13.54	19.23	18.96	13.32	12.26	14.61	7.00	6.96	7.53	7.40	4.79	5.74	7.24	1.60
1974	15.65	21.50	20.30	16.90	15.12	18.90	8.30	5.64	6.51	4.60	7.37	7.97	4.08	−1.83
1975	18.12	18.86	28.75	13.70	11.15	18.85	9.04	10.24	8.91	10.76	3.61	5.15	7.01	0.90
1976	8.32	12.89	17.01	8.79	6.07	15.09	8.06	1.78	3.04	−3.04	−0.20	1.87	5.22	2.37
1977	8.86	10.07	16.06	7.06	8.74	12.57	8.77	3.24	−0.53	1.93	0.92	5.47	3.13	2.14
1978	5.68	10.37	14.47	5.79	6.95	13.21	8.73	1.52	1.12	6.52	1.37	4.32	4.09	1.46
1979	5.38	11.31	15.53	4.44	6.53	13.26	8.52	0.85	0.87	0.63	−0.42	2.36	2.50	−0.48
1980	7.21	11.43	21.18	4.65	8.51	15.73	8.70	0.84	0.71	2.59	−2.15	2.69	2.44	−2.16
1981	6.76	9.44	16.49	3.32	7.05	14.97	9.84	−0.86	−2.61	−3.12	−3.03	0.85	1.93	0.89
1982	6.55	9.97	14.46	6.76	5.63	15.76	6.31	0.50	−0.28	−0.47	1.71	0.55	4.23	0.54
1983	4.83	6.61	11.56	2.56	4.02	9.85	3.87	1.44	−0.15	2.33	−0.31	0.82	0.19	−0.68
1984	3.63	4.70	10.45	1.18	3.31	8.47	4.08	−1.97	−1.68	3.10	−0.76	0.79	0.76	0.28
1985	5.70	4.79	8.67	4.89	3.91	7.14	3.81	2.39	0.45	3.70	2.54	2.13	1.38	0.12
1986	4.47	4.74	7.55	1.60	5.05	5.14	2.07	2.55	1.88	2.96	1.31	5.61	2.48	−0.78
1987	4.96	9.35	5.78	1.39	5.08	4.62	1.82	3.99	4.76	3.37	1.17	4.61	1.46	−1.98
1988	3.36	6.45	5.31	1.28	4.22	3.90	2.79	1.92	2.50	−0.12	0.75	2.88	1.25	−1.36
1989	4.49	4.75	4.79	1.35	4.21	4.75	2.90	1.74	0.45	2.31	0.15	1.29	1.31	−1.99
1990	7.20	4.80	5.35	2.94	5.51	4.81	3.30	3.91	2.08	3.25	0.72	2.86	1.97	−1.76
1991	5.94	4.46	5.65	3.84	7.37	5.43	3.26	2.58	2.02	2.73	0.65	3.63	2.26	−0.94
1992	5.83	3.31	4.77	4.33	9.62	4.36	2.43	1.95	1.29	2.24	1.20	4.93	1.97	−0.86
1993	4.92	2.45	5.65	3.25	6.81	3.48	2.52	1.48	2.02	3.80	1.11	2.79	1.25	−0.12
1994	3.82	2.42	2.33	1.85	2.06	3.63	2.75	0.81	0.57	−0.29	−0.87	−0.85	1.51	0.36
1995	4.38	3.86	2.28	1.08	4.20	1.48	2.52	2.12	1.74	0.24	0.17	2.29	−0.08	0.15

Table 2.12 (continued)

Year	Nominal hourly wage growth (manufacturing)							Real hourly wage growth (manufacturing)						
	Austria	Denmark	Ireland	Netherlands	Germany	France	United States	Austria	Denmark	Ireland	Netherlands	Germany	France	United States
1996	3.30	4.08	3.00	1.60	4.38	2.73	3.27	1.37	2.02	1.24	−0.18	2.45	0.95	1.18
1997	2.20	4.30	3.00	2.10	2.00	2.57	3.55	0.20	2.10	1.00	0.30	0.35	1.00	1.32
1998	2.40	4.80	4.00	2.50	2.70	2.33	3.70	0.50	2.10	1.30	0.60	0.95	0.89	1.28
Standard deviation														
1971–80	4.55	4.38	4.32	4.4	3.1	2.74	0.91	3.65	3.39	3.92	2.99	2.22	1.84	1.86
1981–90	1.32	2.21	4.11	1.85	1.09	4.35	2.38	1.91	2.14	2.23	1.55	1.75	1.09	1.08
1990–98	1.43	0.9	1.39	1.14	2.78	1.25	0.5	0.83	0.54	1.33	0.68	1.86	0.72	0.92
1971–98	4.23	5.25	6.99	4.56	3.44	5.55	2.67	2.9	2.59	2.99	2.21	2.32	2.02	1.5

Note: Real wage growth = nominal wage growth – consumer price. n.a. = not available.
Source: Calculations based on OECD: *Employment Outlook*, CD-ROM.

Table 2.13 Indices for real hourly earnings, real household disposable income, real household disposable income per capita (aged 15–65) and productivity

Year	Austria	Denmark	Ireland	Netherlands	Germany	France	United States
Real hourly earnings (manufacturing)							
1970	64.8	n.a.	68.9	80.3	63.4	66.0	91.4
1980	100.0	100.0	100.0	100.0	100.0	100.0	100.0
1990	116.3	107.4	118.1	104.3	124.3	117.0	93.7
1994	124.1	113.8	128.1	106.4	137.2	125.2	92.3
1998	129.3	122.9	133.0	107.3	145.4	128.7	95.9
Real household disposable income							
1970	69.6	88.5	n.a.	73.4	72.8	72.1	73.2
1980	100.0	100.0	100.0	100.0	100.0	100.0	100.0
1990	131.4	108.7	116.7	121.3	124.2	120.9	132.6
1994	143.3	121.1	134.5	125.6	150.2	128.2	142.0
1998	147.6	137.9	161.2	137.9	159.6	136.6	160.3
Real household disposable income per capita (15–65 years)							
1970	73.4	92.4	n.a.	84.3	77.0	78.2	86.8
1980	100.0	100.0	100.0	100.0	100.0	100.0	100.0
1990	122.3	104.1	108.8	110.2	115.4	111.0	121.4
1994	128.3	114.4	118.4	111.6	110.4	116.1	125.7
1998	n.a.	n.a.	n.a.	n.a.	n.a.	n.a.	n.a.
Productivity (GDP per employed person)							
1970	74.4	83.6	69.1	77.4	77.7	76.2	92.7
1980	100.0	100.0	100.0	100.0	100.0	100.0	100.0
1990	121.0	116.4	144.6	114.1	118.3	122.7	111.3
1994	127.2	129.3	161.0	118.2	113.4	129.2	115.6
1998	137.0	136.1	187.6	121.3	125.5	138.2	120.0

n.a. = not available.
Source: Calculations based on OECD Labour Force Statistics, *Economic Outlook*, OECD CD-ROM.

skyrocketed by 1998 to 190 per cent of its 1980 level. This compares to productivity increases of about 20 per cent in the Netherlands and the United States. It is important to point out, however, that productivity is measured as GDP per employed person, and the average number of hours worked fell in the Netherlands, but not in the United States. Productivity per hour worked is therefore understated for the Netherlands (and for most European countries compared with the United States). This means that the difference between real-wage growth (per hour) and productivity in the Netherlands is even more remarkable. So in general productivity growth remained much higher in Europe than in the United States. There may, however, be statistical reasons for this, such as the underestimation of real growth in service industries (compare with the discussion on the consumer price index in the *Journal of Economic Perspectives*, 1997).[15]

Wages are one thing, but disposable household income is what actually matters to most people. Per capita income depends both on the wage rate and on the employment-to-population ratio. Disposable income is also influenced by tax rates and thus, at least indirectly, again by the employment-to-population ratio. Even with constant wages, per capita income can increase if a larger proportion of the population becomes employed, and this trend may be reinforced by declining taxes, or offset by rising taxes (for a more systematic discussion, see Schettkat, 1992).

Comparing the figures in the second and third panels of table 2.13 clearly shows that the successful European economies achieved a substantial part of their income growth through increasing labour input. Real household disposable income rose much more than real household disposable income per capita, reflecting the rising employment-to-population ratios discussed above. With respect to real per capita household disposable income, Denmark, the Netherlands and Ireland do not perform particularly impressively, but actually very similarly to the rest of Europe. The United States achieved quite high growth in real per capita household disposable income, but differences in working time trends must be taken into account when comparing this with European performance. If average working hours decline in accordance with preferences (see Bell/Freeman, 1996), "working less" represents as much of an "income increase" as "earning more".

Notes

[1] Labels used include "Celtic Tiger", "Fully-Fledged Tiger" (*International Herald Tribune*, 15/16 Aug. 1998), "Dutch Miracle", "Polder Model", "Dutch Lion" and "Danish Miracle", "Northern Star" (*Financial Times*, 30 Nov. 1998).

[2] For a summary of these debates, see Freeman (1995), Wood (1993).

[3] The first may be called "traditional Keynesian" and the second "new-classical macroeconomics".

[4] Most economists accept the broad thrust of the "Lucas critique", which essentially says that people learn from experience, and that predictions of policy effects cannot simply be based on econometric estimates of historic data. However, Lucas closed the model with the assumption of rational expectations, which is an extreme assumption (Blinder, 1989; Schettkat, 1997).

[5] Blinder (1989) argues that the Phillips curve is very stable once external demand shocks are controlled for.

[6] The natural rate of unemployment and the NAIRU are often used as synonyms, although there is a distinction between the two concepts (see Franz, 1991).

[7] Short-term does not mean that the positive effects of a expansionary policy are negligible. But in the long run small economies cannot disconnect their economic development from that of their main trading partners through expansionary fiscal policy to a significant degree (cf. Nowotny, 1999).

[8] In open economies with free capital flows, the impact of the public deficit on the national capital market should be negligible.

[9] It is traditionally argued that wage contracts are nominal contracts and that real wages are only determined after price setting. This is formally correct but actually unions take inflation into account when they set their wage demands.

[10] Although the Bundesbank is required to orient its policy towards general economic policy requirements, this task is explicitly subordinate to its mission to safeguard the stability of the currency. This is usually interpreted as domestic price stability (low inflation) and less as external

stability (exchange rate). The United States Federal Reserve, which is as independent as the Bundesbank, has to take employment and the stability of the currency into account (see Blinder, 1998). The European Central Bank (ECB) is designed along the same lines as the Bundesbank and thus has price stability as its primary objective.

[11] Nominal exchange rates (E) are defined as: E = domestic currency/foreign currency.

[12] The real exchange rates (ε) are here defined as: ε = domestic currency/DM * German price level/domestic price level. Price levels used are GDP price deflators. Since GDP price trends relate to the economy as a whole (i.e. not only to industries producing traded products but also to "sheltered" industries), the real exchange rates probably underestimate actual depreciation since inflation in traded products can be expected to be lower.

[13] For a real depreciation to result in trade balance improvements, the Marshall-Lerner condition must hold, i.e. domestic demand for foreign goods (imports) and foreign demand for domestic goods (exports) must be price elastic.

[14] There are remarkable inter-country differences in employment thresholds (see: Boltho/Glyn, 1995; Appelbaum/Schettkat, 1996).

[15] Germany's low productivity level largely reflects a "reunification effect" since most data are only available for the united Germany after 1990. Similar caveats hold for changes in income, which is upward biased if presented in absolute figures (see second panel from top in table 2.13) compared to the per capita figures (next panel).

Bibliography

Alesina, A.; Summers, L.H. 1993. "Central bank independence and macroeconomic performance: Some comparative evidence", in *Journal of Money, Credit and Banking*, Vol. 25, pp. 151–162.

Appelbaum, E.; Schettkat, R. 1996. "The increasing importance of institutions for employment performance", in G. Schmid et al. (eds.): *International Handbook of Labour Market Policy and Evaluation* (London, Edward Elgar), pp. 791–810.

Arrow, K. J. 1987. "Rationality of self and others in an economic system", in R. M. Hogarth and M. W. Reder (eds.): *Rational Choice* (Chicago, IL, and London, University of Chicago Press).

Bell, L. Freeman, R.B. 1996. "Why do Americans and Germans work different hours", in F. Buttler, W. Franz and D. Soskice (eds.): *Institutional frameworks and labour market performance* (London and New York, Routledge), pp. 101–131.

Blanchard, O. 1997. *Macroeconomics* (New Jersey, NJ, Prentice-Hall).

Blinder, A. S. 1989. "The rise and fall of Keynesian economics", in *Economic Record*, pp. 278–294.

——. 1998. *Central banking in theory and practice* (Cambridge, MA, MIT Press).

——; Solow, R. 1973. "Does fiscal policy matter?", in *Journal of Public Economics*, Vol. 2, pp. 329–337.

Boltho, A.; Glyn, A. 1995. "Can macroeconomic policies raise employment?", in *International Labour Review*, Vol. 134, No. 4–5, pp. 451–470.

Bruno, M. Sachs, J.D. 1985. *Economics of worldwide stagflation* (Cambridge, MA, Harvard University Press).

Buttler, F. et al. 1995. *Institutional framework and labour market performance* (London, Routledge), pp. 1–19.

Carlin, W. ; Soskice, D. 1990. *Macroeconomics and the wage bargain: A modern approach to employment, inflation and the exchange rate* (New York, Oxford University Press).

Dehejia, V.H.; Genschel, P. 1998. *Tax competition in the European Union* (Cologne, Max Planck Institute for the Study of Societies).

Eatwell, J. 1997. "Effective demand and disguised unemployment", in J. Michie and J. Grieve Smith (eds.): *Employment and economic performance* (New York, Oxford University Press), pp. 76–94.

Fazzari, S.M. 1994. "Why doubt the effectiveness of Keynesian fiscal policy?", in *Journal of Post Keynesian Economics*, Vol. 17, No. 2, pp. 231–248.

Franz, W. 1999. *Arbeitsökonomik* (Heidelberg, Springer).

Freeman, R. B. 1988. "Labour markets", in *Economic Policy,* Apr., pp. 64–80.

——. 1995. "Are your wages set in Beijing?", in *Journal of Economic Perspectives,* Vol. 32, No. 9, pp. 15–32.

——. 1998. "War of the models: Which labour market institutions for the 21st century?", in *Labour Economics*, Vol. 5, No. 1, pp. 1–24.

Freeman, R. B.; Schettkat, R. 1998. *From McDonald's to McKinsey: Comparing German and US employment and wage structures* (Washington, DC, National Bureau of Economic Research).

——; ——. 2000. "Low wage services: Interpreting the US–German difference", in M. Gregory and W. Salverda (eds.): *Labour market inequalities* (Oxford, Oxford University Press).

Giavazzi, F.; Pagano, M. 1990. "Can severe fiscal contraction be expansionary?", in *NBER Macroeconomic Annual*, (Washington, DC, National Bureau of Economic Research), pp. 75–110.

Glyn, A. 1997. "Paying for job creation", in J. Michie and J. Grieve Smith (eds.): *Employment and economic performance* (New York, Doubleday), pp. 221–233.

Harcourt, R.B. 1997. "Economic policy, accumulation, and productivity", in J. Michie and J. Grieve Smith (eds.): *Employment and economic performance* (New York, Oxford University Press), pp. 194–204.

Hartog, J. 1998. *ILO Country Employment Policy Review: The Netherlands* (Amsterdam, Universiteit Amsterdam).

Hunt, J. 1996. "The effect of unemployment compensation on unemployment duration in Germany", in *Journal of Labour Economics*, Vol. 13, No. 2, pp. 88–120.

Journal of Economic Perspectives. 1997. Supplement to Vol. 11, No. 3.

Kongshoj Madsen, P. 1996. *The self-organizing economy* (Cambridge, MA, Blackwell Publishers).

——. 1998. *ILO Country Employment Policy Review: Denmark* (Geneva, ILO).

——. 1999. *Denmark: Labour market recovery through labour market policy*, Employment and Training Paper No. 53 (Geneva, ILO).

Layard, R.; Nickell, S. 1987. "The labour market", in R. Dornbusch and R. Layard (eds.): *The performance of the British economy* (New York, Oxford University Press), pp. 131–179.

——; Nickell, S.; Jackman, R. 1991. *Unemployment: Macroeconomic performance and the labour market* (Oxford, Oxford University Press).

Lucas, R. E. J. 1976. "Econometric policy evaluation: A critique", in K. Brunner and A. Meltzer (eds.): *The Phillips curve and labor markets*, pp. 19–46.

——. 1998. "Unemployment: Questions and some answers", in *Economic Journal,* Vol. 108, No. 4, pp. 802–816.

——; Sargent, T. 1978. *After the Phillips curve: Persistence of high inflation and high unemployment* (Boston, MA, Federal Reserve Bank of Boston), pp. 43–72.

Nickell, S. 1997. "Unemployment and labor market rigidities: Europe versus North America", in *Journal of Economic Perspectives*, Vol. 11, No. 2, pp. 55–74.

——; Bell, B. 1996. "Changes in the distribution of wages on unemployment in the OECD countries", in *American Economic Review*, Vol. 86, No. 5, Papers and Proceedings, pp. 302–308.

Nowotny, E. 1999. "The role of macroeconomic policy in overcoming slow economic growth", in W. Filc (ed.): *Makrooekonomische Ursachen der Arbeitslosigkeit* (Berlin, Springer).

O'Connell, P. 1998. *ILO Country Employment Policy Review: Ireland* (Dublin, Economic and Social Research Institute).

Organisation for Economic Co-operation and Development (OECD). 1996. *Employment Outlook 1996* (Paris).

——. 1997a. *Economic Surveys: Austria 1996–1997* (Paris).

——. 1997b. *Economic Surveys: Denmark 1996-1997* (Paris).

——. 1997c. *Economic Surveys: Ireland 1996–1997* (Paris).

——. 1998. *Economic Surveys: Netherlands 1997–1998* (Paris).

——. Various years. *Statistical Compendium* (Paris).

Pichelmann, K.; Hofer, H. 1998. *ILO Country Employment Policy Review: Austria* (Geneva, ILO).

Robinson, P. 1997. "Is there a pay problem?", in J. Michie and J. Grieve Smith (eds.): *Employment and economic performance* (New York, Oxford University Press), pp. 177–193.

Scharpf, F.W. 1997. *Globalisierung als Beschränkung der Handlungsmöglichkeiten nationalstaatlicher Politik* (Cologne, Max Planck Institute for the Study of Societies).

Schettkat, R. 1992. *The labor market dynamics of economic restructuring: The United States and Germany in transition* (New York, Praeger).

——. 1996. "Labor market flows over the business cycle: An asymmetric hiring cost explanation", in *Journal of Theoretical and Institutional Economics*, Vol. 16, No. 3, pp. 641–653.

——. 1997. "Employment protection and labour mobility in Europe: An empirical analysis using the EU's Labour Force Survey", in *International Review of Applied Economics*, Vol. 11, No. 1, pp. 105–118.

——; Reijnders, J. 1998. *The disease that became a model. The economics behind the employment trends in the Netherlands*, EPI paper (Washington, DC, Economic Policy Institute).

Siebert, H. 1997. "Labor market rigidities: At the root of unemployment in Europe", in *Journal of Economic Perspectives*, Vol. 11, pp. 37–54.

Singh, A. 1997. "Liberalization and globalization: An unhealthy euphoria", in J. Michie and J. Grieve Smith (eds.): *Employment and economic performance* (New York, Oxford University Press), pp. 11–35.

Steiner, V. 1997. *Extended benefit–entitlement periods and the duration of unemployment in West Germany*, Discussion paper, Centre for European Economic Research (Brussels).

Teulings, C.; Hartog, J. 1998. *Corporatism or competition, labour contracts, institutions and wage structures in international comparison* (Cambridge, United Kingdom, Cambridge University Press).

Walter, S. 1998. *Taxation and the labour market* (Geneva; mimeo).

Wood, A. 1993. "Low wage competition from the South", in *Journal of Economic Perspectives,* Vol. 32, No. 9.

WORKING TIME: FROM REDISTRIBUTION TO MODERNIZATION

3

*Gerhard Bosch**

3.1 INTRODUCTION

Working time has become highly differentiated in all developed industrialized countries. Until the end of the 1960s, the single male breadwinner was the predominant family structure and policy on work redistribution was confined solely to a reduction in weekly working time or longer holidays. In both manufacturing and services, work organization in firms was based on the 8-hour day. The considerable reductions in working time were brought about by extending the weekend (no work on Saturdays) and increasing holiday entitlement, leaving work organization fundamentally unchanged. This traditional form of working time was assumed, almost unconsciously, to be the self-evident foundation of work organization. Thus standard individual working time was not just an externally imposed regulation but also found its counterpart in work organization at plant or establishment level and became second nature to both employees and firms.

Today, much has changed. There are now considerable differences in working time between women and men, and between young, old and prime-age (24–45 years) employees. There are three principal reasons for these changes. First, the structure of labour supply has changed. A growing proportion of workers is willing and able to work part time. The main driving forces here are increasing rates of economic activity among women and the growing numbers of young people combining work with education or training. Second, the rigid Taylorist forms of work organization have now become more flexible. The reasons lie in the growing importance of the service sector and in changed market conditions. Third, the working-time preferences of both employees and firms have become differentiated as a result of policies pursued not only by the State but also by the social partners. These policies are both a reaction to changed conditions (for example, the promotion of paid work for women or more flexible working hours) and an attempt to

* Institut Arbeit und Technik, Wissenschaftszentrum Nordrhein-Westfalen, Gelsenkirchen.

shape the conditions under which specific working-time preferences among both employees and employers have evolved in the various countries.

This chapter begins by examining the link between unemployment, employment and working time. Their connection is more complex than appears at first sight. The following effects can be identified:

- *Redistribution:* The reduction of collective or individual working time is intended to distribute the volume of work among a greater number of people.
- *Increase in the labour supply:* The differentiation of working-time forms makes it possible for individuals not in a position to work the hours traditionally worked by full-time employees to enter the labour market.
- *Reduction in the labour supply:* Certain forms of organizing working time over the life cycle (extension of education system, parental leave, early retirement) have the effect of reducing the labour supply.
- *Productivity effects:* Shorter working hours may lead to a reorganization of work, and productivity may rise due to higher work intensity or longer operating hours.
- *Effects on household production:* The duration and scheduling of working time influence the demand for goods and services in the market. Just as firms take "make or buy" decisions, so do households, choosing between "do-it-yourself" and purchasing goods and services on the market. Such decisions depend, of course, on the extent to which the market can provide acceptable alternatives to household production.

To date, research has focused primarily on short-term links between working time and employment/unemployment. However, the short-term perspective is inadequate, since labour market effects can occur with very different time lags. Thus when part-time work is expanded rapidly, as has recently happened in the Netherlands, the redistribution effect may predominate in the short term, but in the longer term labour supply may be considerably increased as a result of women being drawn into the labour market in greater numbers. As a result, the employment effect will depend crucially on the induced structural changes in labour supply. The shifting of household production into the market can lead to the creation of new jobs that absorb the increased labour supply. This link is the basis for certain theories of the service sector in which the "outsourcing" of household production as a result of changed family structures is regarded as the most important force driving the development of this sector.

Such long-term effects may mean that many of the current links identified between working time and employment are merely snapshots taken in the immediate aftermath of the change, just as certain working-time patterns caused by changes in labour market behaviour may be merely historical episodes. The title of this chapter is intended to suggest that today's working-time structures are not sustainable indefinitely, but will have to be adjusted to suit new patterns of labour market behaviour and changes in economic conditions. In this respect, all European countries are in a transitional phase.

The long-term development of working-time patterns will also depend crucially on how other spheres of economic and social policy evolve. A policy of work redistribution, for example, could be thwarted if incentives pushing in the opposite direction are created in other policy areas. Failure to take these reciprocal influences into account could lead to incompatibilities between different employment policy instruments, rendering them ineffective. Yet to a large extent they have been ignored by economists. In studies of the employment effects of collective working-time reductions, for example, the instrument is frequently examined out of context and out of time. Like any other instrument of economic policy, however, it can be ineffectual if implemented under certain conditions and very effective under others. Researchers need to investigate in much greater detail the conditions under which working time and employment interact with each other.

These wide-ranging connections can only be partially addressed here. A more detailed investigation would properly be the subject of a larger research project. Nevertheless, comparison of the evolution of work in the four selected countries provides a good starting point for gaining insight into some of the interactions and their dynamics. In all these countries, working time in recent years has been considerably reduced, albeit in very different ways and with a range of different instruments. Three of the four countries belong to the group with the shortest working hours in the world.

The working-time profiles of four countries (Austria, Denmark, Ireland and the Netherlands) and some of the factors shaping their specific profiles are outlined below. As far as possible, all four countries are compared. In some cases, however, data are not available for all countries. The linkage between the redistribution of work and employment, and between work organization and working time, is then examined. Particular attention is paid to the link between work organization and working time because it is only at the micro level of the plant or establishment that it becomes clear how the new economic challenges associated with globalization, the introduction of new technologies, or the expansion of the service sector influence working-time patterns. The results of this investigation are then summarized.

3.2 WORKING TIME IN AUSTRIA, DENMARK, IRELAND AND THE NETHERLANDS

Working-time profiles of the four countries

In order to sketch the working-time profiles of these four countries, it does not suffice to compare the average duration of working time. As it can be distributed very differently among different categories of workers, the distribution of working time must be investigated in tandem. Since decisions on working

Table 3.1 Normal working hours per week, per employee, 1996

Country	Full time			Part time			Total		
	Men	Women	Total	Men	Women	Total	Men	Women	Total
Austria	40.2	39.8	40.0	22.3	22,0	22.1	39.6	34.7	37.5
Denmark	39.4	39.3	38.7	13.5	21.2	19.1	36.5	31.9	34.3
Ireland	42.0	38.0	40.4	20.5	18.5	19.0	40.9	33.8	37.7
Netherlands	39.5	39.0	39.4	19.3	18.5	18.7	36.3	25.0	31.6
EU 15	41.3	39.0	40.4	19.3	19.8	19.7	40.1	32.8	36.9

Source: European Commission, 1996a–d. © IAT 1998

time are largely taken in households, the distribution of working time among both individuals and households also needs to be explored. Finally, it is necessary to analyse the evolution of the duration and distribution of working time, in order to be able to distinguish short-lived trends from possible longer-term developments.

Duration and distribution of individual working time

The normal weekly working time of employees in Denmark and the Netherlands is considerably lower than the average for the European Union as a whole (36.9 hours), while it is slightly higher in Austria and Ireland (table 3.1). Aggregating working time to the annual level reveals somewhat greater differences between the Netherlands and Denmark, on the one hand, and Ireland, on the other (data on Austria are not available), which can probably be attributed to longer holidays in the first two countries.

To grasp the extent to which a country's potential labour force is being utilized, the average working hours of all people of working age should be measured, so that not only employees but also the economically inactive population are included. This will thus reflect not only the average duration of employees' working hours, but also different participation rates.[1] On this basis, Ireland has the shortest average annual working time, since the long annual working times in that country are combined with a low participation rate. In the Netherlands, a virtually identical average annual working time is achieved with a higher participation rate and a significantly shorter working time per employee (table 3.2).

Gender gaps

In all four countries, women work considerably shorter hours than men. In Ireland and the Netherlands, the inequality of the distribution of working

Table 3.2 Annual hours per employee and per person of working age (15–65), 1994

Country	Average annual working hours per employee	Employment rate	Employment rate of women	Average annual hours per person of working age
Denmark	1 568	72.4	67.1	1 130
Ireland	1 747	52.3	39.9	914
Germany	1 590	64.8	54.9	1 017
Netherlands	1 447	63.8	52.7	923
Sweden	1 537[a]	71.5	70.6	1 099
United Kingdom	1 683	68.8	62.1	1 159
United States	1 947	72.0	65.2	1 402

[a]Total employment.
Source: OECD, 1998, and author's calculations.

time between women and men is more marked than in the other two countries. Women in the Netherlands work on average 11.3 hours less per week than men, while the difference in Ireland is 6.9 hours. In Austria and Denmark, on the other hand, the difference is around 5 hours (table 3.1). The differences in the employment rate are consistent with those in working time. The gaps between male and female employment rates are greater in Ireland and the Netherlands than in the other two countries (table 3.3). If the employment rate is expressed in terms of full-time equivalents, effectively combining the employment rate and average working time in a single indicator, the differences are even more marked. In particular, the high share of part-time employment among Dutch women forces the gender gap up from 21.4 per cent to 34.8 per cent.

The distribution of working time by sex in figures 3.1, 3.2, 3.3 and 3.4 shows broadly similar peaks in the distribution of average normal working

Table 3.3 Employment rates for men and women, 1996

	Employment rate			Employment rate in full-time equivalents		
	Men	Women	Gender gaps	Men	Women	Gender gaps
Austria	78.9	60.7	18.2	77.3	52.6	24.7
Denmark	82.3	68.6	13.7	76.3	58.1	18.2
Ireland	69.1	43.3	25.8	67.3	38.5	28.8
Netherlands	75.7	54.3	21.4	68.9	34.1	34.8
EU 15	70.4	50.2	20.2	68.3	42.1	26.2

Source: European Commission, 1997a.

Figure 3.1 Distribution of usual weekly working hours, Austria, employees, 1996

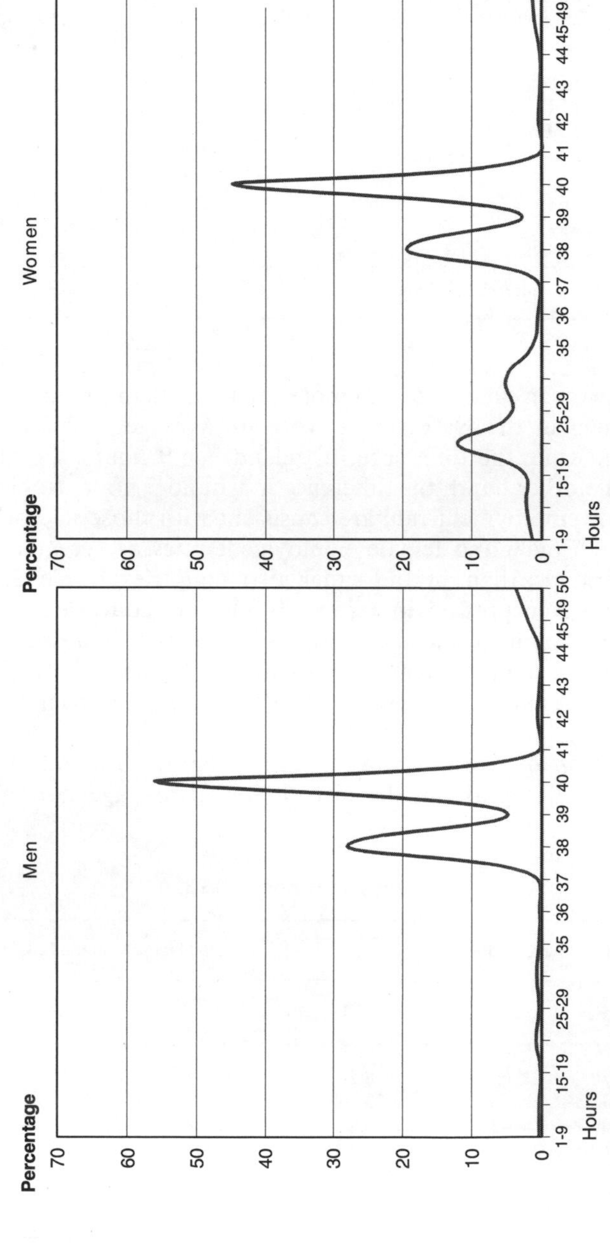

Source: Disk data supplied by Eurostat.

Figure 3.2 Distribution of usual weekly working hours, Denmark, employees, 1987 and 1996

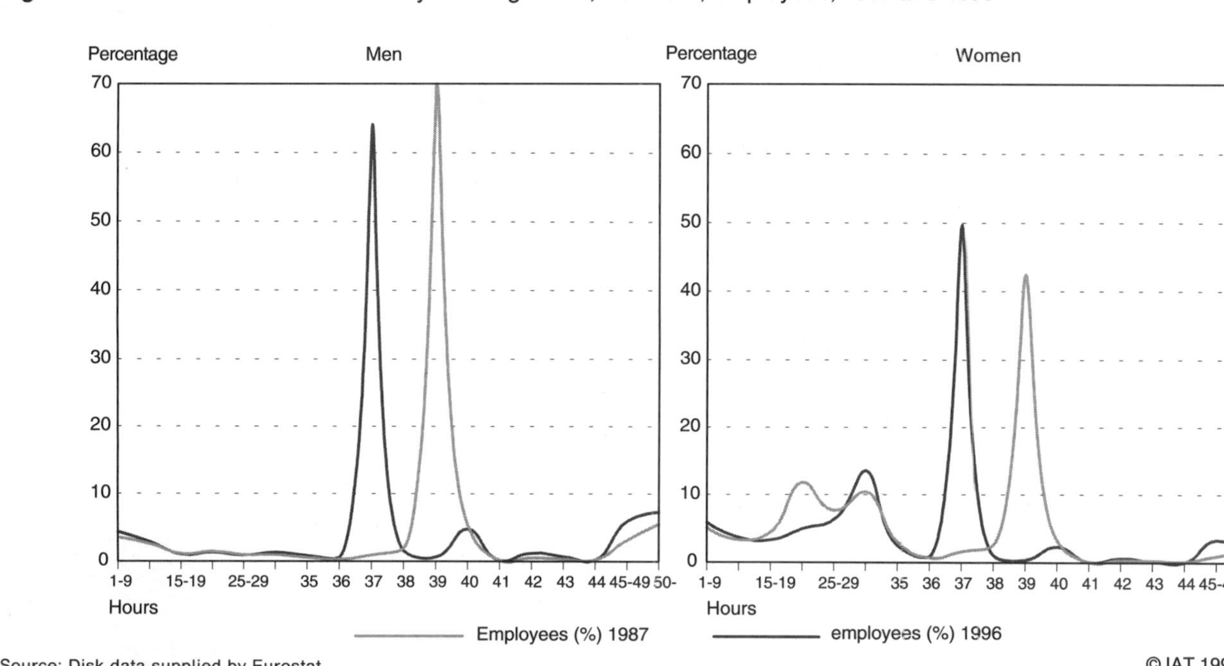

Source: Disk data supplied by Eurostat.

Figure 3.3 Distribution of usual weekly working hours, Ireland, employees, 1987 and 1995

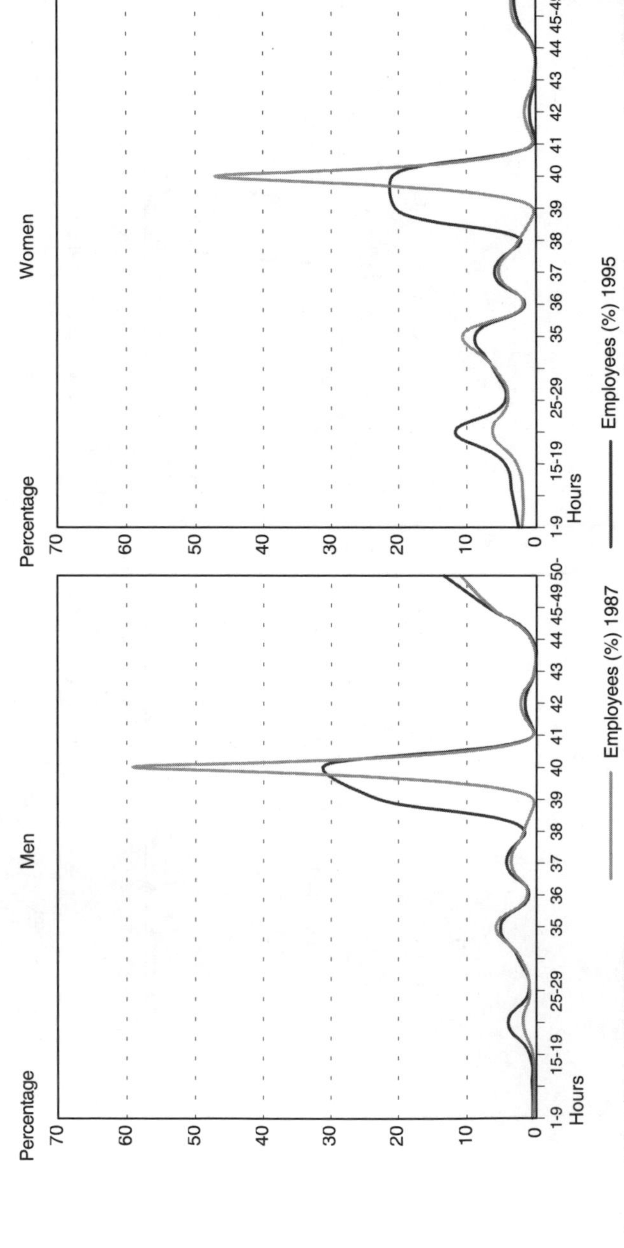

Source: Disk data compiled by Eurostat.

Figure 3.4 Distribution of usual weekly working hours, Netherlands, employees, 1987 and 1996

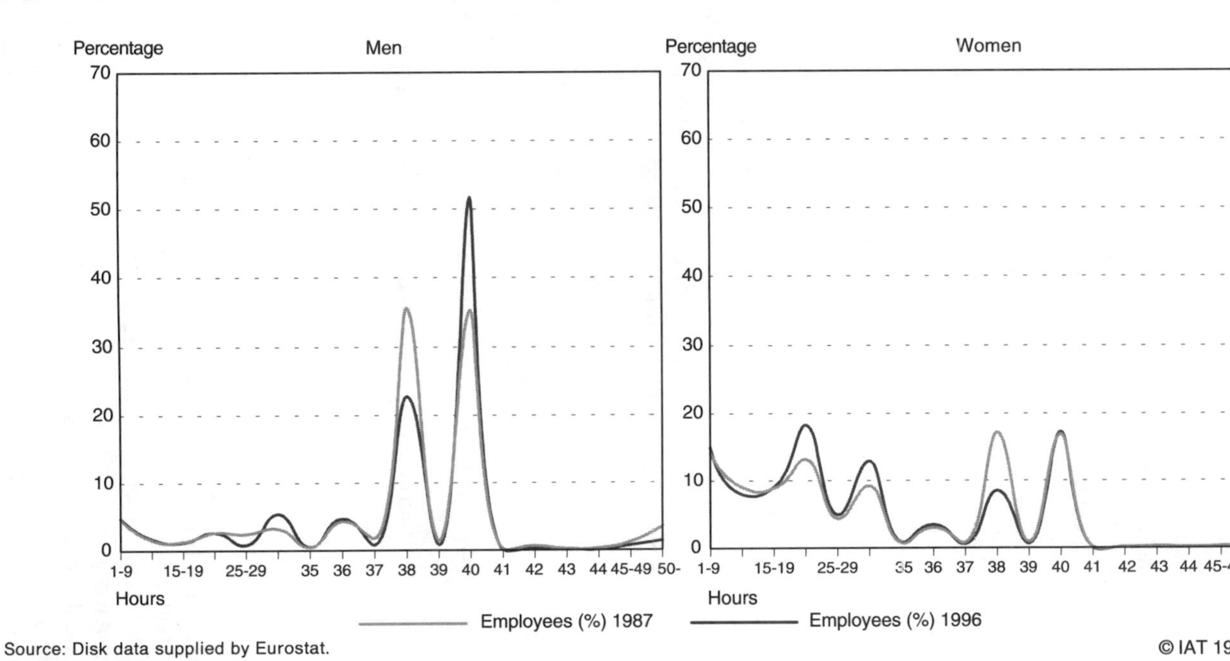

Source: Disk data supplied by Eurostat.

time in the four countries, although they vary in magnitude. Male working time is most homogeneous in Denmark, where more than 60 per cent of men normally work about 37 hours per week. As a result of the general working-time reductions of recent years, this peak has shifted to the left. In the Netherlands and Austria, two peaks around the 37- and 40-hour marks can be discerned. This is due to differences in contractual working time in the various sectors of the economy, and reflects a decentralized, industry-level approach to working-time policy that contrasts with the more centralized approach adopted in Denmark. In Ireland, on the other hand, male working times are the least homogeneous and the differences have widened further in recent years, with increases in both very short and very long working times. In Austria, Denmark and the Netherlands there is still a clearly delineated standard working time for men; in Ireland, such a norm has lost much of its importance.

The differences in women's working time both within and between countries are much more marked than for men. These differences are the consequence of very disparate working times for female employees with and without children and for the various age cohorts (see Chapter 4). Denmark can be regarded as the country with the most clearly delineated standard working time for women. About 50 per cent of Danish women employees work a 37-hour week, and there is a second peak for part-timers at around the 30-hour mark. In Austria as well there are peaks of similar magnitude round the 37- and 40-hour marks and one for part-timers around the 20-hour mark. For Dutch and Irish women, on the other hand, the usual working time is distributed between 0 and 45 hours without any pronounced peaks, whereby Dutch women tend to work fewer hours and Irish women somewhat longer hours. In Ireland, the standard working time for women employees of 40 hours, which was still discernible in 1987, has lost some of its importance. This is mainly due to increased female participation rates, which have risen from 32.1 per cent in 1985 to 43.3 per cent. Many women with children have entered the Irish labour market, and are unable to work the long hours required of full-timers.

The distribution of paid and unpaid working time in households

The differing distribution of individual working times between men and women is the consequence of working-time decisions taken at household level. Traditionally women have been responsible for work associated with reproduction and men for paid work. This division of labour can be analysed only if the time budgets for both types of work are examined. Goldschmidt-Clermont and Pagnossin-Aligisakis (1995), in a report to the United Nations, summarized the attempts made to gather data on paid and "do-it-yourself" work in 14 industrialized countries. They make a distinction between economic and non-economic (personal) activities such as personal care, education, social activities and hobbies. Economic activities are further subdivided into paid work and unpaid economic activities such as the production and preparation of food, childcare, care of dependent adults, civic work and building, repair and household work. The distinction between personal activities and the two categories of economic activities is made on the basis of the "third person criterion", which stipulates that an economic activity can be delegated to a third person, whereas a personal activity cannot. This applies, for example, to preparing a meal but not to listening to music or sleeping. This "third person criterion" discloses the potential substitutability of monetized and non-monetized activities. Unpaid work can be converted into paid work, and vice versa.

The most important findings from the studies of 14 industrialized countries are summarized below.[2]

- The total time devoted to economic activities by individuals over the age of 15 varies between 6 hours 16 minutes and 7 hours 34 minutes; the method of calculation included every day of the year (including weekends, public holidays and vacations).
- The total time devoted to "do-it-yourself" work is about the same as that given over to paid work in all countries.
- Men devote more time to paid work than women. For them, the share of paid work in their total time budget for economic activities is between 52 and 79 per cent; for women, the figure is between 19 and 58 per cent.
- Measured in terms of time input, the value of "do-it-yourself" work is equivalent to 43 per cent (+/−10) of GNP.[3]
- In the last 30 years, the time spent on paid work as well as on "do-it-yourself" work has declined.
- The time devoted by men and women to paid work and "do-it-yourself" work is falling very slowly, although women still spend considerably more time on household production activities than men.
- Within the "do-it-yourself" category, the time given over to activities related to food, clothing and housing is declining, while that devoted to shopping and organization (paperwork and services) is rising.

These time studies confirm the great importance of household production to the economic well-being of society. Furthermore, they show that such "do-it-yourself" work is a predominantly female domain, although the time devoted to it by men has risen slightly. Since the data gathered in every country are based on different definitions, unfortunately the findings listed above cannot be used for international comparisons. Despite this limitation, it should be noted that the substantial difference in the time devoted to paid and unpaid economic activities by Danish and Dutch women – almost equal at around two hours in each country – clearly reflects the difference in female participation rates (table 3.4).

Table 3.4 Time devoted to paid and unpaid economic activities in six countries (average time per person per day in hours and minutes)

Year Age	Austria 1992 (10+)		Denmark 1987 (–58)		France 1985–86 (15+)		Germany 1991–92 (16+)		Netherlands 1987 (12+)		United States 1985 (15+)	
Sex	M	F	M	F	M	F	M	F	M	F	M	F
Time for paid economic activities												
Hrs:mins	4:40(a)	2:17(a)	6:00	4:19	4:00	2:10	4:28(a)	2:12(a)	2:58(a)	1:13(a)	4:31	2:47
%	71	31	79	58	62	30	61	30	52	19	63	37
Time for unpaid economic activities												
Hrs:mins	1:53(b)	5:01(b)	1:38	3:10	2:28(a)	4:59(a)	2:53	5:08	2:47(b)	5:03(b)	2:37	4:46
%	29	69	21	42	38	70	39	70	48	81	37	63
Total time in all economic activities												
Hrs:mins	6:33	7:18	7:38	7:29	6:28	7:09	7:21	7:20	5:45	6:17	7:08	7:33
%	100	100	100	100	100	100	100	100	100	100	100	100

Notes: Because of rounding and the transformation of time units, percentages may not always sum to 100 nor time to 24 hours.
Austria: (a) including travel time; (b) excluding travel time.
France: (a) including travel time.
Germany: (a) time in SNA activities (productive market activities as defined by the United Nations System of National Accounts): including paid work, travelling because of work, other job-related time; excluding lunch break.
Netherlands: (a) excluding "travelling because of work". (b) including "travelling because of work"; excluding "reading, talking with children; indoor and outdoor playing with children".
Source: Goldschmidt-Clermont/Pagnossion-Aligisakis, 1995.

The evolution of working time

It cannot be said that there is currently an unambiguous trend towards shorter working times. The joint international "convoy" that for 100 years steamed steadily, albeit at differing speeds, towards the goal of the 8-hour day and then the 40-hour week has now broken up into several individual groups operating independently and with little radio contact. In some industrialized countries, such as Great Britain[4] and the United States, full-timers' working time has increased in recent years (table 3.5). In these countries, deregulation has led to a sharp increase in income inequalities, and the question of earnings has come to the fore for employees. Clearly, reductions in working time depend on certain preconditions on the income distribution side, of which more later in section 3.3.

The four small open economies belong to that group of countries in which overall working time was reduced between 1983 and 1993, though in very different ways. In Austria and Denmark, weekly working time for full-timers fell considerably.[5] In Ireland and the Netherlands, by contrast, working time was reduced largely as a result of an increase in the share of part-time employment.

The data on the effect of part-timers on duration reveal just how complex the dynamic of changes in working time now is. In Denmark, Sweden and the

Table 3.5 Contribution of part-timers to recent changes in average annual hours of employees (average change in hours from year to year)

	Change attributable to:				
Country	Period	Overall change	Change in hours of full-timers	Change in hours of part-timers	Change in share of part-timers
Belgium	1983–93	−7.5	−2.5	0.2	−4.9
Canada	1983–93	−1.1	0.7	0.5	−2.3
Denmark	1985–93	−6.6	−7.1	−0.9	1.4
France	1983–93	−4.1	0.4	0.7	−4.4
Germany	1983–93	−10.9	−6.1	−0.9	−3.9
Great Britain	1983–93	−1.5	3.8	−0.5	−5.0
Greece	1983–93	−1.0	−1.6	−0.4	1.3
Ireland	1983–93	−7.4	−1.0	−0.4	−6.0
Italy	1983–93	−3.7	−3.0	0.4	−0.9
Luxembourg	1983–93	−2.1	−0.9	−0.1	−1.1
Netherlands	1987–93	−6.6	0.0	3.2	−11.3
Portugal	1986–93	−6.9	−6.5	0.6	−0.3
Spain	1987–93	−6.0	−3.8	−0.4	−1.8
Sweden	1987–94	7.7	1.8	3.6	2.3
United States	1983–93	7.3	4.7	1.3	1.2
Unweighted average	**1983–93**	**−3.1**	**−1.4**	**0.5**	**−1.7**

Source: OECD, 1998.

Figure 3.5 Percentage of involuntary part-time workers

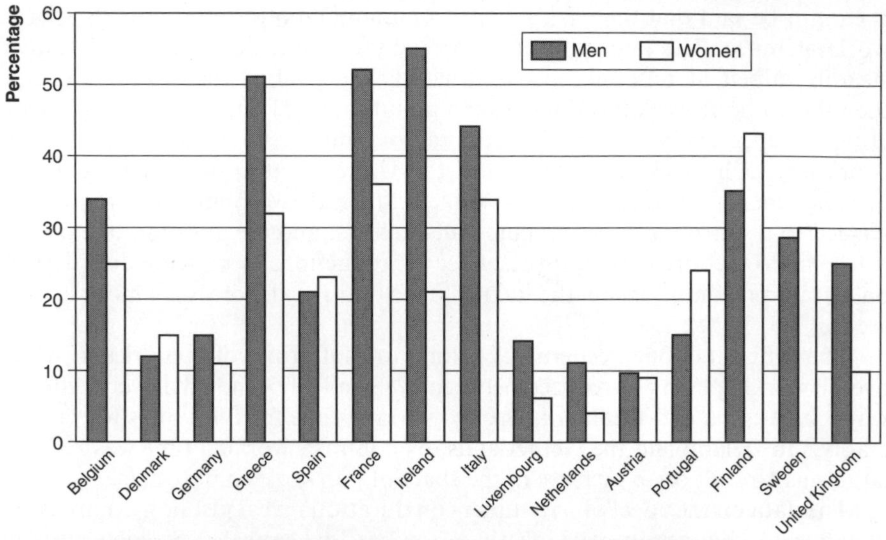

Source: Eurostat: *Erhebung über Arbeitskräfe*, 1996, p. 86.

United States, the share of part-time workers actually fell between 1983 and 1993; in the Netherlands, Sweden and the United States, the number of hours worked by part-timers rose. Thus countries which, for employment policy reasons, seek to expand part-time work may fall into a "part-time trap" (Lehndorff, 1998), because in the long term it is possible that the share of part-time employment will decline and the number of hours worked by part-timers will expand. This part-time trap can be assessed in terms of the share of involuntary part-timers, that is, the proportion of workers who have had to accept part-time employment for lack of a full-time job. The share of involuntary part-timers in Ireland is currently considerably higher than in the other three small open economies (figure 3.5). In Ireland a large majority continues to prefer wage increases over reduced hours, whereas in Denmark and the Netherlands the majority of employees give priority to reduced working time; no figures are available for Austria (table 3.6).

It is not only annual working hours but also the total time worked over the life cycle that has been reduced, albeit at differing rates, in the four small open economies. In particular, the participation rate for men aged between 55 and 64 has been reduced through statutory or company early retirement programmes. In 1995, only slightly more than 42 per cent of men aged between 55 and 64 were still economically active in Austria and the Netherlands. In the Netherlands, the participation rate in this group fell between 1968 and 1995 by 38.3 per cent (table 3.7). The decline in the participation rate in this group was considerably

Table 3.6 Workers' preferences on working hours and earnings, European Union, 1985 and 1994[a] (percentage of employees)

Country	More earnings			Fewer hours		
	1985	1994	Ratio 1994–95	1985	1994	Ratio 1994–95
Belgium	58	48	0.83	36	40	1.11
Denmark	38	32	0.84	51	66	1.29
France	62	53	0.85	34	40	1.18
Germany	56	54	0.96	30	34	1.13
Greece	68	84	1.24	26	14	0.54
Ireland	78	59	0.76	19	37	1.95
Italy	55	54	0.98	39	39	1.00
Netherlands	46	43	0.93	47	52	1.11
Portugal	82	58	0.71	11	35	3.18
Spain	64	70	1.09	31	24	0.77
United Kingdom	77	62	0.81	19	32	1.68
Unweighted average	**62**	**56**	**0.90**	**31**	**38**	**1.20**

[a] Figures exclude workers unable to choose between more earnings and fewer hours, and non-responders.
Source: European Commission: *Employment Outlook*, 6/1998, p. 67.

less rapid in the other two countries. In Austria and the Netherlands, the opportunities provided in law for early retirement were extended. In Ireland there was no generalized programme of this kind but, at most, individual agreements were concluded at firm or industry level. In Denmark early retirement schemes exist

Table 3.7 Participation rates of older and younger workers

Country	Year	Male and female, 15–24 years	Male, 55–64 years	Female, 55–64 years	Total	Changes in male participation rates, 55–64 years (% points)	
						1968–88	1988–95
Austria	1994[a]	62.5	41.3	18.5	71.7		
	1995	61.7	42.6	18.8	72.4		1.3[b]
Denmark	1983[b]	65.3	67.2	41.7	79.6		
Ireland	1988	76.0	69.1	42.3	83.8		
	1995	73.2	67.9	40.1	80.1	1.9[c]	−1.2
	1971[a]	63.2	91.9	21.3	65.6		
	1988	52.5	69.5	19.0	61.9		
	1995	45.6	63.9	21.3	63.0	−21.5[d]	−5.6
Netherlands	1971[a]	59.4	80.6	14.9	58.5		
	1988	59.8	46.9	15.8	65.2		
	1995	64.5	42.3	18.6	70.6	−33.7	−4.6

[a] No earlier data available; [b] 1994–95; [c] 1983–88; [d] 1971–88.
Source: OECD, Labour Force Statistics, 1996.

but, as in other Scandinavian countries, early retirement, so popular in Belgium, France, Germany and the Netherlands, has never been used as a policy for tackling unemployment. Employment trends among older workers are dealt with in greater detail in Chapter 4.

The working-time profiles of Austria, Denmark, Ireland and the Netherlands

The working-time profiles of these four countries differ considerably. Table 3.8 summarizes the results obtained using the various indicators outlined in the preceding analysis. Where data are lacking, we have attempted to fill in the gaps with plausible assumptions. Thus our assessment that, in families with children, dual-earner households have now become the dominant household form in Denmark is based on data on the high full-time rate among women with children (see Chapter 4) and the data in figures 3.1, 3.2, 3.3 and 3.4. In contrast, the statements on the level of "do-it-yourself" work are pure estimates. It should be borne in mind, in evaluating the indicators, that the categories low/high/medium denote solely the relationship of these four countries *to one another*. The relativity of these categories would be recognized immediately if countries with completely different working-time structures, such as Great Britain or Japan, were included.

In terms of paid employment, the countries can be characterized as follows:

Austria

In Austria, the outlines of a standard working time for both men and women are clearly discernible. However, the dominant form of economic activity, albeit only by a short head from the single male breadwinner model, is the dual-earner household in which both partners work full time. Austria has the lowest incidence of part-time work of the four countries. Working time has been reduced primarily through cuts in contractual working time and working time over the life cycle. Here too, it is unclear whether and how, after 30 years of early retirement schemes, Austria will succeed in integrating the rising share of older workers. Potential labour supply is utilized to a moderate extent and relatively evenly.

Denmark

The outlines of a new standard working time can be clearly discerned in Denmark. The differences in working time between men and women are minor and the gap is narrowing further. Men's contractual working times have fallen significantly and a growing share of women is now working full time. Working time over the life cycle has been reduced less than in other countries so that, in some respects, Denmark is better prepared for the demographically induced

Table 3.8 Working-time profiles of Austria, Denmark, Ireland and the Netherlands

	Austria	Denmark	Ireland	Netherlands
Contractual working time	Medium	Low	High	Medium
Working time per employee	Medium	Low	High	Low
Working time per person aged 15–64	Medium	High	Low	Low
Difference in working time between men and women	Low	Low	High	High
Is there a standard working time?	M + F yes	M + F yes	M + F no	M yes/F no
Dominant form of working time in households with children	Dual earner both full time (33%)	Dual earner both full time	Male single earner (45%)	Dual earner Male FT/Female PT(44%)
Reduction in working time?	Yes, collective reduction	Yes, collective reduction	Yes, through expansion of part-time work	Yes, through increased part-time work and collective reduction
Participation rate for men aged 55–64	Sharp fall	Slight fall	Slight fall	Sharp fall
Amount of household production	Low	Low	High	High

Note: The high/low/medium categories of the four countries denote only their relationship to one another.

increase in the share of older workers. Long working time over the life cycle, alongside high participation rates and long working hours among women, mean that the potential labour supply is being utilized very fully and, above all, equally. Working times seem to correspond largely to current employee preferences.

Ireland

Ireland has the most traditional working-time structures. The single male breadwinner is still, by a clear margin, the dominant form of economic activity in households with children. Working time is very unevenly distributed between men and women. The notion of standard working time has lost much of its meaning, both for men, most of whom are working longer hours, and for women, most of whom are working shorter hours. Workers tend to be more interested in maximizing their earnings than in reducing their working time. Part-time work has expanded rapidly in recent years, but is not always willingly accepted. Despite lengthy working times over the course of the year and the life cycle, the potential labour supply is utilized only to a limited extent and very unevenly. This would suggest that the volume of paid work will need to be increased in the long term.

The Netherlands

The Netherlands is the first "part-time society" in the world. For families with children the dominant pattern of economic activity is now for the man to work full time and the woman part time. There is no discernible standard working time for women. Working time over the life cycle has been drastically reduced. The potential labour supply is utilized to only a limited extent and relatively unequally. There is a high level of household production. Working-time structures correspond largely to current employee preferences, with a widespread desire for further cuts in working time. It remains unclear how, after 30 years of early retirement schemes, the Netherlands will succeed in integrating the rising proportion of older workers. Equally, it is not certain whether women will continue to accept the unequal utilization of the male and female labour supplies. It can be assumed that the volume of paid work will have to be increased in the longer term.

3.3 CAUSES OF VARIATIONS IN NATIONAL WORKING-TIME PROFILES

The national working-time profiles outlined above have their roots in a number of factors, of which only the following will be investigated here: (1) wage levels and income distribution, (2) the tax and social security systems, (3) the child-care system, (4) education and training policy, (5) working-time policy, and (6) industrial relations.

Wage levels and income distribution

In poor industrialized societies, working hours are usually comparatively long. Short working times – to the extent that they are welcomed by employees – are an indicator of a country's level of economic well-being. One precondition for the acceptance of shorter working hours is an adequate income, meaning that employees and their families can "afford" such working hours. As earnings rise, time becomes relatively more scarce and interest grows in distributing productivity gains in the form of cuts in working time rather than wage increases. Absolute wage levels as well as income distribution are important for the evolution of working time.

GDP per hour, per employee and per capita[6] are used as indicators of income levels. Table 3.9 shows that per capita GDP in Austria, Denmark and the Netherlands is above the EU average. The above considerations suggest why preferences for working-time reductions rather than wage increases might be greater in these countries than in Ireland, where earnings are considerably lower than the EU average. It is also clear from table 3.9 that the Netherlands and, to an even greater extent, Austria and Denmark achieve high per capita GDP from a combination of high hourly productivity and short working times. As far as quality of life is concerned, this is certainly a significantly better combination than achieving a similarly high per capita GDP with much longer working time, as in the United States. Thus GDP per hour worked in Denmark is 66 per cent greater than in the United States, while GDP per employee is about the same, since employees work significantly shorter hours than their American counterparts; per capita GDP is somewhat higher than in the United States, since the participation rate in Denmark is also higher. It can reasonably be assumed that the quality of life afforded by the Danish combination of high hourly productivity with short working times is higher than the American combination of low

Table 3.9 GDP per hour, per employed person and per capita in ECU (in percentages: United States = 100)

	GDP per hour worked		GDP per employed person		GDP per capita	
	ECU	%	ECU	%	ECU	%
Austria	35.61	(153)	45 014	(106)	20 819	(96)
Denmark	38.65	(166)	42 618	(101)	23 768	(109)
Ireland	23.33	(100)	31 508	(74)	12 253	(56)
Netherlands	30.22	(129)	39 741	(94)	18 322	(84)
EU	26.28	(113)	36 796	(87)	16 644	(77)
United States	23.35	(100)	42 419	(100)	21 751	(100)

Source: Cichon, 1997.

Table 3.10 Levels and changes in earnings inequality among advanced OECD countries (measured by the ratio of 90th to 10th decile, male earnings, 1979–95)

	1979 or other initial year	1995 or other end year	Annual change
Major rise in inequality			
New Zealand	2.72 (1984)	3.16 (1994)	0.044
United States	3.18	4.35	0.027
Italy	2.29	2.64 (1993)	0.025
Canada	3.46 (1981)	3.74 (1994)	0.021
Great Britain	2.45	3.31	0.020
Some rise in inequality			
Australia	2.74	2.94	0.013
Japan	2.59	2.77 (1994)	0.012
Austria	2.61 (1980)	2.77 (1994)	0.009
Netherlands	2.51 (1985)	2.59 (1994)	0.009
Sweden	2.11	2.20 (1993)	0.008
Finland	2.44 (1980)	2.53 (1994)	0.006
Denmark	2.14 (1980)	2.17 (1990)	0.003
France	3.39	3.43	0.002
Decline in inequality			
Belgium	2.29 (1985)	2.25 (1994)	−0.004
Norway	2.05 (1980)	1.98 (1991)	−0.006
Germany	2.38 (1983)	2.25	−0.013

Source: Freeman, 1997.

hourly productivity with long working times. The higher standard of living in Denmark compared with the Netherlands is likely to be one factor in explaining why more Danish than Dutch workers give priority to working-time reductions over wage increases (table 3.6). Relatively speaking, Dutch workers pay the price of their lower degree of labour supply utilization with a lower standard of living.

The evolution of income distribution seems to us almost more important than changes in average real wages. If the inequality of income distribution earnings widens, then real wage rises in the lower- and middle-income brackets will be lower than average or possibly even negative. Over the past 20 years, earnings inequality has increased in many countries (table 3.10). In the United States average weekly real wages for men declined by 13 per cent between 1973 and 1995. The wages of a male German worker in the lowest earnings decile have about 2.2 times the purchasing power of his American counterpart; those of a British worker only 1.3 times (Freeman, 1997). Since trade union members are concentrated in the lower and middle income brackets, increasing earnings inequality will make it more difficult for unions or the State to push through a policy of collective working-time reductions. Workers will then seek to make up for their loss of earnings by working longer hours. This

Table 3.11 Average wages of women in industry as a percentage of those of men

Country	Manual industrial workers	Non-manual industrial workers
Austria	n.a.	n.a.
Belgium	75.7	64.9
Denmark	84.5	n.a.
Germany	74.4	68.1
Greece	77.1	69.0
Spain	73.2	60.8
France	80.8	68.4
Ireland	69.7	n.a.
Italy	n.a.	n.a.
Luxembourg	70.6	59.4
Netherlands	77.8	67.8
Portugal	72.7	70.3
Finland	78.3	n.a
Sweden	89.5	n.a.
United Kingdom	68.4	59.7

n.a. = not available.
Source: Jepsen et al., 1997, p. 213.

could explain the increase in full-timers' working hours in Great Britain, New Zealand and the United States. Neo-liberal policies of income differentiation tend to undermine policies seeking to redistribute working time. It is safe to assume that the relative stability of income distribution in Denmark, Germany and the Netherlands over the past 20 years was an important pre-condition for the acceptance of work redistribution policies in those countries. Conversely, it could be said that policies of labour market deregulation that lead to a widening of income inequalities (OECD, 1996, 1997b) are not compatible with strategies for work redistribution.

Differences of varying magnitude in men's and women's working time have been observed. The question is whether these differences are linked to gender-specific wage gaps. Table 3.11 shows that the gender pay gap for manual industrial workers in Denmark is less marked than in Ireland, in particular, but also than in the Netherlands. Thus Danish households are more easily able to "afford" increases in the woman's labour supply and a reduction in the man's labour supply; in the other countries, this would be associated with significant losses of earnings.

Tax and social security

Tax and social security systems can provide incentives for firms and employees to take certain decisions on working time. In fact, the diversity of these incentives is so wide that they can be only partially dealt with here. Let us begin by examining the incentives for firms, taking social security contributions

Figure 3.6 Social contributions in relation to wages in the Netherlands, 1994

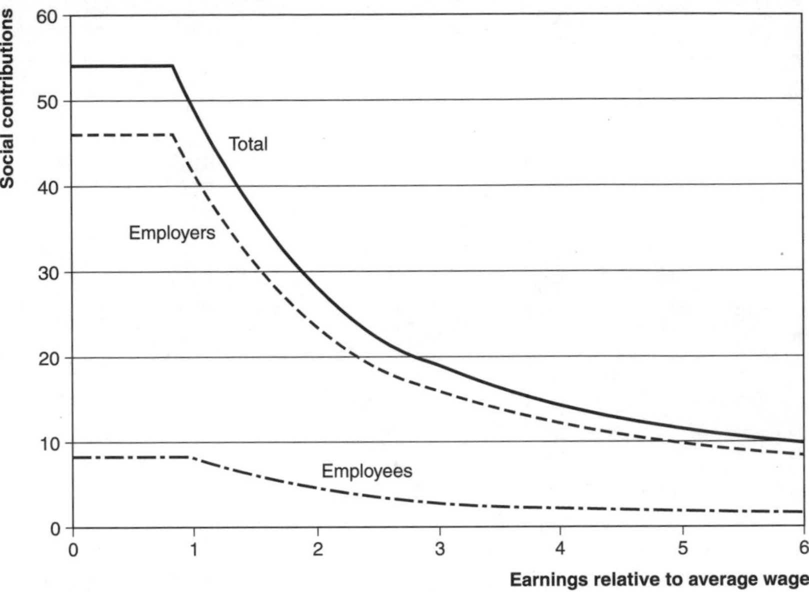

Source: Ward, 1996.

as a starting point. If social security contributions are a high percentage of labour costs and are paid only up to a certain income ceiling, they become fixed costs once that limit is reached, which makes long working hours attractive to employers in terms of cost. Social security contributions in the Netherlands are high (figure 3.6) and they work regressively, since contributions are paid only up to a certain threshold. In Ireland, by contrast, contributions are lower and are only slightly regressive (figure 3.7). In Denmark, social security contributions are very low, since social protection is financed primarily out of taxation. As a result, the fixed-cost problem is of very little significance there.

In reality, however, this has only a minor effect on working time. Ward (1996) has established that there is no linkage in the EU between indirect labour costs – the most important element of which is social security contributions – and working times:

> Indeed, for industry, there seems if anything to be an inverse relationship, with those countries with the lowest level of indirect cost having the highest average hours worked per year (the UK and Ireland, in particular), while the two countries with the shortest average working hours, Belgium and Sweden, have the highest level of (adjusted) indirect cost.... Moreover, the two countries with the most regressive schedules of employer contribution rates, the Netherlands and Germany, also had among the shortest working hours.[7]

Figure 3.7 Social contributions in relation to wages in Ireland, 1994

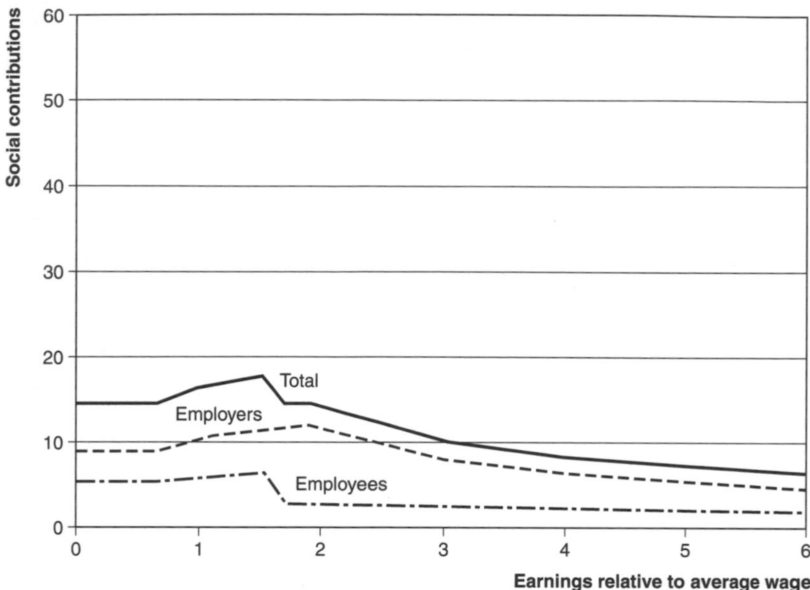

Source: Ward, 1996.

What incentives are there in the tax systems for households to take particular working-time decisions? Some data are available on this question for Austria, Denmark and the Netherlands.[8]

In the past, the tax systems in most industrialized countries have tended to favour the single male breadwinner model, which until recently was the dominant model and the dominant form of family life. Many countries have changed their tax systems in recent years. Thus Austria (1992), Denmark (1970) and the Netherlands (1984) have switched from joint to individual assessment, although the tax systems in these three countries are not completely individualized, since allowances can still be claimed in respect of economically inactive partners. Table 3.12 shows that Denmark is the only country where the single breadwinner model is associated with tax advantages. This is not the case in Austria or the Netherlands and, in Ireland, couples can decide whether they wish to be assessed jointly or separately. If the wife is not economically active, or works only a few hours, then there are considerable advantages to be gained from joint assessment. Although table 3.12 reflects not only the tax effects but also the income effects – the wage gaps between women and men on which the calculations were based – even if equal wages are assumed, the characterization remains more or less the same.

Table 3.12 Average tax rate (including social security contributions) applying to average income for different household situations as a percentage of gross household income (applied: average male earnings for men and women)

	Single person	Married couple, man in full-time employment and woman in ...		Single breadwinner
	Full time	Full-time job	Part-time job	Full time
1. Countries with a high tax burden, in which sole earners receive little, if any, tax advantage				
Netherlands	35.3	35.3	32.2	32.8
Sweden	35.8	35.8	34.0	35.8
2. Countries with extremely high and moderate tax burdens, in which sole earners receive significant relief in respect of tax and social security contributions				
Denmark	44.0	44.0	41.4	36.8
Germany	45.6	45.6	41.7	36.0
Belgium	37.8	40.0	35.4	29.0
3. Countries with relatively low tax burdens, in which the tax reliefs for a particular marital status are of little, if any, consequence				
France	29.2	29.2	26.7	22.9
Austria	29.5	29.5	26.1	28.1
Spain	26.7	30.3	26.8	26.7
Portugal	21.4	22.0	28.0	19.0
United Kingdom	27.1	26.4	23.8	25.7

Note: the tax burdens on single people and single breadwinners do not agree with the high values in table 3.13.
Source: Dingeldey, 1998b.

In practice, however, the incentive structures in national tax and social security systems clearly exert only limited influence on household patterns of economic activity. In Denmark, a pattern of labour market behaviour is rewarded that in reality no longer dominates. However, marginal tax and social security rates can be important for working-time decisions. In Denmark and the Netherlands, for example, marginal tax rates are very high when working time increases, whereas in Great Britain they are very low. This may explain the low share of employees who work very long hours in the first two countries and the high share of those in Britain.

The structure of social security benefits may also offer specific incentives for particular working-time decisions. The pension insurance system in the Netherlands, based on universal benefits, is frequently adduced as a reason for the high level of acceptance of the Dutch part-time model. If this were a decisive factor, however, part-time work would be even more widespread and popular in Ireland than in the Netherlands: the gross replacement rate of part-timers' retirement benefits in Ireland is the highest in Europe (Jepsen et al., 1997, p. 52). There are several reasons why no one-to-one relationship exists between these figures and actual labour market behaviour.

First, the level of the basic pension for many workers is too low to meet basic needs. Second, it is unclear how many workers actually consider their future pensions when taking their decisions on labour market behaviour or, indeed, whether they have the information on which to base such decisions. Third, many part-timers are only temporarily employed on a part-time basis, so that it is necessary to analyse not only rates but, more particularly, longer-term employment records. Fourth, for many workers (especially women), it is not individual pension entitlements but household entitlements that are decisive, including the derived pension entitlements that are maintained if the spouse dies. Finally, working time is "chosen" not in a vacuum but under the pressure exerted by social norms and institutional arrangements.

Childcare

As female participation rates rise, the public provision of childcare is increasingly important among the institutional arrangements that constrain working time.[9] It is in Denmark that such provision is most highly developed: 48 per cent of children up to age 3 have a place in crèches with long opening hours, compared with 8 per cent in the Netherlands, 3 per cent in Austria and 2 per cent in Ireland (see Chapter 4, table 4.17). There are also differences, albeit less pronounced ones, in the provision of nursery places for children aged between 3 and 6. Two-thirds of Danish schoolchildren have access to out-of-school care and recreation services, compared with 6 (and less) per cent in the Netherlands, Austria and Ireland (CEC, 1997).

Thus a significantly greater share of the burden of social reproduction is assumed by households in Ireland and the Netherlands, which reduces women's time budget for paid work. The consequence is the very uneven distribution of working time between men and women described above. In Denmark, many of the activities associated with social reproduction have been shifted out of households into the market or the public sector, and the time devoted by men and women to paid work has become much more equal. This has been possible only because of the virtuous circle created by an expanding labour supply and the emergence of new jobs in the service sector. As a result, much greater use – in terms of paid employment – has been made of the potential labour supply than in the Netherlands or Ireland.

The public provision of childcare is more important than the incentives emanating from the tax system, since it directly increases the degree of freedom enjoyed by households in taking their decisions on working time. The Central Planning Bureau in the Netherlands seems to have realized this link: some sectors of the Dutch economy are currently experiencing labour shortages, and attempts are being made to increase participation rates, whereby the provision of childcare is regarded as an important starting point (*Handelsblatt*, 1998).

Table 3.13 Labour force participation rate by level of educational attainment, 1992 (aged 24–64)

	Early childhood, primary and lower secondary education		Upper secondary education		Non-university tertiary education		University education		Total	
	Men	Women	Men	Women	Men	Women	Men	Women	Men	Women
Austria	71.6	42.8	83.6	61.1	n.a.	n.a.	93.1	82.0	81.7	54.7
Denmark	78.8	68.3	90.8	86.6	94.1	92.8	94.9	92.3	87.1	79.4
Ireland	82.4	29.2	93.4	54.3	94.3	71.4	93.6	79.8	86.5	43.9
Netherlands	77.1	38.4	88.5	63.2	n.a.	n.a.	91.3	77.4	85.0	53.8
OECD total	80.2	49.6	90.2	69.8	92.7	81.8	93.9	84.6	86.8	61.6

n.a. = not available.
Sources: OECD: *Bildungkompakt*; *OECD-Indikatoren*, 1995, pp. 33–35.

Education and training policy

One of the most important factors influencing individual labour market behaviour is educational level. As educational levels rise, so the participation rate goes up. This connection can be clearly discerned in these four countries (table 3.13). Comparison of male and female participation rates by educational level reveals that certain groups of women now have higher participation rates than men of low educational attainment. In two of the four countries (Austria and Denmark), the participation rate for female university graduates is significantly higher than that for men whose educational attainment does not go beyond lower secondary level. In the Netherlands the rates are about the same, and it is only in Ireland that male rates continue to be higher, albeit only by a short head.

Table 3.14 shows that the stock of human capital in the economically active population in Austria and Denmark is significantly greater than that in Ireland

Table 3.14 Human capital in international perspective

	Average time spent in education by 25–64 year-olds	Human capital per person aged 25–64 in $ purchasing power	Per capita GDP 1993–94 in $ purchasing power
Austria	12.1	72 600	19 200
Denmark	11.4	65 800	19 200
Ireland	9.6	30 000	13 800
Netherlands	11.3	46 100	17 700
Germany	13.2	74 200	18 500
United States	12.6	85 500	25 400

Source: Schuhmacher, 1997.

Figure 3.8 Educational level of men aged 25–54 in EU Member States, 1995

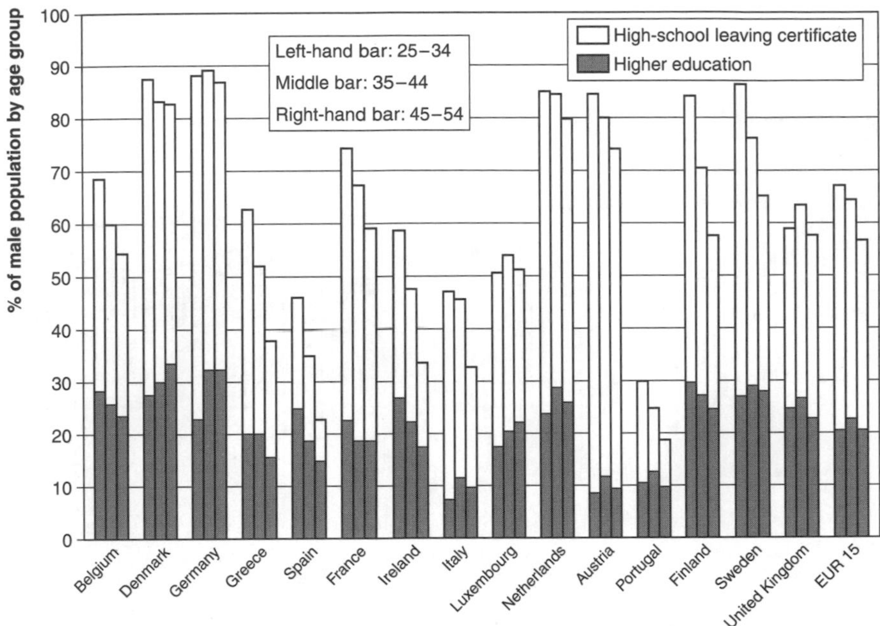

Source: European Commission: *Employment and Social Affairs, 1996*, p. 68.

and the Netherlands. This is probably one of the factors that explains why less use is made of the potential labour supply in the latter two countries. However, figures 3.8 and 3.9 reveal the dynamic of educational expansion by comparing various age cohorts and show that the educational attainment of the younger age groups in Ireland is now fast approaching that of other countries. On the basis of this expansion of education, it is reasonable to expect an increase in participation rates in Ireland in the next few years. The level of educational attainment in the Netherlands, which is higher than in Ireland and is to be further improved in the medium term through the injection of considerable extra resources (*Handelsblatt*, 1998), would suggest that participation rates will also rise there in the longer term; on this basis, at least, it is unlikely that the current low utilization of the potential labour supply will be a permanent feature of the Dutch economy.

There are several reasons for the linkage between education and participation rates that has been established here. They are located at both the micro and the macro levels. Individuals with higher levels of education have access to more interesting and better-paid jobs, with the result that their incentive to work and level of commitment, which are already high because of their

Figure 3.9 Educational level of women aged 25–54 in EU Member States, 1995

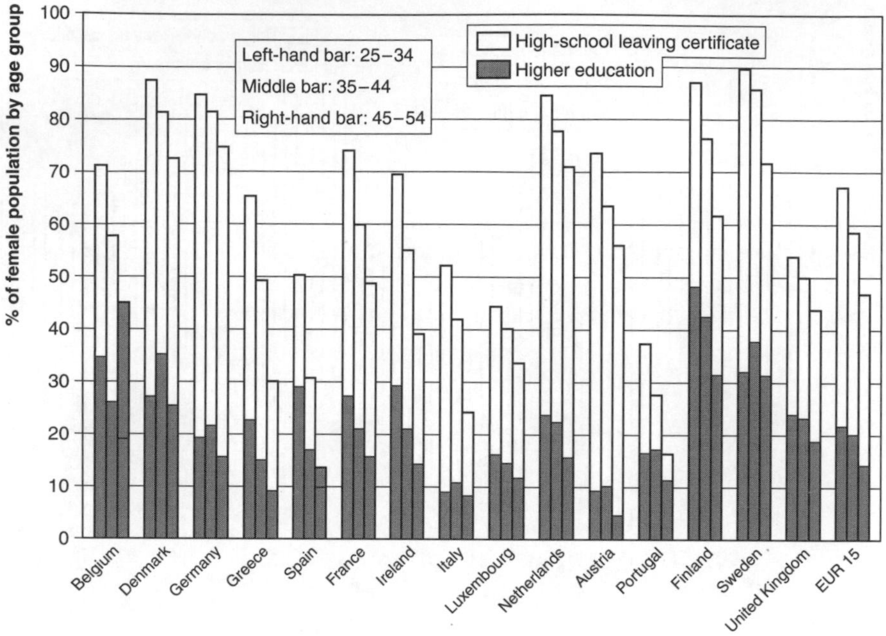

Source: European Commission: *Employment and Social Affairs, 1996*, p. 68.

considerable investment in education, is further strengthened by their rather positive experience of work and earnings potential:

- To remain in such high-skilled jobs, which are usually integrated into occupational or firms' internal labour markets, workers require continuous work records and ongoing training and/or learning. Unlike unskilled jobs, which it is possible to leave and re-enter without penalty, discontinuities are penalized in skilled occupations.
- More highly skilled workers are more likely to gain access to new areas of employment in periods of structural change. The ability to undertake further training is particularly important in this respect. This connection between education/training and structural changes has already manifested itself in early retirement policy. It is primarily older unskilled workers who have left the labour market early.[10]
- In periods of high unemployment, firms have more opportunities to select the most highly qualified workers, so that unemployment becomes increasingly concentrated in low-skilled groups.
- Investment in education is a decisive factor in growth. The existence of a well-educated labour force plays an important role in determining investment

decisions. The expansion of education in Ireland is undoubtedly one of the reasons why the country has attracted so much foreign investment. The potential for endogenous growth is also strengthened, since firms are able to market new or higher-value goods and services.

- A high educational level is also a precondition for a redistribution of work. Only if there are sufficient skilled workers in the labour market can the hours of work left "vacant" by individual or collective working-time reductions be redistributed among a greater number of people. The fact that the Dutch part-time policy and the high labour turnover in Denmark caused by workers claiming their entitlement to parental leave or part-time employment did not lead to labour market shortages can only be explained by the high level of education and training in the two countries.[11]
- Thus an expansion of education can produce a virtuous circle of a rising labour supply coupled with increased demand for labour. Evidence for this is provided by the close link between the level of GDP and national stocks of human capital. Once depreciations have been taken into account, the stock of human capital provides a measure of investment in education (DIW, 1998).

Working-time policy and industrial relations

The regulation of working hours by law or collective agreement reflects, on the one hand, the changing interests and needs of both workers and employers; on the other, it conditions and constrains the realization of such interests. In all four countries we can observe both common trends in working-time regulations as well as differences. The latter reflect the different choices made and the strategies pursued in these countries, and the varying development of the welfare State (European Commission, 1996a–d).

The common trends are:

- In all four countries the working hours of full-time employees were reduced in the late 1980s or early 1990s through collective agreements. In Austria and in the Netherlands the normal working hours set out in collective agreements varied between 36 and 40 hours per week. In Ireland working time became an issue in national tripartite bargaining in 1987. The Programme of National Recovery provided scope for local negotiations on working time. Most blue-collar workers now have a standard week of 39 hours while white-collar workers enjoy a standard of between 35 and 37.5 hours. While in Austria, Ireland and the Netherlands the standard working hours vary between sectors, in Denmark the 37-hour week applies to the entire workforce (table 3.15).
- The trade-off for shorter working hours was greater working-time flexibility and a decentralization of working-time decisions to the plant level. The

Table 3.15 Statutory limits on normal weekly hours of work and overtime work

	Legal maxima			Premium for overtime hours	Normal weekly hours set by collective agreements
	Normal weekly hours	Weekly overtime hours	Maximum weekly hours		
Austria[a]	40	5 (10 during 12 weeks per year)	50 (60 in some circumstances)	50%	36–40
Denmark[b]	37	None	48	50% for 1 hour; rising to 100%	37
Ireland	48	12	60	25%	38–40
Netherlands	45	15	60 (maximum average over 13 weeks is 48)	No legislation on premium	40

[a] Collective agreements may permit up to 10 additional overtime hours (e.g. in hotels and restaurants or transport services). Work agreements may permit hours of supplementary overtime for up to 12 weeks up to a weekly working time of 60 hours to prevent severe economic detriments, and provided other measures are not feasible. The Labour Inspectorate may permit a greater number of overtime hours. There are many exceptions to the maximum weekly hours rule, which allow 60 hours and more. The average maximum weekly working time must not exceed 48 hours over a reference period of four months, which may be extended by collective agreement up to one year.

[b] Normal weekly hours of 37 and overtime premiums have been established through collective bargaining.

Source: OECD, 1998, p. 168. © IAT 1998

working-time laws in Austria and the Netherlands, for example, increased the maximum working hours per day and extended the calculation periods for flexible working hours (table 3.16). Deviations from the legal standards are possible through collective agreements (Austria, Netherlands) or written agreements between employer and works councils (Netherlands). The new laws shifted responsibility for working time to the social partners in both countries. Collective agreements in all countries now allow the introduction of flexible working-time schedules (for example, annualized hours), although the rules vary with respect to maximum daily or weekly hours, overtime supplements, or consultation with works councillors.

- Part-time work is becoming more and more regulated. Part-timers are now paid equal rates per hour (Austria, Denmark, the Netherlands) and discrimination in other areas such as dismissal protection, unemployment benefits, and public and private pensions are partially abolished (table 3.17).

The following differences can be observed:

- Only in Austria, the Netherlands and Denmark do we find regulations which go beyond a "defensive" ban on discrimination against part-time work to an "offensive" approach. This means that decisions on working hours are made not solely by employers, but that the rights of employees

Table 3.16 Provisions for averaged/annualized hours of work[a]

	Date of legislation	Working-time unit used in averaging	Reference period[b]	Limitations
Austria	1997	Legal week (40 hours) or any shorter normal weekly working time which is provided for under a collective agreement	Unlimited; averaging schemes have to be permitted by collective agreement; if the reference period is more than one year, time off in lieu has to be granted in blocks of several consecutive weeks	9 hours per day; 10 hours if time off in lieu can be taken in blocks of several consecutive days or, in case of reference periods of more than one year, in blocks of several consecutive weeks; 48 hours per week or 50 hours per week if the reference period does not exceed 8 weeks
Denmark	1990	Collective agreement Legal week (37 hours)	6 months	Must be agreed by employees on each occasion
Ireland	1997	Legal week (48 hours)	3 weeks[c]	56 hours per week
Netherlands	1996	40-hour week	13 weeks or 4 weeks	10 hours per day, 50 hours per week over 4 weeks; 9 hours per day, 45 hours per week over 13 weeks[d]

[a] Maxima as laid down by labour legislation and by collective agreements at the national level.
[b] The maximum period of reference may be lower in certain branches.
[c] Flexibilization is only possible when associated with shift work.
[d] The basic legislated limit is that no more than 520 hours may be worked over 13 weeks. Under discretionary requirements, which require an agreement between the parties, a maximum of 200 hours can be worked per four-week period and 585 hours per 13-week period.
Source: OECD, 1998, p. 171.

to reduce working hours temporarily are extended. In the Netherlands the social partners agreed in the Stichting van de Arbeid (Foundation of Labour)[12] to guarantee part-timers a statutory right to part-time work (see box 3.1). Bills incorporating such a regulation have, however, not yet been passed in both chambers of Parliament.

- In Austria, Denmark and the Netherlands parental-leave schemes permit parents to take leave or work part time until the children reach a certain age (see Chapter 4, table 4.16). One of the most innovative elements in Danish working-time and labour market policy was the introduction in 1994 of different forms of paid leave. Leave is not only used to harmonize the working hours and individual needs of parents, but also to integrate

Table 3.17 Legal position of part-time employment

	Legal basis	Form of contract	Pay	Overtime provision	Dismissal protection	Including worker representation threshold	Information and consultation	Right to full-time work
Belgium	Law of 30 Mar. 1990	Written	(a)	Employee has to agree	(a)	Includes those working less than 75% of normal hours counted as half	Annual report by employer to works council on employment situation	No legal provision
Denmark	No statutory provisions	(b) 15 hours contract	No legal provision	No legal provision	<15 hours weekly	(a)	No legal obligation to consult works council	No legal provision
France	Specific law defining part-time as less than 4/5 of normal hours	Written	(a)	Premiums after >full-time hours	(a)	Included pro rata	No provision	Priority in recruitment
Germany	Empl. prom. art. 1985	No specific form	(a)	>full-time hours	(a)	(a)	Obligation to inform, co-determination right	Employer must take account of employee wishes to work full time
Greece	No specific provision	No specific form	(a)	>full-time hours	(a)	(a)	No specific provision	(a)
Ireland	Law of 1990	(b) >18 hours weekly written contract	No requirement for proportional pay	>full-time hours	<8 hours weekly and service of 13 weeks	Not included	No specific provision	Priority right to full-time vacancies

Italy	No specific legal provision	Written	(a)	Forbidden	(a)	Not laid down	Obligation to consult enterprises with 20 or more employees	Priority for new recruitment
Luxembourg	No specific legal provision	No specific form	(a)	> Normal	(a)	Fully for those working >24 hours: otherwise not included	Employer may not refuse to bargain with the worker representative	No legal provision
Netherlands	No specific legal provision	No specific form	(a)	> full-time hours	Domestic workers working less than 3 hours weekly	Includes only those working more than 1/3 of normal hours	Obligation to inform works council	No legal provision
Portugal	No specific legal provision	No specific form	(a)	(a)	(a)	(a)	Obligation to consult and negotiate with employer representation	Priority for new recruitment
Spain	No specific legal provision	Written	(a)	(a)	(a)	Included pro rata	Obligation to consult works council	No legal provision
United Kingdom	No specific legal provision	(b) <16 hours written evidence	No requirement for proportional pay	No provision	< 8hours weekly16 hours for less than 5 years	(a)	No specific provision	No legal provision

(a) no difference compared with full-time employment;
(b) difference compared with full-time employment.
Source: Delsen, Huijgen, 1994, p. 3.

Box 3.1 "Considerations and recommendations to promote part-time work and differentiation in patterns of working time" of the Stichting van de Arbeid, the Netherlands.

In October 1992, the Minister of Social Affairs and Employment sent the Labour Foundation a letter asking the Foundation, among other things, to take initiatives aimed at the promotion of part-time work in all posts of employment and sectors. In September 1993, the Foundation of Labour sent its "Considerations and recommendations to promote part-time work and differentiation in patterns of working time" to the Minister. The starting point of the analysis was that there are demand- and supply-side needs for a differentiation of working hours. For employers this will lead to more efficient business management, while it will allow enterprises to fine-tune business hours and working hours. It will also enable employees to match working hours and working times with individual circumstances. "The key is to reach a balance between the individual wishes of employers and employees... In the past decades, part-time work has increased considerably in the Netherlands and reached a record high from an international point of view. However, this development should be prevented from coming to a halt in the future. This is not unrealistic considering that part-time work remains concentrated in a limited number of sectors (mainly in the service industries) and jobs (especially lower-qualified work) and, because of its small size, produces too limited an income and a vocational perspective (the majority of the present part-time jobs are for less than 20 hours a week). ... the Foundation recommends parties in the collective bargaining and enterprise to lay down rules for the employer to honour in principle a request from the employee to adjust his or her hours, unless this cannot be reasonably asked of the employer, on the basis of important business interests. The basic assumption of such an arrangement should be that, in principle, every job at every job level and in every sector lends itself to a working-hours pattern deviating from regular (full-time) working hours."

Source: Stichting van de Arbeid, 1993.

the unemployed and promote further training (box 3.2 and table 3.18). This is a step towards lifelong flexible working hours where flexibility of working hours is linked with social security.

Obviously, there is still a lag in terms of "offensive" working-time strategies in the different countries. The Dutch part-time policy may come to an end if a statutory right for employees to reduce working hours is not introduced. A new balance between employers and employees has to be found in the decisions over part-time work. Only in Denmark has working-time policy been linked to further training policy. If we are to go beyond mere rhetoric on lifelong learning, then employees must be given time for further training during their working life.

Box 3.2 Denmark: The introduction of paid-leave arrangements

Paid-leave arrangements were introduced in Denmark in 1992 (table 3.18). They were tested for two years and then became part of Danish labour market policy. The idea is that companies replace an employed person on leave by an unemployed person. The chances of an unemployed person getting a job improve if he or she has temporary work experience, so leave taken by the employed is linked with incentives for companies to recruit an unemployed person. These arrangements are also known as job rotation schemes. In the sabbatical leave scheme, the employment of a substitute is mandatory. In educational and childcare leave, this is not a formal requirement but is promoted in various ways (there are agreements between firms, training centres and the employment offices).

The leave schemes are very popular in Denmark. In 1996, 121,000 people took leave; of this total, 72,700 persons went on educational leave, 46,999 were on childcare leave, and 1,500 on sabbaticals. Half of the people taking leave are unemployed. On average about three-quarters of the vacant jobs are filled by substitutes. The replacement rate is higher in small firms and in the public service. Forty-six per cent of the substitutes had been employed before and only 54 per cent were unemployed. In total it is estimated that the leave schemes reduced open unemployment by 60–70,000 in 1995. However, two-thirds to three-quarters of this figure is the result of unemployed persons taking leave and therefore not being counted as unemployed (Madsen, 1998).

Table 3.18 Denmark: Paid-leave arrangements under the 1994 labour market reform

	Educational leave	Sabbatical leave	Childcare leave
Target group	1. Employed 2. Unemployed 3. Self-employed	1. Employed	1. Employed 2. Unemployed 3. Self-employed
Applicant must be eligible for unemployment benefits?	Yes	Yes	No
Maximum duration	1 year	1 year[a]	26 weeks/1 year[b]
Right for the applicant?	No	No	Yes (up to 26 weeks)
Mandatory substitute?	No	Yes	No
Amount paid as share of unemployment benefit	100 %	60 %[c]	60 %[c]

[a] From 1995, the minimum duration of a sabbatical is 13 weeks. [b] From 1995, the right to leave for child-minding is reduced to 13 weeks if the child is older than one year. [c] Benefits for sabbatical leave and child-minding leave were originally set to 80 per cent of unemployment benefits. In 1995, they were reduced to 70 per cent and were further reduced to 60 per cent in April 1997.

Source: Kongshoj Madsen, 1998, p. 66.

3.4 WORK-SHARING, EMPLOYMENT AND WORK ORGANIZATION[13]

The full employment policy by means of investment is only one particular application of an intellectual theorem. You can produce the result as well by consuming more or working less. Personally I regard the investment policy as first aid ... Less work is the ultimate solution ... How you mix up the three ingredients of a cure is a matter of taste and experience, i.e. of morals and knowledge (Keynes, 1945, p. 384)

It is generally taken for granted that without working-time reductions, the productivity gains of the past 150 years would have led to high and persistent levels of unemployment (Drèze, 1986, p. 36). John Hicks described the reduction in working time as a means of avoiding "secular unemployment" (Hicks, 1946, p. 301). However, what is regarded as self-evident over the long term is controversial in the short term. Some of those prepared to accept the role of work-sharing in reducing unemployment over the long term argue that such reductions have no place in the armoury of medium-term employment policy. Rigidities in work organization or higher wage costs are frequently adduced as evidence in support of this position (Drèze, 1986, p. 44).

It seems necessary to close the gap in the argument between the short- and long-term perspectives and to ask: Under what conditions might work-sharing lead to higher employment? How might these conditions be incorporated into policy strategies on working time? The debate on working time is often very unsatisfactory in this respect, since it all too frequently becomes bogged down in quasi-religious exchanges of articles of faith between supporters and opponents of work-sharing. However, working time can be shared in very different ways and under very different conditions. Like any other instrument of employment policy, it may be used successfully or unsuccessfully.

It cannot be argued that a reduction in working time is not a suitable instrument of employment policy simply because it has not led to higher employment in a particular country. It may be that this effect was produced by certain peripheral conditions, such as excessive wage increases, traditional management styles or labour shortages in certain segments. Under different conditions, working-time policy may be very successful. We need to identify these peripheral conditions not only to enable us to discuss whether working time should be reduced but also give us much greater insight into how such a reduction might be implemented.

The starting assumption is that reductions in collective working time can no longer be regarded as the only means of implementing work-sharing. It can also be realized in the form of cuts in individual working time, as the Netherlands example shows. We begin with a brief survey of the historical evolution of working time, productivity and work organization. We then deal with the major studies of the employment effects of collective working-time reductions over the past 15 years, so as to establish the conditions under which positive and negative employment effects have been produced. Other forms of working-time reduction, such as the expansion of part-time work, and the link between working time and work organization, are examined more closely.

The long-term evolution of working time, productivity, growth and pay

One of the phenomena that accompanied the economic development of the industrialized countries was a considerable reduction in working time. Increased prosperity was redistributed in the form not only of wage increases but also of a reduction in working time. About 120 years ago, workers in what are now regarded as the industrialized countries worked more than 3,000 hours per year. Since then, average working time has declined by almost 50 per cent (table 3.19). It is true that these figures include the effects of part-time work, which did not begin to make a significant impact until the 1960s. Nevertheless, it can be argued that, from the standpoint of the last century, most full-time workers in the Western industrialized countries today work part time. Gross national product (GNP) per capita, which we shall take as a very rough indicator of the evolution of material well-being, has risen five- to ten-fold over the same period.

A great deal of often qualitative evidence has been put forward by industrial sociologists and economic historians suggesting that firms that cut working time also change their system of work organization. At the beginning of the Industrial Revolution, labour was used extensively, that is, by making working time as long as possible. Deutschmann (1985) has shown in his historical analysis just how non-intensive production systems were in the early stages of the Industrial Revolution. Production was still dependent on natural energy sources, such as water and wind, and stoppages were frequent. Work was badly organized, with plenty of opportunities for unauthorized breaks. As working-time reductions were pushed through by trade unions and parliaments,[14] constraints were placed on the extensive utilization of labour, making it necessary to make more intensive use of labour and machinery.

Table 3.19 The evolution of working time, productivity per hour worked and GNP per capita, 1870-1992 (percentages)

	United States	Germany	Japan	France	Great Britain
Working time	−46.3	−46.9	−36.3	−47.6	−50.0
Productivity per hour worked	+1 287.6	+1 734.7	+4 352.2	+2 127.9	+918.8
GNP per capita	+918.6	+998.3	+2 632.0	+967.1	+501.7

Source: Maddison, 1995.

The introduction of scientific management (Taylor, 1947) divided the work process into standardized tasks, each with an allotted time. The mechanization of production gave firms control over work rates. Scientific studies of the work process proved that if tasks were highly concentrated, productivity declined considerably when working time was long. Daily, weekly and annual recovery periods are required (Semmer et al., 1995). Continuity of production was closely linked with stable demand, which became more independent of fluctuations in local markets. The extension of markets to the national and, increasingly, international level became the precondition for mass production. Product standardization led to reduced costs when output volumes were high, and the development of storage techniques made it possible to buffer the production process from short-term market fluctuations (Deutschmann, 1985).

Denison (1962), in a long-term study from 1929 to 1957, estimated that at the beginning of this period, when weekly working time was over 48 hours, working-time reductions were compensated for by higher productivity at a rate in excess of 100 per cent; at the end of the period, when weekly working time was already down to 40 hours, the rate of compensation was about 60 per cent. Comparable results have been obtained by German studies which show that, at the end of the last century, working-time reductions were compensated for by productivity increases at a rate of more than 160 per cent; after the First World War, the rates of compensation were between 60 and 140 per cent and from the end of the Second World War until 1970 they were between 30 and 70 per cent (Hacker, 1970). Thus working-time reductions were a precondition for more efficient work organization and a crucial source of growth. However, since the opportunities for further intensification of work dwindle in the long term, this productivity effect is eventually exhausted.

The standardization of tasks was also a fundamental precondition for allocating several workers to the same job, thereby making it possible to decouple individual working times from operating hours by introducing shift work. In the case of the United States, Foss (1995) shows that, in the course of development, the industrial capital stock was used both more intensively (fewer stoppages) and more extensively (longer operating hours). Thirty-nine per cent of the increase in machine operating times between 1929 and 1963 can be explained by an increase in operating hours, while the rest is accounted for by a reduction in machine stoppage times (table 3.20).

Foss also calculates the capital-saving effects of changes to the organization of operating hours in American firms between 1929 and 1976. During this period, the gross capital stock in the United States rose by 166 per cent, an annual growth rate of 2.1 per cent. The annual increase in operating hours of 0.46 per cent amounted to about 22 per cent of this increase in the capital stock. Without an increase in operating hours during this period, American manufacturing industry would have had to increase its capital stock not just by 265.9 per cent but by 331.6 per cent (an additional 200 billion dollars) in

Table 3.20 Annual rates of change in machine utilization times and operating hours in the United States, 1929–63 (percentages)

Year	Annual machine utilization times	Weekly operating hours	(1) as % of (2)
	(1)	(2)	(3)
1929–63	1.17	0.46	0.39
1929–54	1.00	0.51	0.51
1954–63	1.65	0.35	0.21

Source: Foss, 1984, p. 23.

order to achieve the level of output produced in 1976 (Foss, 1995). Shorter working times did not prove to be an obstacle to more extensive utilization of the capital stock; all that was necessary was a reorganization of the shift system. In the nineteenth century, continuous (seven-day) production plants operated a two-shift system; at the beginning of the twentieth century there was a changeover first to a three-shift system and then, after the Second World War, to four-shift operation. In countries in which working time has been further reduced in recent years, five- and even six-shift systems are now being introduced.[15]

This connection between working time and work organization has also been exploited by policy-makers. For example, some years ago Singapore placed legal restrictions on working time in order to force firms to introduce more efficient forms of work organization and to encourage modernization of the economy. Conversely, there are cases in which increased working time has made it possible to return to traditional, extensive forms of work organization. The sweatshops in the United States come immediately to mind, as does the current regressive trend in work organization in many German construction firms, where a plentiful supply of cheap, illegal labour is forcing the abandonment of a form of organization based on team work and high skill levels, and a return to a hierarchical form based on wide differences in skill levels.

Thus the reduction in working time over the past 100 years was not only part of a policy of redistribution, but also an important factor in economic growth. It is true that the working-time reductions of the past 100 years were largely forced upon employers by legislation and collective agreements; nevertheless, they caused firms to introduce new forms of work organization that have benefited employers and not just workers. The 8-hour day and the 40-hour week became fixed points of reference for firms around which they developed the paradigms of work organization. This aspect has not been adequately considered in the economic debate.[16] The reduction in working time is regarded primarily as a defensive policy in conflict with the proactive growth policy that is held to be necessary (Neifer-Dichmann, 1991).

Working-time reductions as employment policy: Some experiences from the past 15 years

The 40-hour week became the norm in most Western European countries in the mid- to late 1960s. From the mid-1970s onwards, following the rise in unemployment in the wake of the oil crisis, many trade unions sought, often successfully, to reduce working time below this rigid limit (Bosch/Dawkins/Michon, 1994). The initial pace was set by Belgium, which is still, with Denmark and Germany, one of the countries with the shortest collectively agreed average working times. Other countries followed, including Great Britain (39-hour week in the engineering industry in 1981), France (legislation introducing the 39-hour week passed in 1982), the Netherlands (38-hour week introduced in many industries between 1983 and 1986), and Germany, where, after major strikes in the engineering and printing industries, the process of reducing working time below 40 hours in many parts of the economy began in 1985. Germany and the Netherlands were two of the few European countries where collective working-time reductions continued into the second half of the 1980s and during the recession of the first half of the 1990s, although at an increasingly slow pace. In the Netherlands, the theme of industry-wide collective agreements on working-time reductions resumed in 1996, particularly in certain parts of the service sector. In the banking industry, for example, weekly working time has now been reduced to 36 hours (ATOS, 1997). In Belgium and France, the State has provided incentives for such agreements to be concluded: social security contributions are reduced when working time is cut. These arrangements now apply even when jobs are not at risk, provided that working time is reduced in order to create new jobs.

These developments have left their mark on European working-time statistics. In 1983, 87 per cent of male dependent employees in Germany were still working a collectively agreed 40-hour week; by 1992, that figure had fallen to 19 per cent. The comparable figures for the Netherlands are 80 per cent and 32 per cent, and for Denmark 75 per cent and 6 per cent (European Commission, 1994). The average number of hours actually worked per week also fell noticeably between 1983 and 1992, although not in all countries. In Great Britain, because of the high volume of overtime worked, there has even been an increase in the effective annual working time of full-time workers. The Government of France has already introduced the 35-hour week, while the Government of Italy plans to do so over the next few years. This might mark the beginning of further working-time reductions in Europe.

The working-time reductions of the 1950s and 1960s were essentially an attempt to improve working and living conditions. This objective has not been wholly ignored in the past 20 years, but the main purpose of the reductions during this period has undoubtedly been to combat unemployment. The employment effects of these cuts in working time have been investigated in many studies. The major problem in all empirical studies of the employment effects of working-time reductions lies in the difficulty of isolating the influences exerted by growth, productivity and working time from each other. In theory, it is impossible to make a clear distinction on either the macroeconomic or microeconomic level. However, the range of expected employment effects can be narrowed down by ensuring that the assumptions on which any estimates are based are as well founded as possible, both theoretically and empirically. Most studies, using a range of different methods (regression analyses, surveys of firms and case studies, macroeconomic simulations, decompositions), put the positive employment effects at between 25 and 70 per cent of the arithmetically possible effect. Only a few studies estimate the effects to be neutral (Hunt, 1996) or even negative (König/Pohlmeier, 1987).

We cannot refer here to all the studies known to us and will therefore confine ourselves to a few examples:

- Surveys of firms and works councillors have been carried out in several European countries. The results are heavily influenced by who asks the questions and who answers them. Works councillors tend to give more positive assessments than managers. The actual questions asked also matter. An employment effect cannot be defined solely in terms of new recruitment, but may also be reflected in a reduction or avoidance of redundancies, the conversion of part-time jobs to full time, or a reduction in short-time working; yet surveys frequently ask only about the new jobs created. Despite differences in the questions asked and the persons interviewed, all the surveys with which we are familiar show that the working-time reduction in question had a positive employment effect (table 3.21).
- Surveys often underestimate the employment effect, since they only produce snapshots taken soon after the reduction in working time has been implemented. Macroeconomic simulations and case studies carried out after a longer interval show that in many cases employment does not rise for some time.
- Thus the 1985 reduction in weekly working time in the German engineering industry from 40 to 38.5 hours initially triggered a rise in the volume of overtime in many plants (Bosch et al., 1988; cf. in table 3.21 the company survey conducted by the employers' association in Germany). The Deutsche Institut für Wirtschaftsforschung has estimated that one-third of this 1.5-hour cut was initially offset by a short-term increase in overtime; only later did the volume of overtime begin to decline: "It was not until the next downturn in the economy that the increased volume of overtime was further reduced and the job-saving effect thereby achieved" (Stille/Zwiener, 1997, p. 90).
- In France, the immediate reaction of many firms to the introduction of the 39-hour week was to intensify the work process (e.g. by reducing cycle times) in a way that could not be sustained over the medium term. As has been estimated by means of macroeconomic simulations, the ensuing productivity increase fell gradually from an initial 75 per cent to about 50 per

Table 3.21 Selected company surveys on the employment effects of collective working-time reductions

Country	Working-time reduction	Nature of investigation	Employment effects found
France	39-hour week, 1982	Company survey carried out in 1983 by the government statistical service, INSEE	26% of firms: new recruitment; 11%: reduction in job losses; 59%: no change in employment
Germany	Reduction of working time in 3 stages to 38½, 37½ and 37 hours (engineering industry)	Surveys of works councils at each stage by IG-Metall (about 5,000 plants)	Employment effects of 70%, 58% and 70%, respectively
Germany	First stage in the reduction of weekly working time to 38½ hours in 1985 (engineering industry)	Company survey by engineering employers' association (about 5,000 plants)	Employment effect of 21% (plus 14% extra overtime, which was later reduced)
Germany	Reduction of weekly working time to 39 hours (public service)	Establishment and staff council survey by market research institute, Infratest	Employment effect of 52%
Netherlands	Industry-wide collective agreements on 38-hour week (shorter in some cases), 1982–85	Company survey carried out by Loontechnische Dienst	15% of firms: new recruitment (with employment effect of about 20–25%; 3.5%: existing jobs safeguarded; 78%: no change in employment
Germany	First stage of reduction in weekly working time to 38½ hours in 1985 (printing industry)	Survey of works councils by IG Druck trade union (450 plants)	Employment effect of 66%

Sources: ATOS, 1997; Cette/Taddei, 1994; Seifert, 1991.

cent, so that the employment effect of the working-time reduction made itself felt only by degrees (Cette/Taddei, 1994, p. 147).

- Similar developments can be observed in the Netherlands. Many of the cuts in weekly working time from 40 to 38 hours in the Dutch private sector took place during the recession of 1983-84. The fairly modest employment effects recorded in the first statistical survey conducted by the labour market authorities were accounted for by the surplus capacity that existed at the time of the reductions. Furthermore, case studies ascertained that staff shortages were initially filled by means of overtime, fixed-term contracts and subcontracting

Table 3.22 Employment effects of collective reductions of working hours in the Netherlands, 1983–87 (thousands)

	1983	1984	1985	1986	1987	Total
Private sector	3	8	9	10	4	34
Public sector/subsidized	3	7	8	19	4	41
Total	6	15	17	29	8	75

Sources: Ministerie van SZW; ATOS, 1987, p. 20.

(de Lange, 1989). It was not until a later assessment, based on an econometric estimate, was undertaken by the Ministry of Labour that a considerably more positive picture emerged for the longer period between 1983 and 1987 (table 3.22).

- Thus the employment effects of working-time reductions are, first, distributed over the economic cycle. Second, there is a time lag, since firms have to adapt their work organization and also need time to recruit new workers. Since adjustment times are not involved in employment protection agreements such as that concluded at Volkswagen, the employment effect makes itself felt immediately, albeit in the form of redundancies avoided rather than new jobs.

It is evident from case studies that the employment effects vary according to type of plant and occupational category. The effects are much less marked among white-collar workers than among manual workers (Bosch et al., 1988; Lehndorff, 1995). There are two main reasons for this. First, the potential for work intensification is greater in white-collar occupations, since rationalization programmes in the past were directed mainly at manual jobs. Second, working-time standards, such as arrangements for breaks or overtime payments, are observed more closely in manual than in white-collar jobs. In all countries, the degree of unpaid overtime is higher among white-collar than manual workers. At Volkswagen, where the 28.8-hour week was introduced without wage compensation, those white-collar employees not covered by the collective agreement – and some who are – now work the same long hours as before, despite the cut in working time, and are being paid less for doing so. This is why only 15.5 per cent of senior managers and 39.5 per cent of those white-collar workers covered by the collective agreement welcome the working-time reduction, compared with 52.4 per cent of manual workers (Hartz, 1996). These differentiated effects on employment, working conditions and living standards, together with the influence of pay already noted above, go a long way towards explaining the differing assessments of working-time reductions made by the various occupational categories.

Two general conclusions can be drawn from this brief outline of the employment effects of collective working-time reductions. First, the considerable methodological problems mean that precise results are not possible; the best that can be hoped for is an estimate of the range within which the employment effects might lie. Second, most empirical studies confirm that collective working-time reductions can be expected to produce positive employment effects. However, the broad range of possible effects that can be derived from the various sets of assumptions on which the models are based merely reflects the fact that the circumstances under which working time is reduced are just as important as the working-time reduction itself (Cette/Taddei, 1994, p. 91). These circumstances are not laws of nature, but the product of human choices. This is why the most important thing is to agree on the *conditions* that have to be *created* if the working-time strategy pursued is to be as successful as possible in creating jobs. The key factors to be taken into account here are (a) wages and compensatory wage increases, (b) skill shortages, (c) fixed labour costs and (d) work organization.

Wages and compensatory wage increases

When cuts in working time are combined with compensatory wage increases, so that monthly pay remains the same despite shorter monthly working time, it is commonly assumed that the cake is being distributed twice, meaning that the compensatory wage increase is being paid in addition to the usual pay rises. If this were the case, then working-time reductions would indeed lead to unit cost increases. However, cuts in working time and pay increases can of course be negotiated as part of a total package. In this case, the wage increase paid in compensation for the working-time reduction can be offset by lower pay rises. If a package of this kind ensures that the increase in costs does not outstrip the gain in productivity, then unit wage costs will remain constant. If the aim is to reduce working time quickly and in larger steps than can be achieved by reducing working time in line with the expected gain in productivity, then the compensatory wage increase will have to be abandoned altogether (as in the Volkswagen model, for example). If longer-term package deals can be agreed on, then larger cuts in working time can be combined with compensatory wage increases while at the same time ensuring cost neutrality.

This is precisely the kind of long-term package deal that was agreed in the Netherlands and which underpinned working-time reductions in the German engineering industry. Employees finance the working-time reductions themselves by accepting lower wage increases. In the Netherlands, it was even possible, within a concerted wages policy, simultaneously to implement a policy of wage moderation, to bring about a decline in wage levels, particularly relative to German rates (DIW, 1997)[17] and to achieve considerable reductions in working time. In Germany the share of wages in GNP fell, since the long-term collective agreements concluded in the 1980s underestimated future rates of productivity growth and prices, and the balance of distribution between productivity gains and rises in real wages even shifted in favour of company profits.

However, there are counter-examples where the cake was, so to speak, divided up twice. In Norway, working time was reduced in 1986 from 40 to 37.5 hours per week, first in the engineering industry and then in the rest of the economy. However, this cut in working time was accompanied neither by coordinated pay negotiations nor by agreements on more flexible forms of working-time organization. This omission contributed greatly to the rise in overtime and inflationary pressures (Bosch, 1997).[18]

Skill shortages

One of the most important arguments against a policy of work-sharing is that it will lead to considerable skill shortages (figure 3.10). If skill shortages develop in the labour market, work cannot in fact be redistributed. In that event, cuts in working time will either reduce growth or be buffered by increased overtime. Some indication of the importance of skills can be obtained from a comparison between Germany and Great Britain. In Germany, working time was cut during a period of rapid economic upturn. However, skill shortages did not occur in Germany between 1982 and 1992: the volume of overtime even declined, from 80.2 hours per employee in 1980 to 65 hours in 1992. This was unique for a boom period. The most important reason for this happy state of affairs was probably the fact that, in the years preceding the reduction in working time, many firms operating within the German vocational training system had been training more skilled workers than their immediate needs required. Firms had responded to political pressure by declaring themselves willing to help those youngsters born in years with very large cohorts to enter the labour market. It also proved fortuitous that this same period also saw an increase in training

Figure 3.10 Interference with production through skill shortages in manufacturing

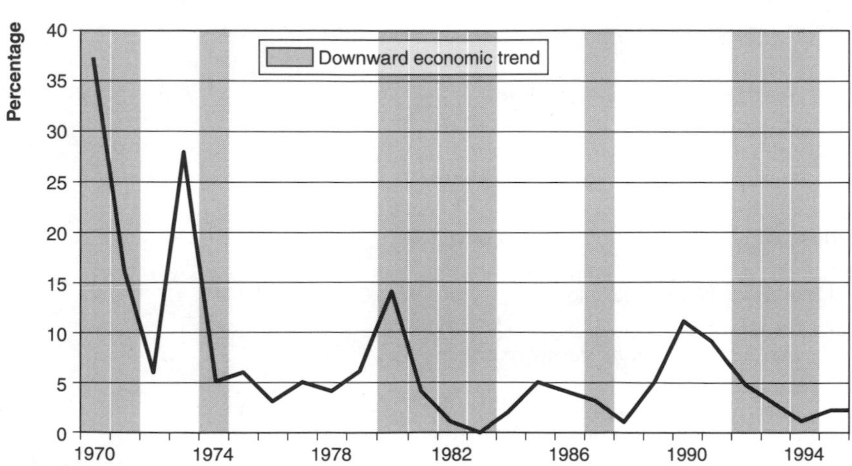

Source: Stille/Zwiener, 1997, p. 29.

Table 3.23 Vocational training in Great Britain, France and Germany (distribution of vocational qualifications in the economically active population, percentages)

	Great Britain (1989)	France (1988)	Germany (1988)
Higher education qualifications	11	7	11
Technician	7	7	7
Skilled worker	18	33	56
No vocational qualification	64	53	26

Source: OECD, 1995, p. 53.

provision for the unemployed as part of active labour market policy. As a result, the fears of skill shortages proved unfounded, except in a few isolated cases. During the implementation of the working-time reductions, firms complained less about shortages of skilled workers than in the early 1980s. The situation in Great Britain is very different. There, 64 per cent of employees have no formal vocational qualifications, compared with 26 per cent in Germany (table 3.23). One reason for the higher volume of overtime worked in Great

Table 3.24 Trends in paid overtime work

	1980	1985	1990	1995	1996
A. All industry					
Germany					
Weekly overtime hours per employee	1.5	1.3	1.3	1.3	1.2
Japan					
Weekly overtime hours per employee	3.1	3.4	3.6	2.6	–
United Kingdom					
Weekly overtime hours per male employee	3.8	3.5	3.6	3.2	3.1
B. Manufacturing					
Finland					
Weekly overtime hours per wage and salary earner	–	0.96	0.94	1.01	0.90
Italy					
Overtime working hours as proportion of total hours	3.2	3.7	–	5.5	5.0
Japan					
Weekly overtime hours per employee	3.8	4.2	4.5	3.1	–
United Kingdom					
Weekly overtime hours per male employee	5.6	5.3	5.9	5.6	5.3
United States					
Weekly overtime hours per employee (Production or non-supervisory worker)	2.8	3.3	3.6	4.4	4.5

Source: OECD, 1998.

Britain than in Germany (table 3.24) certainly lies in the inadequate supply of skilled workers in the British economy.[19] One British personnel manager, in a conversation with the author, put his finger on the problem: "We don't have skill shortages, we call it overtime". Thus a policy of work redistribution will be more difficult in countries with an inadequate supply of unemployed skilled workers than in those in which the supply of skilled workers is plentiful thanks to an active labour market and training policy.

Fixed labour costs

If social security contributions are calculated as a proportion of pay, then they constitute variable costs. The recruitment of additional workers does not lead to an increase in social security costs if the volume of work remains unchanged. The situation is quite different if the contributions are paid only up to a set ceiling or on a flat-rate basis and thus become fixed costs per employee. In this case, there are increased incentives to make greater use of overtime and fewer incentives to hire new workers for whom new insurance policies would have to be taken out. This fixed-cost problem can be observed in the United States, for example, where firms contract into health and pension insurance schemes that are normally paid for on a per capita rather than on an hourly basis. It has been shown that working time is longer in those firms that have contracted into insurance schemes for their employees than those that have not (Cutler/Madrian,1996). Most European countries have statutory social security systems. Contributions are paid as a proportion of earnings or the systems are financed out of general taxation, so that the fixed-cost problem is of no great significance for full-time employees. The privatization of social security systems, now being discussed in many European countries, could lead to the erection of new barriers to a policy of work redistribution.

Company training expenditure can be a further element in fixed costs. If firms invest heavily in raising the skill levels of their workforces and they, rather than employees or the State, bear the cost, then employers clearly have an interest in extending the working time of their skilled employees. If the half-life of skills declines as the pace of technical change quickens, and if skills also become less divisible or give rise to additional communication costs, then the problem becomes even more acute. Just as capital-intensive firms seek to extend their machine operating times as far as possible, so they are becoming increasingly keen to extend "brain operating times". This is one of the reasons why the actual working time of highly skilled employees has risen in recent years, despite a fall in their contractual working time. Figure 3.11 reveals a widening gap between actual and contractual working time for this category of the workforce. Thus the transition to a "knowledge society", with its attendant increase in skill levels, also creates barriers to work-sharing. The interests of individual firms and those of the wider economy may diverge at this point. Efficiency in the economy as a whole will rise if a

Figure 3.11 Working times of high-skilled employees in Western Germany

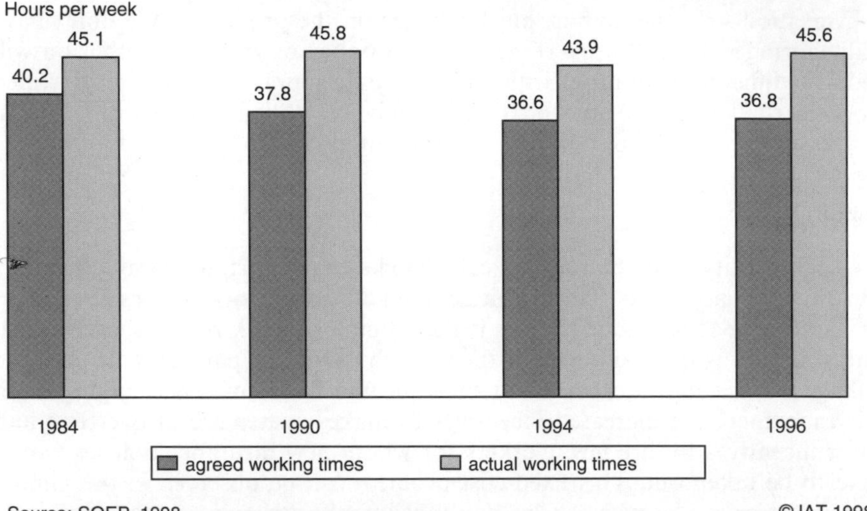

Source: SOEP, 1998. © IAT 1998

large part of the skill reservoir – forced to lie fallow or even waste away because of unemployment – can be brought back into production through work-sharing; for firms, however, this may give rise to higher costs.

Work organization

Larger cuts in working time generally require an accompanying change in work organization. Firms that cling to their old system must either resort to the use of overtime, so that the reduction produces no employment effect but only a wage increase, or they can try to fit the working-time reduction into their outdated system of work organization designed for longer working hours, which can give rise to considerable productivity problems. Thus when weekly working time was cut in Germany, the Netherlands and Norway, many companies initially retained their shift systems based on the 40-hour week, and did not seek to make changes until difficulties became apparent. The following problems arose: The volume of overtime went up and firms sought to economize on overtime premiums. To compensate workers for the shorter working hours, too many days off had to be granted and the frequent periods of absence made it difficult to ensure that employees communicated with each other. The old systems became too inflexible and working time could no longer be adjusted adequately to demand; moreover, new shift systems with shorter working times opened up new opportunities for extending operating hours.

Such organizational changes have undoubtedly been made easier by agreements introducing greater flexibility into working-time arrangements (Bosch,

Table 3.25 Percentage of firms that have changed their use of flexible forms of working time in the past three years

	Finland	Denmark	France	Western Germany	Italy	Ireland	Norway	Netherlands	Spain	Great Britain
Increased	62	16	19	55	32	25	23	43	35	30
Unchanged	24	53	46	27	22	27	59	38	52	31
Reduced	0	1	1	1	0	1	1	0	1	1
Not used	12	25	24	14	36	31	10	14	10	32

Source: Cranfield School of Management, 1995.

1997; ATOS, 1997). In the past 20 years, trade unions in many countries have traded shorter working times for greater flexibility, and governments have established the preconditions for a more flexible distribution of working time. Of fundamental importance in this respect are the opportunities for extending operating hours and distributing working time more flexibly over the year, which is why the dividing lines between weekly and annual working-time reductions are becoming fluid. In Austria, for example, the metal and engineering industry extended the equalization period for the flexible distribution of working time to one year; the legal framework for this was established by the Working Time Act which came into force in the same year (1997). Previously, Austrian working-time legislation had permitted an equalization period of only a few weeks.

Working-time reductions create the necessary scope and incentives for an active policy of *working-time management at firm level* that can lead to considerable increases in efficiency. Table 3.25 shows that in those countries with an active working time policy (Finland, the Netherlands, Germany), firms have in recent years introduced flexible working times on a wider basis. In many cases, the entire system of work organization had to be rethought, resulting in considerable organizational innovations (see below).

The employment effects of extending part-time work

In a number of countries, the creation of part-time jobs is seen as an opportunity for work-sharing and the reduction of unemployment. In other countries, the part-time rate is declining and the opportunities for creating additional part-time jobs seem to be limited. In the United States, the share of part-time employees has been static since 1983, and in Denmark it declined from 19.5 per cent in 1983 to 16.5 per cent in 1996; in the Netherlands, on the other hand, it rose from 18.5 per cent in 1993 to 29.3 per cent in 1996 (OECD, 1997b).

The question of whether new jobs can be created by dividing work up into part-time jobs cannot be answered in the abstract. Part-time work means different things in different countries and even in the various segments of national labour markets. These varying conditions have first to be identified before any plausible statements can be made. To this end, it is useful to enquire into the reasons why part-time work has expanded rapidly in some countries and is stagnating or even declining in others. We suspect that the following factors play some part:

Wage differentials between full-timers and part-timers

If the differential is more than 100 per cent, as at United Parcel Service (US$20 per hour, compared with US$8–9), then volunteers for reduced hours will be thin on the ground. The gender pay gap is also important. If men in Great Britain earn £7 per hour, they are unlikely to be enthusiastic at the prospect of restricting their overtime if their wives are earning only £3 in the service sector. It can also be argued that decisions on part-time work depend on the distribution not only of individual but also of household earnings. In the Netherlands, household incomes in the lowest decile of the income range are 61.5 per cent of average household earnings; the equivalent figure for the United States is only 34.7 per cent (Atkinson et al., 1994). The high level of acceptance of part-time work in Scandinavia is probably not unconnected with the low pay differentials between the various sectors of the economy, as a result of the wage solidarity policy pursued there.

Differences in social security arrangements for full-timers and part-timers

The legal and actual thresholds for social security entitlements are equally important. In Germany, the thresholds for entitlement to health and old-age insurance are a working time of 15 hours per week or monthly earnings of DM 610. The limit in Japan has been reduced from 30 to 20 hours per week, but this is still the highest threshold in all the OECD countries. In the United States, many part-timers do not qualify for company health insurance and pension schemes. These thresholds act as an incentive for firms to create precarious part-time jobs that are cheaper for employers, but such jobs are scarcely acceptable to employees. No employees will voluntarily reduce their working time if they have to give up their entitlement to social security benefits.

Career downturn or cultural acceptance

One of the most formidable barriers to the voluntary reduction of working time is the damage it can do to careers. In a culture that places a high value on full-time work and a willingness to do overtime, employees seeking to reduce their working time are regarded as without ambition and can more or less write off their career prospects. Part-time work will not gain lasting cultural acceptance unless firms cease to be the sole arbiters of decisions on part-time work, and part-time work ceases to be confined to marginal activities, as has happened in the Netherlands. If employees are given a right to work part time, as in

Scandinavia, or an entitlement to work part time is enshrined in law, as is currently being discussed in the Netherlands, then part-time work will not only be imposed through the "market" but can also be a matter of free choice. The Dutch and Scandinavians are trying to change the culture by strengthening the rights of employees to reduce their working time. In the Scandinavian countries, mothers and fathers of young children have the right to convert to part time and subsequently return to a full-time position.

The level of women's integration into the labour market

A high level of part-time work, particularly among women, may possibly be a transitional phase between the single male breadwinner model and men's and women's integration into the labour market on an equal footing. This could explain why the Netherlands – initially a late starter in terms of integrating women into economic activity – now has a very high part-time share, which is likely to decline in future; and why the part-time share in Denmark is also now falling, particularly among women, who are increasingly aspiring to full-time employment and regard part-time work merely as a temporary interlude. In Denmark, the female part-time rate fell between 1983 and 1996 from 34.5 per cent to 24.2 per cent; in the Netherlands, it rose over the same period from 44.7 per cent to 55.4 per cent (OECD, 1997b).

Since the conditions under which part-time work can be introduced vary so much, it is difficult to make any general statements on the employment effects. The following observations can claim a degree of plausibility:

- If female participation rates in a country are very low, the initial effect of an expansion of part-time work will be an increase in the labour supply. Employment will rise without unemployment necessarily falling.
- If part-time work is introduced solely on the initiative of employers and spreads mainly within the service sector, where there are considerable fluctuations in demand that can be dealt with more easily with smaller time-units than with the large blocks of time worked by full-timers, then full-time employment will be displaced by part-time work. The number of employees may remain the same, but the volume of paid work – taking this effect on its own – will fall.
- If employees are given the right to work part time, either temporarily or permanently, and part-time work spreads to a wide diversity of jobs, then the employment effects will be positive, since the potential for rationalization will be limited.
- As more and more women enter the labour market, the scope for expanding part-time work diminishes. It is more likely that working time will begin to rise again. Such a "part-time trap", caused by an increase in the labour supply and leading possibly to rising unemployment, can be avoided only if men's working time is also reduced.

Work organization and working time

In the past, cuts in working time have always been linked to changes in work organization. This remains the case today. However, the impetus for changes in work organization emanates not only from changes in working time but also from changes in the structure of the labour supply, and in market and competitive conditions. Shifts in labour supply have already been examined, with the increase in female participation rates highlighted as one of the main changes. We will now focus on the consequences of changed market and competitive conditions. The main point to be made here is that firms are seeking to adjust their working times and operating hours in increasingly more sophisticated ways, a trend which can be characterized as the "fine tuning" of working time.[20]

One of the reasons for this fine tuning in manufacturing industry is that today's firms are increasingly less able to cope with seasonal fluctuations by holding extensive stocks and, consequently, need to adjust production much more closely to demand. Such demand-oriented workforce assignment is a familiar characteristic of the service sector and is now spreading to manufacturing, implying a "tertiarization of working time".

The diversity of product variants has increased to such an extent that it has become too expensive to keep large stocks. As a result, the order situation and disruptions to the production and supply chain impact directly on working time. In consequence, working time replaces keeping extensive stocks as the source of flexibility and employees become buffers in the production process.[21] In production departments, therefore, working times are becoming more customer oriented and in some cases are drawing close to those in the service sector. In many European countries, the restrictions on opening hours in the retail trade and other service industries have been reduced or eliminated, so that employees' working time is distributed over a greater proportion of the week. It is more cost-efficient to deal with fluctuations in orders by distributing working time flexibly over the year than by alternating periods of overtime and short time. This is why firms are increasingly adopting the year (or, for longer order cycles, periods of several years) instead of the week as the reference point for their working-time planning. Surveys of firms have shown that only a small proportion of firms in EU Member States have introduced annualized working times. However, these surveys tend to be misleading, since there are functional equivalents for annualized working hours. Through the skilful distribution of days off, holiday scheduling, the extension of their flexitime systems or the delegation of working-time decisions to teams with output rather than input (i.e. working-time) targets, many firms effectively introduced annualized working times long ago – without actually using the term – which in many countries is extremely conflictual (Bosch, 1997).

Firms are reacting in very different ways to the new demands. Some that rely on specialist knowledge and competences are trying to increase working-time flexibility in their core workforce and to take their employees' interests into account as much as possible. These firms are breaking with the Taylorist tradition and introducing flat management structures, self-responsibility, employee participation, teamwork and stable employment. The "fine tuning" of working time decisions is being decentralized and in some cases organized by the employees themselves. In other firms, however, particularly in labour-intensive service industries facing tough price competition, Taylorism is actually being reinforced. Competences are concentrated in a small proportion of the workforce and flexibility is achieved by increasing the size of the peripheral workforce. Decisions on working time are handed down from above. Little account is taken of employee interests.

In the European Union today, there is a range of very different combinations of work organization and working time. It is true that many European firms are moving towards decentralized organizational forms with a less rigid division of labour. Such firms are shifting away from mass production towards production-to-order and quality products. However, rumours of the death of Taylorism or Fordism are premature, since a process of re-Taylorization can be observed in both new service industries and traditional craft industries, such as construction. These industries are very labour-intensive, subject to tough price competition, and demand is very cost-elastic.

Unlike the Taylorism that prevailed in manufacturing industry nearly a century ago, the process of neo-Taylorism is driven not by production requirements but by the labour market. It is possible only because of the existence of wage differentiation and the availability in the labour market of a large pool of workers who can be deployed flexibly. This pool varies in size from country to country. It gets larger the wider the wage dispersion, the lower the level of labour market regulation, the lower the share of skilled workers, the higher the unemployment rate, the higher the level of migration of unskilled workers into Europe, and the lower the level of female integration into the labour market.

If it is assumed that in future women will be more fully integrated into the labour market, that the migration of low-skilled workers will decline as Eastern Europe develops economically, that more is invested in training and that new labour market regulations in areas such as minimum wages are introduced, then it is unlikely that some of the Taylorist organizational forms that are becoming widespread today will survive for very long. This should make us cautious about prematurely accepting such new forms of work organization as the necessary consequence of tertiarization. As the pool of part-time workers shrinks, certain forms of work organization may eventually be regarded as historical episodes. It is also possible, however – in conjunction with a neo-liberal policy of wage differentiation and the impoverishment of sections of the population – that such forms of work organization will predominate for many years to come.

3.5 CONCLUSIONS

Working-time patterns and work organization are changing in all European countries. Analysis is inevitably like taking a snapshot of a moving object. In just a few years current working-time structures may be regarded merely as a historical episode. We have tried not only to describe the current situation but also to analyse the change factors in order to gain an idea of the direction of change and the institutions that influence working-time structures.

The major change on the supply side of the labour market is the increasing workforce participation of women, especially married women with children. The two most important causal factors are: younger women are much better educated and less willing to accept traditional housewife roles; and the number of high-wage jobs for men in the manufacturing sector is decreasing, so that families increasingly need two salaries. The household is the locus where individuals are deciding on their working hours. We assume that the participation of women in the labour market starts with low-hour part-time work and might end in a newly defined standard working time. It could mean a much shorter working week for both partners, or traditional full-time work with a lot of flexibility over the life cycle. Of course this new standard might vary between countries and is clearly "path-dependent".

The working-time patterns in the four countries analysed reflect different stages of this development. Ireland and the Netherlands are latecomers; Austria and, to a much greater extent, Denmark are ahead in the degree of women's integration in the labour market.

The major change on the demand side of the labour market is the new need for a more flexible work organization, in which flexible working hours are an important element. The number of product variants has increased dramatically; companies can no longer hold extensive stocks; the expanding service sector is leading to changes in the demands on workers, especially regarding their working hours; and the increased cost sensitivity of companies requires "fine tuning" of working hours. Companies need to learn to develop new forms of work organization based on shorter and more highly differentiated individual working hours.

These critical developments on the supply and the demand side of the labour market require a proactive response by the institutions that influence working-time structures.

The necessity of modernization can be understood best when we try to envisage a scenario of no institutional change. In the absence of the introduction of parental leave, an improvement in public childcare and equal legislative treatment of part-time work, women would either be trapped in marginal jobs or be impelled to forgo motherhood. The potential labour force would be underutilized, and the incompatibilities between work and family life would reduce individual well-being. In the absence of changes in work organization, corporate flexibility would mainly be based on the traditional instruments of overtime and external flexibility, especially the use of peripheral workers as buffers. Both would increase polarization in the labour market. The range of possibilities to redistribute working hours will diminish because firms have not learned to manage shorter working hours and employees get used to working overtime, so that both are locked in "overtime cultures".

A proactive approach has to take into account the different needs of employees, as well as employers, and find ways to reconcile them by implementing four strategies:

1. The social partners should both promote new types of flexible, post-Taylorist work organization, which increases the scope for individual workers to manage their own working time and adjusts working hours to fluctuating demands at the same time.

2. Individual options for flexible lifelong working hours (the right to work part time as discussed in the Netherlands; parental or training leave as in Denmark) should be extended to create a balance between the flexibility requirements imposed by the market and the flexibility needed by individual workers.

3. Public childcare should be extended (as in Denmark) and the tax and social security system be adjusted to new working-time patterns (such as the basic pension in the Netherlands, which helps part-timers especially).

4. Education and vocational training must be improved. In flexible types of work organization, firms need more multifunctional workers. The increased frequency of workers' transitions into and out of the workforce (resulting from leave schemes, for example), would be managed by employers and employees much more easily if they had higher training and qualifications. Perhaps even more importantly, working time can only be redistributed if there are no skill shortages on the labour market, implying the need for intensive public support for training.

We have found that working-time reductions are an instrument to create employment, but that success is contingent on certain conditions. It is important, in particular, that wage compensation and wage increases are negotiated together and ensure cost neutrality; that wage differentiation is low so that a reduction of working hours is more readily acceptable; that skill shortages on the labour market are avoided through an active training policy; that fixed labour costs are low; and that work organization is changed to avoid cuts in machine-operating hours and to adapt work organization to shorter and more flexible individual working hours. If working time is to be successfully redistributed, with positive employment effects, through an increase in part-time working, two further conditions are required: hourly pay differentials must be minimized and discrimination against part-time work in the social security system and labour legislation must be abolished.

In all four countries, standard working hours have been reduced and part-time work extended. In Ireland the percentage of workers working long hours is rising, in spite of a fall in average hours, which leads to some question marks as to whether the reduction of standard working time led to creation of jobs. The increase of part-time work in Ireland has helped many women find jobs. In Austria, Denmark and the Netherlands reduced working hours did not result in an increase in overtime and long working hours. Workers are today working fewer hours than in the 1980s and this seems to have had a positive impact on the labour market. In recent years the Netherlands has enjoyed a higher proportional job increase than the United States, with a constant volume of working hours. This was the result of the enormous expansion of part-time work, which made it possible for many women to enter the labour market.

Although we did not analyse the employment effects of the reduction of standard working hours and the increase of part-time work in these four countries, it seems that their recent employment performance cannot be explained without the work-sharing policies. The most important employment effect can definitely be found in the Netherlands. In the longer run labour supply in the Netherlands will increase further because better-skilled young women will no longer accept marginal part-time jobs. The long-term effects of such forms of work-sharing are particularly complex because a higher female labour supply will go hand in hand with an increase in demand for services which were previously produced in households. In the best case, a virtuous circle might be created between the increase in hours worked by part-timers and an increase of jobs in the service sector.

Notes

[1] Such a measure calculated on lifelong working hours would also reflect early retirement, all types of leave (parental or educational) and the later entrance into the labour market due to higher education.

[2] The methods used are questionnaires or self-reporting; in some, but not all cases, commuting time is included in working time. This and other differences prompt the authors to issue the warning that the data they present should not be used for any kind of transnational comparison. In future the situation may improve because coordinated surveys are planned for the European Union. Table 3.4 comprises only the results for six countries. For further information see Goldschmidt-Clermont/ Pagnossin-Aligakis, 1995.

[3] In Western Germany in 1992, the share was between 33 and 55 per cent, depending on the method of calculation. However, the work input was recorded without any evaluation of its economic efficiency. Thus it cannot be concluded from these figures that GNP would be doubled by the conversion of non-monetized into monetized work. As soon as domestic and personal work is converted into paid work, it is rationalized and shrinks in volume.

[4] Great Britain refers to England, Scotland and Wales.

[5] According to data on Austria (European Commission, 1996a), working time in some industries was reduced through collective agreements to between 36 and 38.5 hours. Such agreements covered about one-third of all employees.

[6] It would be even better to convert these values into purchasing power parities, since they are "distorted" by exchange rates.

[7] In the United States there is a strong link between fixed costs and working hours (see section 3.4). Probably this effect is neutralized in Europe by the influence of other intervening variables such as wage structure and trade union influence.

[8] These data were gathered during a research project, conducted at the Institut Arbeit und Technik, which focused on the financial incentives contained in tax and social security systems for particular patterns of household working time. The following observations are based on the findings of this project (Dingeldey, 1998a).

[9] The social organization of sick and elder care, an issue not addressed here, is also highly important.

[10] This is probably the most important reason why participation rates for unskilled men are lower in the Netherlands and Austria than in Denmark and Ireland.

[11] The connection between work redistribution and education/training is examined in greater detail.

[12] The role of the Stichting van de Arbeid in the Dutch system of industrial relations is described in Visser (1998).

[13] This section is based in part on studies conducted with Steffen Lehndorff (cf. Bosch/ Lehndorff, 1997).

[14] Even before statutory or collectively agreed working-time reductions were implemented, individual firms had already recognized that production could be more efficient with shorter working times. However, the vast majority of firms did nothing until the collective working-time reductions were introduced.

[15] In France and the Scandinavian countries, working time for continuous shift workers has been reduced in some cases to 35 hours per week; this has created the impetus for the development of new shift systems.

[16] One exception is the outstanding work by Görres (1984).

[17] Since 1984, the Dutch guilder has been pegged to the DM. With a fixed exchange rate, competitive price advantages can be achieved only through a policy of wage restraint. In the Netherlands, a policy of strict wage restraint was pursued. While unit wage costs in Germany rose between 1979 and 1996 by 48 per cent, they rose in the Netherlands by only 27 per cent (DIW, 1997).

[18] Empirical experiences with the relationship between reductions in working time and labour costs have been summarized by Cette/Taddei (1994, p. 45) as follows: "Historically all the compromises achieved have ultimately ended in the same financing mechanism: over the long term, the bill is ultimately always paid for by productivity gains, even if at the outset the negotiating partners have always been much exercised by the needlessly mythical question of wage compensation."

[19] In Germany and Great Britain, skilled workers work more overtime than unskilled workers. A differentiated comparison between the two countries would show that the volume of overtime worked by unskilled workers in Great Britain is also much higher than in Germany. Thus skill shortages are only one reason for the differences between the two countries. Others include the more uneven earnings distribution in Great Britain and different national traditions in trade union policy.

[20] In addition, firms are often interested in replacing expensive forms of working time with cheaper ones. Their main objective here is to avoid paying bonuses for night, Saturday and Sunday work, or for any hours worked over and above the standard 8-hour day.

[21] Until two years ago, for example, one large European car plant still held sufficient stocks for six days' production. This represented a capital commitment of DM 150 million. The stocks have now been reduced to less than two days' production. The objective over the next few years is to reduce their value to six hours of output.

Bibliography

Anxo, D. et al. (eds.). 1995. *Work patterns and capital utilization. An international comparative study* (Dordrecht, Kluwer).

Atkinson, J. et al. 1994. *Income distribution in OECD countries: The evidence from the Luxembourg Income Study (LIS)*. Paper presented at the American Economic Association Meeting, Boston, MA.

ATOS Beleidsadvies en -onderzoek bv. 1997. *Reduction of working hours in the Netherlands 1988-1995. Study contract concerning company policies with regard to the reduction of working time* (Amsterdam; manuscript).

Bosch, G. 1995. "Flexibility and work organization", in *Social Europe*, Suppl. No. 1. European Commission, Directorate General for Employment, Industrial Relations and Social Affairs (in English, French and German).

——; 1997. "Annual working hours: An international comparison", in G. Bosch, D. Meulders, and R. Michon. (eds.): *Working time: New issues, new norms, new measures* (Brussels, DULBEA, Université Libre de Bruxelles), pp. 13–36.

——; Dawkins, P.; Michon, F. (eds.). 1994. *Times are changing. Working time in 14 industrialized countries* (Geneva, ILO).

——; Lehndorff, S. 1988. *Arbeitszeitverkürzung und Beschäftigung – Erfahrungen in Europa und wirtschaftspolitische Empfehlungen,* DIW-Vierteljahreshefte, No. 4.

——; ——. 1997. "Réduction du temps de travail et emploi", in *Travail et Emploi,* No. 74, pp. 125-143.

——; et al. 1988. *Arbeitszeitverkürzung im Betrieb. Die Umsetzung der 38,5-Stundenwoche in der Metall-, Druck- und Holzindustrie sowie im Einzelhandel* (Cologne).

Bosworth, D.; Cette, G. 1995. "Capital operating time: Measurement issues", in Anxo et al., pp. 89-120.

CEC (Commission of the European Communities). 1997. *Equal opportunities for women and men in the European Union: Annual report 1996* (Luxembourg).

Cette, G.; Taddei, D. 1994. *Temps de travail, modes d'emplois: vers la semaine de 4 jours* (Paris, Editions du Seuil).

Cichon, M. 1997. "Can Europe afford the future financing of the welfare states?", in A. Bosco and M. Hutsebaut (eds.): *Social protection in Europe. Facing up to changes and challenges* (Brussels, European Trade Union Institute).

Cranfield School of Management. 1995. *Price Waterhouse Cranfield Project 1995 Survey Results* (Cranfield, Cranfield School of Management, Centre for European Human Resource Management).

Cutler, D.M.; Madrian, D.C. 1996. *Labour market response to rising health insurance costs: Evidence on hours worked,* National Bureau of Economic Research, Working Paper 5525 (Cambridge, MA).

De Lange, W. 1989. *Configuratie van arbeid* (Zutphen, Buin).

Delsen L.; Huijgen, F. 1994. *Analysis of part-time and fixed-term employment in Europe using establishment data* (Dublin, European Foundation for the Improvement of Living and Working Conditions).

Denison, E.F. 1962. *The sources of economic growth and the alternatives before us*, Suppl. Paper No. 13 (New York, Committee for Economic Development).

Deutschmann, C. 1985. *Der Weg zum Normalarbeitstag. Die Entwicklung der Arbeitszeiten der deutschen Industrie bis 1918* (Frankfurt/New York, East-West).

Dingeldey, I. 1998a. "Steuern durch Steuer- und Sozialversicherungssysteme?", in *Jahresbericht 97/98 des Institut Arbeit und Technik* (Gelsenkirchen, Institut Arbeit und Technik).

——. 1998b. *Work, the family and the tax and social security system: The rewards and penalties of various patterns of household economic activity and working time. A comparative study of ten European countries* (Gelsenkirchen, Institut Arbeit und Technik).

DIW (Deutsches Institut für Wirtschaftsforschung). 1997. "Die Niederlande: Beschäftigungspolitisches Vorbild?", in *Wochenbericht*, No. 16.

Drèze, J.H. 1986. *Work-sharing: Why? How? How not...?* CEPS Papers, No. 27 (Brussels, Centre for European Policy Studies).

European Commission. 1994. *Employment in Europe* (Luxembourg).

——. 1995a. *Employment in Europe* (Luxembourg).

——. 1995b. *European Economy Reports and Studies*, No. 3 (Brussels).

——. 1996a. *Labour Market Studies: Austria*, Report by L&R Sozialforschung und ECOTEC Research and Consulting Ltd. (Brussels, Luxembourg).

——. 1996b. *Labour Market Studies: Netherlands*, Report by the Netherlands Economic Institute (Luxembourg).

——. 1996c. *Labour Market Studies: Denmark*, Report by PLS Consult and P. Jensen (Luxembourg).

——. 1996d. *Labour Market Studies: Ireland*, Report by J.J. Sexton, P.J. Connell (eds.) (Luxembourg).

——. 1997a. "Equal opportunities for women and men in the European Union", in *Annual Report 1996* (Luxembourg).

——. 1997b. *Youth in the European Union. From education to working life* (Luxembourg).

Europäische Gemeinschaft. 1996. *Erhebung über Arbeitskräfte, Ergebnisse 1996*, Statisches Dokument No. 3C (Luxembourg).

Eurostat. 1995. *Work organization and working hours 1983–1992* (Luxembourg, Statistical Office of the European Union).

Foss, M. 1984. *Changing utilization of fixed capital. An element in long-term growth* (Washington, DC, London, American Enterprise Institute for Public Policy Research).

——. 1995. "Operating hours of US manufacturing plants, 1976–1988, and their significance for productivity change", in Anxo et al., 1995, pp. 160–171.

Freeman, R.B. 1997. *When earnings diverge. Causes, consequences, and cures for the new inequality in the U.S.*, Report commissioned by the Committee on New American Realities of the National Association (Washington, DC).

Goldschmidt-Clermont, L.; Pagnossin-Aligisakis, E. 1995. *Measures of unrecorded economic activities in fourteen countries* (New York, Human Development Report Office).

Görres, P.A. 1984. *Die Umverteilung der Arbeit. Beschäftigungs-, Wachstums- und Wahlfahrtseffekte einer Arbeitszeitverkürzung* (Frankfurt, New York, East-West).

Hacker, J. 1979. "Beeinflussungsmöglichkeiten der Arbeitslosigkeit in der Bundesrepublik Deutschland durch Senkung des Arbeitsvolumens", in *Beiträge zur Arbeitsmarkt- und Berufsforschung*, Vol. 39, pp. 175–219.

Handelsblatt. 1998. (Düsseldorf), 16 Sep.

Hartog, J. 1998. *ILO Country Employment Policy Review: The Netherlands* (Geneva, ILO).

Hartz, P. 1996. *Das atmende Unternehmen. Jeder Arbeitsplatz hat einen Kunden* (Frankfurt, New York, East-West).

Häußermann, H.; Siebel, W. 1995. *Dienstleistungsgesellschaften* (Frankfurt, Goddar).

Hicks, J. 1946. *Value and capital* (Oxford, Oxford University Press, 2nd ed.).

Hunt, J. 1996. *Has work-sharing worked in Germany?* (Yale University; manuscript).

Jepsen M., et al., 1997. *Individualisation of the social and fiscal rights and the equal opportunities between women and men*, DGV report (Brussels, European Commission).

Keynes, J.M. 1945. *Collected writings*, ed. D. Moggridge, Vol. 27 (Cambridge, Cambridge University Press).

Kirsch, J., et al. 1998. *Arbeitszeitarrangements und Beschäftigung im Dienstleistungssektor am Beispiel des Einzelhandels – ein europäischer Vergleich* (Gelsenkirchen, Institut Arbeit und Technik).

Kleinfeld, R. 1997. *Das niederländische Modell. Grundzüge und Perspektiven einer Modernisierung des Sozialsstaates, Studie im Auftrag der Enquetekommission "Zukunft der Erwerbsarbeit" des Landtags, Nordrhein-Westfalen.*

König, H.; Pohlmeier, W. 1987. "Arbeitszeit und Beschäftigung: eine ökonometrische Studie", in G. Bombach, (ed.): *Arbeitsmärkte und Beschäftigungs -Fakten, Analysen, Perspektiven* (Tübingen, Müller).

Kongshoj Madsen, P. 1998. *ILO Country Employment Policy Review: Denmark* (Geneva, ILO).

Lehndorff, S. 1995. "Working time and operating time in the European car industry", in Anxo et al. (eds.): *Capital operating time– An international comparison* (Deventer, Europäische Verlagsanstalt).

——. 1998. "Von der 'kollektiven' zur 'individuellen' Arbeitszeitverkürzung? Arbeitszeitrends- und -erfahrungen in der Europäischen Union", in *WSI-Mitteilungen,* Issue 9.

——; Bosch, G. 1993. *Autos bauen zu jeder Zeit? Arbeits- und Betriebszeiten in der europäischen und japanischen Automobilindustrie* (Berlin, Springer).

Lindecke, C.; Lehndorff, S. 1997. *Beschäftigungssicherung und Neueinstellungen durch neue Arbeitszeitmodelle*?, documentation of the workshop held on 7 Mar., Gelsenkirchen, Institut Arbeit und Technik.

Maddison, A. 1995. *L'économie mondiale 1870–1992, Analyse et Statistiques* (Paris, OECD).

Mishel, L.; Schmitt, J. 1995. *Beware the US model. Jobs and wages in a deregulated economy* (Washington, DC, Economic Policy Institute).

Neifer-Dichmann, E. 1991. "Working time reduction in the former Republic of Germany: A dead end for employment policy", in *International Labour Review*, Vol. 130, No. 4, pp. 511–522.

OECD. 1994. *The tax/benefit position of production workers. Annual Report 1990–1993* (Paris).

——. 1995. *Economic Surveys – United Kingdom* (Paris).

——. 1996. *Employment Outlook* (Paris).

——. 1997a. *Historical Statistics 1960–1995* (Paris).

——. 1997b. *Employment Outlook* (Paris).

——. 1998. *Employment Outlook* (Paris).

Schuhmacher, D. 1997. "Immaterielle investitionen in Deutschland und im internationalen Vergleich", in Deutsches Institut für Wirtschaftsforschung: *Viertelsjahreshefte zur Wirtschaftsforschung*, Vol. 66, No. 2.

Seifert, H. 1991. "Employment effects of working time reductions in the former Federal Republic of Germany", in *International Labour Review*, Vol. 130, No. 4, pp. 495–510.

Semmer, N.; Baillod, J.; Bogenstaetter, Y. 1995. "Kürzere Arbeitszeiten fuehren zu hoeherer Produktivitaet", in *Management Zeitschrift*, Vol. 64, No. 6.

SOEP. 1998. *Deutsches Institut für Wirtschaftsforschung, Socio-economic Panel* (Berlin).

Spitznagel, E.; Kohler, H. 1993. "Kann Arbeitszeitverlängerung zur Lösung der Arbeitsmarktprobleme beitragen?" in *IAB Werkstattbericht*, No. 14.

Stichting van de Arbeid. 1993. *Considerations and recommendations to promote part-time work and differentiation in patterns of working hours*, 1 Sep., No. 7.

Stille, F.; Zwiener, R. 1997. "Arbeits- und Betriebszeiten in Deutschland: Analysen zu Wettbewerbsfähigkeit und Beschäftigung" in *DIW-Sonderheft* (Deutsches Institut für Wirtschaftsborschung), Vol. 1.

Taylor, F.W. 1947, *Scientific management* (New York, Prentice-Hall).

Van Deelen, H. 1987. *Kostenoptimale Arbeits- und Betriebszeiten. Zusammenhänge, Methoden und Anwendungsbeispiele* (Berlin, Springer).

Visser, J. 1998. *Organizational conditions for social dialogue in Europe. The state of the unions and the employers' associations in the 1990s*, CESAR Working Paper (Amsterdam, Centre for the Study of European Societies and Labour Relations).

Ward, T. 1996. *Indirect labour costs and employment*, Contribution to DGV, European Commission, Expert Group on key areas for employment policy identified at the Essen European Council Meeting (Brussels).

Zwiener, R. 1993. "Zu den effekten der Arbeitszeitverkürzung in den achtziger Jahren", in P. Hampe: *Zwischenbilanz der Arbeitszeitverkuerzung* (Munich, Mehring), pp. 91–103.

EQUAL OPPORTUNITIES AND EMPLOYMENT POLICY

4

Jill Rubery[*]

4.1 INTRODUCTION

The Copenhagen Declaration in 1995 committing governments to promote full, productive and freely chosen employment, in line with the ILO's Employment Policy Convention, 1964 (No. 122), provided the context for this book, which is a review of employment policy in relatively successful European countries. The inclusion of a specific chapter on the equal opportunity dimension is particularly relevant for three reasons. First, the World Summit for Social Development (1995) was, by definition, concerned with social as well as economic issues, and therefore the promotion of employment was seen as a means of improving social conditions and social integration, and not solely or simply as a means of meeting economic or political objectives. Second, the interpretation of "full", "productive" and "freely chosen" employment requires an equal opportunities perspective. While the terms of the Declaration appear to be straightforward, they in fact force us to address fundamental issues relating to both the objectives and the outcomes of employment policy. For example, who is to be included under the terms "full employment" and what levels of open or disguised unemployment are compatible with that term; how should employment in low-paid or short-hours jobs be interpreted, as productive or as unproductive; and where do the boundaries lie between active labour market policies that require participation in work for receipt of benefits, and employment which is not freely chosen? Third, an equal opportunities perspective complements the ILO's role in establishing international labour standards and principles; this review needs to identify where employment policies might reduce or increase the likelihood that other key international labour Conventions would be complied with, such as the Equal Remuneration Convention, 1951 (No. 100), calling for the promotion of equal pay between women and men.

We start with a brief definition of an equal opportunities perspective, followed by a description of the key characteristics, from such a perspective,

[*] Manchester School of Management (UMIST), Manchester.

of the employment and societal regimes in Austria, Denmark, Ireland and the Netherlands (section 4.2). We then consider recent employment experience within these four countries from the perspective of equality by sex (section 4.3) and by age and education (section 4.4). In section 4.5 we provide a more general comparison of the extent of both social inequality and social exclusion, from both an individual and a household perspective. In section 4.6 we return to an overview of these four European employment regimes and assess the extent to which the societal systems are generating an employment system compatible with the principles of social justice and equality, and how successfully they are adjusting to new pressures to generate employment opportunities which promote rather than detract from equality. Here we identify the main strengths and weaknesses of the four societies under consideration, with a view to informing future policy proposals within these countries and to identifying lessons that can be learned for reviews of employment policy within the OECD more generally.

4.2 AN EQUALITY PERSPECTIVE ON EMPLOYMENT PERFORMANCE IN OECD COUNTRIES

Assessing employment performance from an equality perspective requires us first to define what we mean by an equal opportunities perspective. Second, we need to consider how to assess whether a country has been performing well or poorly from an equality perspective. This requires a consideration not only of recent trends, but also of different starting points, related to the specific characteristics of the employment and societal regimes.

Defining an equal opportunities perspective

The perspective adopted in this chapter takes equal opportunities to be an essential element of a successful employment policy regime, and not a supplementary (not to mention competing) goal to the overall employment objective specified in the Copenhagen Declaration (1995). The rationale for regarding equal opportunities as integral to employment policy objectives is defined as follows.

First of all, the objective of full employment, by its very name, requires an inclusive approach to employment opportunities. The definition of what constitutes full employment has, however, become increasingly problematic. To a large extent the notion of full employment, applied to any period or country, can be seen in retrospect to apply only with respect to a given definition of which groups are considered to be within the active labour force; full employment in the past has mainly been achieved in a context of social institutions which have limited access to the labour market for certain parts of the population, most notably women. Which groups have rights of access to the labour market is now a more contested issue (Rubery, 1997). In all OECD countries the rationing of employment access to male breadwinners is no longer acceptable either to women or to employers, so that the concept of full employment needs to be redefined to include access for prime-age women as well as men. Yet while the entry of women into the labour force has been offset to some extent by an increasing exclusion of both men and women at the beginning and end of working life, that is, longer transitions into employment and earlier exits, this new system of rationing employment has proved neither socially acceptable nor sustainable.

In particular, there are concerns over the problems of integration faced by those young people not selected for higher education or advanced training and the consequences for family formation of the delayed transition into adult independence. Similarly, rapidly falling effective retirement ages in many OECD countries have led to concerns not only over the potential waste of experience and skill, but also over the problems of financing early retirement for the expanding older generations. Long queues to enter employment and long enforced retirement periods are thus regarded as neither socially equitable nor a sustainable means of rationing access to limited employment. Thus a consideration of the extent to which countries have achieved full employment requires attention to be paid not only to unemployment rates, but also to the employment rates of different demographic and social groups.

This concern with employment rates rather than unemployment rates is not solely motivated by issues of equity, as raising the share of the working-age population in productive employment has been adopted as a principal objective of employment policy in EU countries and, indeed, in the wider OECD community (OECD, 1994a), not least in the interests of providing a sounder base for funding welfare States in the context of an ageing society. To achieve this objective, at least within Europe, most countries will need to expand further the share of the female population within the labour market, as it is differences in female employment rates which primarily explain variations in overall employment rates across OECD countries. The increasing demand for persons with higher qualifications suggests that the rise in young people's participation in education is likely to be permanent. Differences in employment rates for older workers also have some impact on comparative employment rate levels, and some reversal of the downward trends in activity may be necessary both to counter the pressures on welfare expenditures and to reduce the loss to the employment system of accumulated experience. However, it is within the non-employed and underemployed female population that Europe's main reserve of educated labour is to be found (Rubery et al., 1999). If OECD countries are to make full use of their human resource potential (OECD, 1994b), then attention needs to be paid to providing equal opportunities to the female share of the population, which is rapidly achieving the same – if not higher – levels of education as the male population.

Equality issues are central not only to the objective of raising employment levels, but also to the changes taking place in the form and functioning of labour markets. The development of flexible labour markets and a greater diversity of employment opportunities could provide the basis for wider access to employment, or, alternatively, could lead to increased segmentation and stratification, reducing equal opportunities both from a cross-sectional and from a lifetime perspective. Involvement in flexible forms of employment is strongly related to sex, age and labour market position, with women, students and young people and the more disadvantaged providing the main sources of labour for more flexible employment forms (Rubery et al., 1999). Flexible employment may, under some conditions, offer important opportunities to retain or regain contact with the labour market, where the alternative could be permanent exclusion, but it may act not only to concentrate the disadvantaged into ghettos of low-paid or unskilled work, but also to restrict lifetime employment opportunities by limiting access to training or promotion opportunities. The flexibilization of labour markets thus needs to be assessed not only from the perspective of its contribution to the goal of full and productive employment, but also with respect to its impact on segmentation, stratification and social exclusion.

We therefore need to consider whether the developments in the labour market have been leading to higher or lower levels of social and economic inequality, or higher or lower levels of social exclusion. The question of inequality needs to be addressed with respect to both trends in the maintenance of minimum employment and social standards (Sengenberger and Campbell, 1994) and changes across the whole spectrum of the labour market. Social exclusion is concerned not simply with the exclusion of individuals or groups from the labour market, but also with the terms on which disadvantaged workers are offered integration: are the pressures placed upon those without work to enter the labour market compatible with social justice, and are the conditions under which they are expected to work fair and reasonable? Are there still groups who are denied access to active labour market policies even though they wish to work or, alternatively, groups who are under pressure to participate in active policies despite their involvement in other forms of activity, such as care work? The move towards a more active, more fully employed society must not be at the expense of appropriate attention to people's domestic responsibilities and care work.

An equality perspective should therefore seek to shed some light on the extent of complementarities or trade-offs between employment objectives and equality objectives, between the goals of flexibility and those of maintaining reasonable security of employment, ensuring the observance of labour standards and providing access to productive employment opportunities without recourse to coercion. However, an equality perspective also requires us to move beyond the direct consideration of employment trends and patterns to a more general consideration of the social and economic context in which employment policy is conducted. This broadening of perspective is required for at least two reasons.

First, many of the policies which impinge upon equality in the employment sphere are not usually categorized as either employment policies or equal opportunity policies. For example, policies related to the care and welfare of citizens have a potentially greater impact on gender equality at work than many direct employment policy initiatives. Similarly, policies pursued in the interests of macroeconomic stability, such as a squeeze on the public sector, will have implications for specific labour force and social groups. Second, and relatedly, the changes that have been observed within the labour markets of advanced countries over recent years have not been isolated phenomena, but are symptomatic of major social and economic changes in the ways in which we live our lives and structure our relationships. One of the shortcomings of much labour market analysis has been to treat social change as a marginal influence on the labour market, until the changes become so obvious that the basic labour market models, for example of labour supply behaviour, have to be reconstructed (Humphries and Rubery, 1984). The labour market changes observed over recent years – towards a more service-oriented economy, more female employment, more unsocial working hours and more flexible and casual employment, particularly within the youth labour market – are related to changes in lifestyles, and in particular the transfer of activities from the private sphere to that of market or public services, changes in family patterns and household formation towards more single-person households, more unstable couple-households and fewer children, changes in gender relations within the home and within the labour market, changes in the patterns of young people's transition to adult independence and into the labour market, and changes in patterns of retirement from the labour market. These transformations in advanced societies, away from a simple relationship between labour supply and social and household position in which most labour market participants were either young people or household heads, have been relatively slow in their development and, while already institutionalized in some advanced societies, are only now being realized in others.

Thus one of the questions that needs to be asked concerning recent employment trends and developments is the extent to which current labour supply patterns and the underlying social structures leading to these trends can be considered to be stable or are themselves in a process of transition. Where, for example, there has been a major integration of women into the labour market based on part-time work, it needs to be asked whether this is likely to be an acceptable system of integration in the medium to longer term, or whether a further phase of integration into full-time work can be expected. Recent phases of labour market restructuring have been associated with major changes in labour market behaviour, but the latter changes have taken on a form of autonomy that may be independent of further changes in the labour market; for example, the likelihood of a phase of rationalization of clerical and service work, following on from the earlier rationalization of manufacturing work, is unlikely to result in a return to the home for the women drawn into these sections of the labour market during the restructuring of the past two to three decades.

It is, however, not only the stability of the existing patterns of labour market behaviour that needs to be examined, but also the coherence and compatibility between developments in the labour market and the organization of social and family life. The transition from single- to dual-earner households has to some extent forged ahead independently of associated changes in the ways in which labour markets operate, ensuring some reconciliation of work and family life, so as to avoid neglecting children or reducing the fertility rate below acceptable levels. Moreover, welfare States have been adjusting to increasing funding constraints and to changing lifestyles and employment patterns which perhaps will require a more fundamental reassessment of the principles on which the welfare State system is based. Considerations of equality in employment policy thus lead to more general questions of how the emerging employment system fits with the objectives of social stability and social development.

Yet while all OECD countries share common trends towards higher female employment, declining youth and older-age employment and, by and large, towards more flexible employment systems, major differences remain between countries which are related not solely or mainly to stage of development, but to the whole set of interlocking social and economic arrangements that make up a societal system (Maurice et al., 1986) or, in our context, employment regimes or systems. Most comparative research has increasingly come to the conclusion that national labour markets and employment regimes operate under different principles, and that even when societies are adjusting to similar external pressures or influences, the particular forms of adjustment vary, according to the country's own societal logic. These types of logic are rooted, for example, in different approaches to welfare (Esping-Anderson, 1990), different systems of skill formation linked to the institutions both of education and training and of industrial relations, payment systems and rewards. Any assessment of how far, and to what extent, the countries under consideration have made a successful adjustment to external and internal pressures in the labour market, must recognize these divergences and alternative logics and cannot impose some notion of universal welfare, or that of the one best practice system of employment organization.

However, the adoption of a societal system perspective should not become a rationale for the maintenance of the status quo; all societies are under pressure to change and those that place too much stress on the specificities and peculiarities of their system may fail to address the changes that are happening before these changes start to undermine the coherence of the traditional system. These problems apply particularly to those societies which cling to the idea of a traditional gender order in their rationales for social and employment policy. While variations are likely to continue in gender relations between societies, it is arguable that all should be paying more attention to the consequences of the shift from the single- to the dual-earner household as the new social norm. Similarly, even those societies that have had a relatively successful and strongly embedded training system to ease the path for young people into work still need to adjust to the new patterns of employment and the new aspirations of young people for higher education, if these key features of the societal systems are to assist rather than hinder the overall objectives of employment policy. Thus the approach adopted here will be to retain the societal system or employment regime model, but to recast it into a more dynamic perspective, where the issues are how each model is adjusting or has adjusted to meet current and anticipated challenges.

Equality, as is well known in the literature, has both a relative and an absolute dimension. In this chapter we adopt both perspectives. First we need to assess the employment regimes according to the absolute level of equality, for example in earnings and employment opportunities. In particular, we will consider the extent to which the societies in four national regimes (Austria, Denmark, Ireland and the Netherlands) allow women to move away from the traditional roles of financially dependent housewife and disadvantaged worker. Second, we retain the relative, or in this case the societal-regime, perspective. The logic of the societal system and the continuing differences in societal norms prevent us from establishing a full universal model of equality against which to benchmark these four national regimes. The differences which women are likely to continue to express in their preferences for combining wage and care work, for example, preclude universal policy prescriptions as to desired labour market outcomes, at least in the short term. Similarly, whether young people's unemployment is dealt with through greater investment in training or greater efforts to integrate them into work through subsidized employment will depend in part on the relative value attached to training in the particular employment regime, and cannot be decided against some universal criterion of the right amount of training that young people should receive.

Employment regimes in comparative perspective

Four key areas of employment regimes can be identified as having particular significance for equality in employment. Yet under each dimension we find diverse institutional arrangements and societal traditions across the four countries, reinforcing the notion of differences in starting positions with respect to equality. Moreover, there are significant inter-linkages and inter-relationships between the four dimensions, which reinforce the differences in societal paths or trajectories.

Labour market regulation and industrial relations

The systems of labour market regulation and industrial relations influence the level and form of labour standards and their application to different labour market groups.

Three of the countries have strongly centralized and coordinated collective bargaining systems as their main method of regulation. Ireland has a more decentralized tradition but has recently been moving towards a form of social partnership and centralized bargaining. However, the coverage of collective bargaining remains weaker than in the other three countries. Austria and Denmark rely on collective agreements to provide minimum wage protection, while the Netherlands combines a national legal minimum wage with strong collective bargaining. Only Ireland is left with a largely unprotected sector, although there are now plans to introduce a minimum wage (Eurostat, 1998). Austria and the Netherlands tend to combine collective bargaining with legal regulation, but Denmark has adopted a policy of very limited legal regulation, relying instead on high trade union membership for protection. Ireland also has a weak tradition of legal regulation but has been active over recent years, certainly in comparison with the United Kingdom, in developing individual employment rights at work.

Education and training regimes

Education and training systems have to meet the objectives of maintaining both competitiveness and employability. The form that the system takes has implications both for equality of access to employment and for segregation within employment.

The four countries represent perhaps the whole spread of different approaches to initial education and training. Austria is characterized by the dual training system, with a high share of young people in apprenticeship training and traditionally a relatively small share in higher education. The Netherlands also has a reasonably extensive apprenticeship system but this is increasingly becoming school based. Denmark also relies heavily on education but has a tradition – in part because of the high share of small companies – of providing vocational education outside the organization, arranged by social partners or the State. Ireland, in common with the United Kingdom, has a weak tradition of vocational training but has been rapidly expanding its use of education as a means of upskilling the labour force, from a relatively low educational base.

Flexibility and labour market regimes

Flexible labour markets may allow access but also involve high rates of insecurity and indeed high levels of lifetime inequality. Moreover, the form of flexibility has implications for different labour force groups.

Denmark has very low levels of formal job protection, relying instead on high levels of unemployment benefit to cushion problems related to ease of firing. Austria and the Netherlands have moderate to high levels of job protection, while Ireland is classified along with the southern countries as having rather high levels of job protection. Denmark also has relatively high levels of job-to-job mobility, linked to the large number of small firms in Denmark and to the tradition of stratifying the labour market along educational and training lines, a practice which encourages horizontal rather than vertical mobility within organizations (Boje, 1993, 1994).

With respect to the use of atypical contracts, there are some similarities in that none of the countries makes particularly strong use of temporary contracts, while the incidence of part-time work is at least moderate in three countries and very high in the Netherlands. However, the involvement of labour force groups in part-time work is quite different. In Ireland and Austria part-time work is primarily concentrated among women, particularly in prime age. In the Netherlands and Denmark there are very high shares of young people involved in part-time work, but while in the Netherlands this goes hand in hand with high shares of part-time work among prime-age and older women, and even moderate shares of part-time work for men of all ages, in Denmark the share of part-time work among women of child-rearing age is much lower and has, more importantly, shown a persistent tendency to decline over recent years. The implications of the growth of flexible labour markets for patterns of cross-sectional and lifetime inequalities are therefore likely to differ.

Welfare regimes and gender relations

Welfare regimes shape both the employment system and the pattern of gender relations. Differences in welfare regimes reflect different systems of organizing society, particularly with respect to social reproduction. A recent classification of welfare regimes from a gender perspective located Denmark within the Nordic model based on the principle of "everyone a breadwinner" and where benefits are both individualized and based on universal or citizenship principles (Daly, 1996). Austria belongs to the group following the continental European model based on the notion of the male breadwinner family and built around the principles of family-based insurance. The Netherlands is located as lying between the Nordic and the continental European model, as it embraces the principles of both insurance and universality within its benefit system. Ireland also falls between two systems, between the liberal "more than one breadwinner" regime found in the United Kingdom where the welfare State acts primarily as a safety net or a residual form of security, and the Mediterranean model of the "family as breadwinner", where the welfare system is based on insurance principles but is so low in benefits or patchy in coverage that the family effectively acts as the social safety net for most people. These classifications by "breadwinner type" relate more to the principles of the welfare system than to the actual patterns of labour market behaviour, as there is evidence in all European societies of a trend towards dual-earner households. Ireland still has the highest share of male breadwinner households (see below), but Austria has a relatively high share of dual-earner households and certainly more dual full-time earners than found in the Netherlands, which falls between the Nordic and the continental models. Denmark undoubtedly has moved the furthest away from the dual breadwinner model in line with the classification of its welfare State model. Moreover, with the exception of Denmark, all the countries may be regarded as having relatively traditional systems of gender relations.

Welfare State systems are also expected to have an influence on the availability of public services (Esping-Andersen, 1990; Lewis, 1992; Daly, 1996). A classification of European Union countries by social services (Antonnen and Sipilä, 1996) placed Denmark in the group of countries said to have "abundant social care services", while Ireland fell into the category of countries with "scarce social care services". The Netherlands was classified with those that had abundant services for elderly people but scarce services for children. Austria was not included in the comparison but is known to have rather low levels of services for children, therefore making it likely that it would be classified either in the same group as Ireland or as the Netherlands.

Welfare regimes not only shape gender relations but also relations between those in work and those out of work. Denmark has combined a policy of high benefits and relatively long benefit periods with low levels of job protection although recently it has taken steps to move to a more active labour market policy. The other three countries have lower levels of benefits, especially Ireland, and shorter benefit periods. Nevertheless, all have been moving towards a more active policy, reducing levels of benefits or tightening eligibility.

Interpretation of employment performance

Interpretation of the recent employment performance in the four countries requires consideration of differences in structures and starting points, and not simply outcomes.

Countries with poor equality records could be expected to make relatively strong progress towards a more equal employment system. To be more specific, less might be expected from Denmark during the 1990s than in the other countries in terms of further progress towards female integration, and most progress could perhaps be expected from Ireland. Similarly, Ireland and to some extent Austria lagged behind the other countries in terms of the educational levels of their populations, and again one could expect more progress than in Denmark and the Netherlands.

Comparative assessments also have to remain sensitive to the difficulties of transferring practice from one policy regime to another. Even a brief review of differences between the countries suggests that there are interlocking institutions which support either positive or negative forms of equality and employment performance. High rates of mobility or labour market flexibility in Denmark are linked to the system of transferable skills, high levels of benefit protection and strong trade union organization, and not just to the absence of legal job protection; the part-time work system in the Netherlands is facilitated both by high productivity levels and strong societal preferences for shorter working hours; high gender inequality in Ireland is related to the absence of support for childcare, the perpetuation of a male breadwinner model of welfare and the lack of strong legal or collective bargaining protection in female-dominated sectors. However, these societal systems are not immune to change and indeed are being challenged in many respects; therefore assessment of employment performance takes into account the extent to which the regimes are revealing a capacity to adjust to meet new challenges and to develop new coherent systems capable of delivering both high employment and equality.

4.3 EMPLOYMENT PERFORMANCE FROM A GENDER-EQUALITY PERSPECTIVE

Gender differences in employment and unemployment rates

The main source of labour market divergence between the four countries under consideration arguably lies in the pattern of gender integration and gender equality. Denmark has the highest level of integration of women into the wage economy, with a female employment rate of 68 per cent, some 9 percentage points above Austria, nearly 15 percentage points above the Netherlands and nearly 25 percentage points above Ireland (table 4.1). Denmark also has the smallest gender gap in employment rates, but the differences between Denmark and the other countries are smaller using this measure, reflecting the rather high employment rate for men in Denmark, and certainly as compared with Ireland.

If we look at the gender gap in overall employment rates, we find Denmark with the smallest gap (12 percentage points), followed by Austria (nearly 19

Table 4.1 Employment rates by sex, age and education (in %), and gender gaps (M–F)

	Austria			Denmark			Ireland			Netherlands		
	M	F	M–F	M	F	M–F	M	F	M–F	M	F	M–F
All	77.5	58.8	18.7	80.2	68.0	12.2	68.8	43.5	25.3	79.8	53.4	26.4
15–24	58.4	52.7	5.7	69.7	62.0	5.7	38.0	33.7	4.3	54.4	53.9	0.5
25–54	88.2	70.1	18.1	88.5	75.8	12.8	81.3	51.4	29.9	88.7	62.5	26.2
55–64	42.4	17.3	25.1	58.4	37.0	21.4	58.7	21.8	36.9	40.7	19.4	21.3
Education: Less than upper secondary	70.0	47.0	23.0	65.7	55.5	10.2	67.0	24.4	42.6	70.6	36.2	34.4
Upper secondary	83.9	65.5	18.4	82.1	77.1	4.0	85.3	51.9	33.4	83.7	61.4	22.3
Higher	91.6	84.7	6.9	89.3	87.8	1.5	90.2	74.3	15.9	87.0	74.9	12.1

Source: ILO Country Employment Policy Review (CEPR) databank.

points); Ireland and the Netherlands have almost identical gender gaps (just over 25 and more than 26 percentage points respectively). The position of Ireland partly reflects the low employment rate for men, which arises out of a low employment rate for young people and for prime-age men. The lower employment rates for young people in Ireland compared to the other three countries are in part associated with the greater problems of youth unemployment, but also reflect the lower rates of student involvement in part-time work, perhaps a less serious problem in terms of assessing employment performance. The lower employment rate for prime-age men may seem at first sight less dramatic, representing a gap of only 7 percentage points on the other countries, but indicates a continuing problem of unemployment for Irish men in the prime-age groups.

Taking into account both the gender gaps and the inter-country differences in employment rate patterns and levels, we can see that the rate of employment for working-age women is a product of both gender relations and the overall employment system. Women in Denmark perhaps appear to have narrowed the gender gap more than is really the case, with their overall employment rates boosted by the tendency in Denmark for both younger and older age groups to have relatively high employment rates. Employment rates for elderly men are similar in Ireland and Denmark, but the gender gap among older workers in Ireland is particularly high at 37 percentage points, reflecting the fact that the more recent growth in female employment has been concentrated among younger and better-educated groups. While the gender gaps in the other three countries all lie within the range 21 to 25 percentage points, these similar gender differences arise out of very different levels of employment for older workers, with comparatively low rates found in Austria and the Netherlands, and much higher rates in Denmark.

Table 4.1 also shows the differences in employment rates by educational attainment for both men and women. Employment rates are highly sensitive to education for both sexes, but more so for women, even in the most highly integrated labour market (Denmark). The impact of women's education on labour force participation is particularly strong in Ireland, a significant result because of the high share of this population with a low level of education. However, those with a low educational level are concentrated among the older age ranges, and the progressive replacement of these cohorts by younger groups in the working-age population will be an important factor in bringing about a further equalization between the female employment rates and those of both Irish men and women in the other European countries. Education does more to eliminate the gender gap in employment rates in Denmark and Austria than Ireland and the Netherlands, where the gender gap among the higher educated is still well into double figures, compared to an insignificant gap of 1.5 percentage points in Denmark and under 7 percentage points in Austria.

Table 4.2 Employment rates adjusted for shares of part-time work by sex, age and education (in %), and gender gaps (M–F)

Full-time equivalent employment rates[a]	Austria			Denmark			Ireland			Netherlands		
	M	F	M–F	M	F	M–F	M	F	M–F	M	F	M–F
All												
1–24	57.4	49.1	8.3	56.5	46.2	10.3	35.8	30.0	5.8	40.4	36.9	3.5
25–49	87.7	61.3	26.4	87.3	66.2	21.1	80.0	48.0	32.0	85.6	42.7	42.9
50–64	55.6	25.5	30.1	67.1	41.0	26.1	64.9	22.1	42.8	51.9	17.9	34.0
Education:	58.4	37.5	20.9	62.1	39.5	22.6	54.8	19.3	35.5	59.1	23.6	35.5
Less than upper secondary												
Upper secondary	79.4	56.9	22.5	78.6	59.1	19.5	70.8	46.1	24.7	76.5	43.6	32.9
Higher	86.6	73.5	13.1	88.1	71.4	16.7	85.8	69.0	16.8	78.6	52.7	25.9

[a] A part-time job counts for half a full-time job.
Source: European Labour Force Survey, 1996, special tabulations.

These comparisons of employment rates by sex tend to overstate the equality in employment so far achieved in all countries, as they take no account of the relative extent of part-time employment. Recalculating employment rates in terms of full-time equivalent employment rates (that is, taking one part-time job as equal to half a full-time job) leads to quite a different picture, with wider gender gaps in all cases, but particularly in the Netherlands (see table 4.2). On this basis, the Netherlands takes over from Ireland as having the lowest female employment rates in the prime- and older-age ranges. The differences between Austria and Denmark are also reduced, for although the part-time rates for women in Denmark have been falling, this has been from a relatively high level. Indeed, on this basis there is little difference in the employment rates for highly educated women between Austria, Denmark and Ireland, and Austria even has a higher employment rate than Denmark.

An assessment of employment performance depends not only on how many people are in employment, but also on how many of those who wish to work are unable to find work, and how long they are excluded from the labour market. Even on conventional measures of unemployment – which tend to underestimate the size of the female population which is without work but wishes to work – women have a higher unemployment rate than men in all four countries, although with much more significant gender gaps in Denmark and the Netherlands than in Austria or Ireland. Long-term unemployment rates are also higher for women in all countries except Ireland. Table 4.3 provides perhaps a more useful indicator of the extent of unemployment: unemployment rates are expressed as a share of the working-age population, rather than the labour

Table 4.3 Persons who are unemployed, hidden unemployed or inactive, not wanting work (as a percentage of the working-age population)

	ILO unemployed	Non-ILO jobseekers	Discouraged workers	Other inactive, wanting work	Total unemployed and hidden unemployed	Inactive, not wanting work
Women						
Austria	3.1	0.9	n.a.	n.a.	4.0	38.0
Denmark	6.3	1.4	0.3	6.9	14.9	18.1
Ireland	5.7	1.2	0.2	5.4	12.6	44.4
Netherlands	5.1	2.0	1.1	6.0	14.2	30.8
Men						
Austria	3.2	0.6	n.a.	n.a.	3.8	20.2
Denmark	4.9	0.5	0.1	3.4	8.9	10.1
Ireland	9.3	0.8	0.3	3.3	13.7	19.3
Netherlands	4.9	0.9	0.4	3.5	9.7	14.3

n.a. = not available.
Source: European Labour Force Survey, 1995, special tabulations.

force, and other groups currently excluded from the ILO measure of unemployment but who have indicated a wish to work are identified. These groups include discouraged workers, those who are seeking work but not immediately available for work, and other people classified as inactive but who say they wish to work. Data for Austria are not available for discouraged workers or other inactive people wanting work. The impact of adding these other categories to the standard unemployment measures is further to increase the disparity between male and female unemployment rates, especially for Denmark and the Netherlands. Although in Ireland the share of those wanting work but not included in the conventional unemployment measure is higher for women than for men, expressing unemployment in terms of population rather than the workforce reduces the size of conventional unemployment for women to well below that for men because of the low female participation rate.

In addition to reinforcing the notion that unemployment rates are an inadequate measure of underutilized labour supply in all labour markets, these data on hidden unemployment also emphasize differences in the extent of mobilization of women workers in the wage labour markets across the four countries under review. The integration of women into wage employment is much greater in Denmark; if we take the hidden as opposed to the measured unemployment rate, the size of the female inactive working-age population is reduced to only 18 per cent. Although hidden unemployment is also relatively high in the other two countries for which we have evidence, it is still the case that both Ireland and the Netherlands (along with Austria) have a much higher share of women who show no apparent interest in entering the wage labour market when responding to the labour force survey.

The role of gender in past and future employment change

So far we have considered the differences in the integration of women into the labour market from a cross-sectional perspective. We now turn to recent employment trends and the role that changes in the gender pattern of employment over time have played in the four countries' recent employment success and will continue to play in the future.

Table 4.4 shows that the growth of women's employment has been the dominant feature of recent employment growth in all the countries except Denmark, where the gender differences have been less marked – this is not necessarily surprising given the higher integration of women into the Danish economy at the beginning of the 1980s. The figures also to some extent understate the growth of female employment in Denmark; in contrast to other countries, the recent period has been characterized by a substitution of part-time by full-time work, rather than vice versa. Female employment has grown in all four countries and over most time periods, except for 1990–94 in Denmark and 1996 in Austria; moreover, male employment growth has not only been consistently lower but also more frequently negative, particularly in the 1980s. However, the recent period of relatively good employment performance in all four countries has witnessed positive gains for men as well as for women, certainly if we take the whole of the 1990s into consideration. In Denmark the declines of the early 1990s have given way to positive growth for both sexes in the mid-1990s, while in Austria there was a strong upward trend in the early 1990s giving way to a reduction in employment in 1996. Ireland and the Netherlands both have the strongest upward growth for men in the 1990s and the highest rates of female employment growth. Thus we are looking here at a recent period of expansion of employment opportunities for both men and women, although weighted particularly in favour of women in the

Table 4.4 Rate of growth in employment by sex

Employment growth	Austria		Denmark		Ireland		Netherlands	
	Male	Female	Male	Female	Male	Female	Male	Female
1980–96	12.6	34.1	n.a.	n.a.	−1.7	52.3	16.9	88.5
1980–84	0.8	1.8	0.7	1.8	−1.4	1.0	−0.7	3.6
1985–89	0.4	1.1	1.1	1.4	−0.7	0.8	2.7	6.1
1990–94	1.5	3.3	−0.8	−0.6	0.7	5.1	0.5	3.5
1995	−0.5	2.0	2.5	1.0	4.1	6.0	2.8	3.1
1996	−0.1	−2.9	0.9	1.0	1.9	5.8	1.6	2.8

n.a. = not available.
Source: CEPR databank.

Table 4.5 Projected changes in female employment, 1990–2005: High-growth scenario

	Projected increase in participation rate (percentage point)	Projected percentage growth in female labour force	Projected female share of labour force, 2005 (%)	Projected increase in 1990 (percentage point increase)
Austria	9.8	35.1	45.9	4.0
Denmark	8.0	16.7	48.0	1.9
Ireland	15.9	68.4	41.3	7.6
Netherlands	11.7	40.3	44.5	5.7
EU12	10.2	30.6	44.9	4.8

Source: Institut für Oekonomische Forschung, 1994; 1995.

two countries where the female employment rate was lowest at the beginning of the 1980s.

The significance of female employment for future labour market trends is outlined in table 4.5. According to Eurostat-sponsored projections for future labour supply growth (1990–2005), the increase in the female labour force, assuming a high-growth scenario, should be of the order of 16 per cent in Denmark, 35 per cent in Austria, 40 per cent in the Netherlands and no less than 68 per cent in Ireland. These growth rates are predicted to result in further increases in the female share of the total labour force in all four countries. In Denmark the increase is relatively minor, at just 1.9 percentage points, but the projected outcome, with women representing 48 per cent of the total workforce, is close to what might be expected to be the maximum share of 50 per cent. In Austria the share would rise by 4 percentage points, according to these projections, giving almost a 46 per cent female share of the labour force, while in the Netherlands a 5.7 percentage point rise would result in a 44.5 per cent female share. Ireland's two-thirds increase in the female labour force would raise the female share of the workforce by 7.6 percentage points, but the female share would still be much lower than in the other three countries, at just over 41 per cent.

While these high-growth scenarios can be criticized for exaggerated estimates of future labour supply, the significance of female employment growth is confirmed also by more circumspect projections undertaken by the EWERC research centre (Rubery and Smith, 1999); these are based simply on the assumption that the higher employment rates observed for younger cohorts would be maintained as the population ages (that is, assuming that the employment rates of those over 35 will not be diminished by childbirth and child-rearing and will thus provide a good indicator of employment rates for that cohort up to retirement). These assumptions lead to predictions of a fairly modest rise – compared to the 1995 level – in the female employment rate for all countries except Ireland. However, this rise contrasts with the fall

Table 4.6 Impact of population and cohort effects on female working-age employment rate, 1995–2010

	(1) Female working-age employment rate		(2) Impact of ageing of the 35–39 cohort on female employment rate in 2010		(3) Impact of ageing of the 30–34 cohort on female employment rate in 2010	
	(a) 1995	(b) 2010 Population with 1995 rates	(a) Changes to the 35–55 age group	(b) Changes to the 35–59 age group	(a) Changes to the 35–55 age group	(b) Changes to the 35–59 age group
Austria	59.2	57.3	59.3	61.6	59.8	62.3
Denmark	67.0	65.1	66.6	68.3	66.6	68.3
Ireland	41.3	39.6	43.1	44.9	46.7	49.3
Netherlands	53.2	49.5	51.1	53.0	52.5	54.6
EU 15	49.6	49.4	50.6	52.2	50.6	52.2

Note: Under scenario (2) we assume that the employment rates attained by women aged 35–39 will be at least maintained as women move through their 40s. We assume some fall in employment rates as women move into their 50s, but for column (a) we assume that fall to be only half the percentage point fall in 1995, with the employment rate for those aged 55–59 remaining unchanged at 1995 levels; for column (b) we assume that the drop in employment rates between those aged 50–54 and 55–59 is only half that in 1995. Scenario (3) repeats the assumptions under scenario (2), except that here it is the employment rates attained by 30–34 year olds in 1995 that are assumed to be maintained as the cohort moves through their late 30s and their 40s.
Source: European Labour Force Survey, 1995, and Eurostat population projections (baseline scenario); Rubery, Smith, Fagan (1999).

in employment rates projected to occur by 2010 as a result of a changing population structure, if age-specific employment rates remain constant (table 4.6). The increasing tendency for younger women to maintain higher employment rates may play a very significant role in offsetting tendencies towards declining employment rates implied by changing population structures over the next two decades. For Ireland the impact on projected employment rates of ageing alone is to raise the female employment rate (35–59 age group) from 41.3 per cent in 1995 to 49.3 per cent in 2010.

The vital importance of female labour to the goal of raising employment rates is further illustrated in table 4.7, where the educational levels of the non-employed in the prime-age and older-age categories are explored. This reveals that men with medium or higher education account for less than a fifth of non-employed prime-age people, while women with higher or medium education account for between 36 and 45 per cent. These data also reveal the much lower average educational level of the labour reserve in Ireland, and to some extent the Netherlands, than in Denmark and Austria, although of course the greater size of the labour reserve in the first two countries still provides for a sizeable pool of educated labour, particularly female labour.

The contribution of women's employment to recent strong employment performance is, however, not merely significant in quantitative terms but has

Table 4.7 Educational levels of the non-employed (prime age and older)

	Men			Women			Total
	Low	Medium	High	Low	Medium	High	
Aged 25–49							
Austria	5.1	14.0	1.8	32.9	42.9	3.3	100
Denmark	8.9	15.9	3.9	25.6	34.5	11.2	100
Ireland	10.6	2.5	2.0	49.3	25.9	9.6	100
Netherlands	9.4	5.1	2.6	44.2	30.7	8.0	100
Aged 50–64							
Austria	13.0	21.9	1.0	37.2	25.7	1.3	100
Denmark	11.5	19.1	5.4	32.8	23.7	7.5	100
Ireland	22.2	3.8	2.5	51.2	14.7	5.5	100
Netherlands	17.6	14.6	5.6	41.9	15.5	4.8	100

Notes: Education: low = compulsory secondary or below; medium = post-compulsory secondary; high = tertiary. Some totals may not add up exactly because of rounding.
Source: European Labour Force Survey, 1996, special tabulations.

shaped the nature of recent employment trends and performance. This is evident particularly in the Netherlands and Ireland. In the Netherlands the recent expansion has consolidated the claim that the Netherlands is the first part-time economy, a characteristic primarily based on the market for female labour. In Ireland women have played a central role in the recent expansion of manufacturing based both on new multinationals and on traditional industries. The explanation for the recent boom in investment in Ireland is the availability of large supplies of well-educated but relatively cheap labour. Given a relatively large gender pay gap in Ireland and limited regulation of minimum wages, it is almost certain that the availability of women workers at low wages has been a major factor in that attraction, although lack of wage data on Ireland makes it difficult to pursue the analysis further. These two examples suggest that in part the recent integration of women to the economy has been based not necessarily on "integration through equality", but on "integration through differentiation". In the Netherlands, as we document further below, the employment of women as part-time workers has not been based specifically on low hourly wages or poor working conditions – but part-time work does generate lower incomes, and the development of the part-time economy nevertheless requires a large supply of labour, able to draw on income support from other family members. In Denmark the pattern of recent employment growth has been relatively evenly spread between women and men, perhaps a sign of the greater integration based on equality in Denmark. Moreover, it is significant that women appear to have been able to maintain their employment share despite an expansion of the private –

Table 4.8 The role of public sector employment by sex and working time, and recent growth of the public and private sectors

	Austria			Denmark			Ireland			Netherlands		
	Full-time	Part-time	All	Full-time	Part-time	All	Full-time	Part-time	All	Full-time	Part-time	All
% of men's employment in public sector	18.5	33.5	18.9	22.6	33.4	23.9	21.6	35.0	22.4	22.6	24.3	22.9
% of women's employment in public sector	36.6	24.8	36.1	51.2	59.5	54.1	41.2	49.3	43.0	40.3	47.7	45.4
Employment change: 1980–96 index (1980 = 100)		104.4			108.9			111.5			119.3	
Employment change (000s)		143			211			136			999	
Change in private sector (000s)		65			120			107			997	
Change in public sector (000s)		208			91			29			2	

Note: The definition of the public sector is likely to differ between the two data sets.
Source: European Labour Force Survey, 1996, where public sector workers are defined as employees in: public administration and defence, and compulsory social security; health and social work; other community, social and personal service activities (NACE REV-1 categories L, M, N and O). For employment growth statistics see Pichelman and Hofer, 1998, p. 14, where the data are derived from OECD: *Employment Outlook*, various years.

rather than the public – sector over recent years. In Austria, in contrast, the strong female employment growth in the early 1990s may have been fuelled by the growth of the public sector, a relatively small employer in Austria by international standards (see table 4.8).

Women tend to be disproportionately employed in the public sector and thus the expansion of the public sector, perhaps as part of a process of catching up with other European countries, is likely to have a major impact on women's employment. Indeed the expansion of the public sector can initiate a virtuous circle of female employment growth, whereby more childcare services lead to more women being brought into public services employment to provide the care, and more women entering private or public services employment as they are able to find care facilities for their children. Almost inevitably, any restructuring of the public sector will have a major impact on women, as a consequence of the changes both in the level and form of services provided and in the terms and conditions of employment in the public sector. Another aspect of the growth of the part-time economy in the Netherlands has been a switch within the public sector away from full-time jobs in education and public administration towards part-time work in the health sector (Hartog, 1998). Thus from a sectoral and occupational, as well as a macro growth perspective, the restructuring of employment has had a strong gender dimension, related to the prevailing gender patterns of segregation, unequal pay and different working time arrangements. The significance of these dimensions within the restructuring process depends largely on the level of gender differentiation within the four countries, a topic to which we now turn.

Gender equality in the labour market

There are three main ways in which gender differences manifest themselves within employment:

- in patterns of occupational segregation, both horizontal and vertical;
- in differences in pay, both current and over a lifetime; and
- in differences in working time, both actual hours and contractual arrangements.

Segregation

All European and OECD labour markets have a high level of occupational segregation by sex, and the four countries under consideration here are no exception. Comparison of the extent of segregation over time and between countries is hampered by the prevalence of different systems of occupational classification. Table 4.9 provides the most recent, available estimates of segregation in the four countries, but while the index for Denmark, Ireland and the Netherlands is based on a data set which has been harmonized by Eurostat,

Table 4.9 Indices of segregation for all employment, 1994[a]

	Index of segregation (IS)	Index of dissimilarity (ID)	Karmel and MacLachlan IP index
Denmark	58	58	29
Ireland	51	54	25
Netherlands	52	53	26
Austria[b]	–	57	–

[a] Based on ISCO-88 (COM) three-digit classification. [b] The Austrian index, calculated by Pastner (1996), is based on national data sources and is not comparable with the other three countries.
Source: European Labour Force Survey, 1994; Elias, 1995.

the data for Austria refer to a specific national classification system and thus cannot be directly compared with the results for the other three countries. Segregation is usually measured by an index of segregation which attempts to capture the degree of change necessary within the labour market to bring about equal representation between women and men within occupational categories. There has been considerable debate in recent years over the appropriate index to use for such measurements (see Rubery and Fagan, 1993 for an overview of this debate; and Anker, 1998). This debate has pointed to the potentially very different results according to the choice of indicator, but in the case of European labour markets over recent years there has in practice been little difference in either the ranking of countries or the direction of change whatever index measure is used (Rubery et al., 1999).

For the sake of completeness, we present the results in tables 4.9 to 4.11 from a range of index measures. What we see from this information is that, in line with now well-established expectations concerning Scandinavian countries, Denmark has the highest level of occupational segregation, while Ireland and the Netherlands have comparatively low levels, particularly if the index of segregation rather than the index of dissimilarity is used. It is mainly the southern European countries, in which agricultural employment remains important, where lower levels of segregation are recorded, but this reflects in part the tendency for agricultural occupations to be gender-mixed. We have no harmonized data on changes in segregation between the 1980s and mid-1990s because of the switch from one International Standard Classification of Occupations to another (ISCO-68 to ISCO-88), but from the evidence using ISCO-68 data for the 1980s, and national data in Austria in 1981 and 1991, there appears to have been relatively little change in the overall indices of segregation during the 1980s. Of course, as we have argued elsewhere (Rubery and Fagan, 1993; 1995), this does not necessarily mean no change in segregation, but may instead hide a pattern of desegregation, for example in some higher-level jobs, combined with rising segregation within already female-dominated segments in services and clerical work.

Table 4.10 provides data for 1996 for all four countries, using harmonized Eurostat data on representation within the main occupational groups, regrouped into four main categories: professionals, managers and technical; clerical; services and elementary occupations; and skilled agricultural, craft and plant operative jobs. These data reveal basically similar patterns, with the first category of managerial, professional and technical jobs being relatively mixed, while clerical and service, and elementary, are female dominated, and agriculture, craft and plant operative occupations are overwhelmingly male dominated. The main exception to this pattern is services and elementary work in Ireland, which are still male dominated. More significant variations are found in the shares of part-time work: these shares tend to be lower in higher-level jobs and to take on greatest importance in service and elementary work, with clerical work holding an intermediate position.

Table 4.10 Occupational gender segregation and concentration, full and part time

	Male full-time	Male part-time	Male	Female full-time	Female part-time	Female	Total	Concentration of female full-timers	Concentration of female part-timers
Austria									
Professional, managerial, technical	55.3	3.1	58.4	31.5	10.0	41.6	100	31.3	24.6
Clerical	32.5	1.0	33.5	48.3	18.2	66.5	100	22.4	20.8
Services and elementary	32.3	1.7	33.9	41.7	24.3	66.1	100	29.3	42.3
Agriculture, craft and plant	76.6	2.7	79.4	16.0	4.7	20.6	100	17.0	12.3
Total	**54.2**	**2.4**	**56.5**	**30.9**	**12.5**	**43.5**	**100**	**100**	**100**
Denmark									
Professional, managerial, technical	53.8	3.3	57.0	32.1	10.9	43.0	100	40.3	25.9
Clerical	24.3	3.8	28.1	50.3	21.7	71.9	100	21.5	17.6
Services and elementary	24.4	13.4	37.7	30.4	31.8	62.3	100	27.5	54.5
Agriculture, craft and plant	82.2	3.1	85.3	13.3	1.3	14.7	100	10.6	2.0
Total	**49.1**	**6.0**	**55.1**	**29.4**	**15.5**	**44.9**	**100**	**100**	**100**
Ireland									
Professional, managerial, technical	56.3	1.5	57.8	36.1	6.1	42.2	100	36.7	21.9
Clerical	28.9	1.2	30.0	57.8	12.2	70.0	100	27.3	20.3
Services and elementary	47.4	6.5	53.9	28.1	18.0	46.1	100	23.9	54.0
Agriculture, craft and plant	84.0	2.7	86.7	12.2	1.1	13.3	100	12.0	3.7
Total	**58.6**	**3.1**	**61.7**	**29.9**	**8.5**	**38.3**	**100**	**100**	**100**
Netherlands									
Professional, managerial, technical	54.0	8.0	62.0	14.7	23.3	38.0	100	52.5	39.4
Clerical	28.6	5.5	34.1	23.8	42.1	65.9	100	22.2	18.7
Services and elementary	24.4	14.0	38.4	12.0	49.6	61.6	100	18.6	36.4
Agriculture, craft and plant	77.7	10.8	88.5	4.3	7.2	11.5	100	6.7	5.4
Total	**50.0**	**9.4**	**59.4**	**13.1**	**27.5**	**40.6**	**100**	**100**	**100**

Note: Totals may not add up exactly, owing to rounding.
Source: European Labour Force Survey 1996, special tabulations.

Table 4.11 Indices of segregation for full-time, part-time and all-in employment, 1994

Country	Index of segregation			Index of dissimilarity			Karmel and MacLachlan index		
	Part-time	Full-time	All-in employment	Part-time	Full-time	All-in employment	Part-time	Full-time	All-in employment
Denmark	47	56	58	48	56	58	18	27	29
Ireland	47	45	51	47	53	54	19	23	25
Netherlands	31	45	52	32	50	53	12	17	26

Note: Based on ISCO-88 (COM) three-digit classification.
Source: European Labour Force Survey, 1994; Rubery and Smith,1999.

These data, therefore, point to another dimension to the pattern of segregation by gender – the role of part-time work. Table 4.11 calculates segregation indices for full-timers and part-timers separately and compares them to the index for "all-in employment". Part-time work, considered in isolation, tends to be less segregated than full-time work, but to a large extent this reflects the tendency for male part-timers to work in female-dominated occupations. The impact on the overall segregation of the labour market is better identified through a comparison of the full time and the all-in employment segregation index. In all cases the full-time index is below that for all-in employment, indicating that part-time work adds to gender segregation. However, the difference tends to be relatively small. The only exceptions apply to Ireland and the Netherlands and to some of the index measures; the index of segregation shows a large change for the Netherlands and Ireland, as does the Karmel and MacLachlan index for the Netherlands, but the most widely used index, the index of dissimilarity, only records a small change for both countries.

Pay and income inequality

While the level of segregation in all four countries is fairly similar, the consequences of unequal distribution in the labour market, as revealed by the gender pay gap, are very different. There is a lack of harmonized comparative data and even a lack of national statistics in some countries, particularly Ireland and Austria, but all available sources support the view that Denmark has a relatively narrow earnings distribution and a narrow gender pay gap; the Netherlands has a wider income distribution than Denmark, but stands very much in a middle position for European countries. In contrast, both Austria and Ireland are believed to have both wide earnings distribution and large gender pay gaps, although there is a lack of information for detailed comparisons. As is now fairly well established, gender earnings gaps are positively fuelled by wage systems which result in wide levels of overall wage

Table 4.12 Earnings by education and sex (index: upper secondary = 100)

	Year	Lower secondary	Upper secondary	Non-university tertiary	University level	Total
Men						
Austria	1991	85	100	n.a.	146[a]	
Denmark	1993	86	100	110	142	
Ireland	1993	77	100	121	171	
Netherlands	1993	84	100	n.a.	136[a]	
Women						
Austria	1991	81	100	n.a.	134[a]	
Denmark	1993	86	100	111	133	
Ireland	1993	62	100	123	187	
Netherlands	1993	73	100	n.a.	141[a]	
Women as % of men						
Austria	1991	80	83	n.a.	76[a]	77
Denmark	1993	73	73	74	68	72
Ireland	1993	45	56	57	61	59
Netherlands	1993	44	51	n.a.	53[a]	49

[a] Combines non-university and university-level tertiary education. Mean annual earnings: n.a. = not applicable.
Source: OECD: *Education at a Glance,* 1996, p. 242–243.

inequality (Blau and Kahn, 1992; Whitehouse, 1992; Rubery and Fagan, 1994). Table 4.12 provides OECD data on earnings by both education level and sex. These confirm that Denmark has the most egalitarian structure by education (the earnings of the higher educated in the Netherlands are reduced through the amalgamation of university and non-university tertiary education), and also reveal the much greater earnings inequality in Ireland. The data are based on mean annual earnings, a factor which could explain the rather surprising finding of higher gender equality in Austria than Denmark, where the part-time employment rate is still higher. The data also reveal the very large gender gaps in annual earnings in both Ireland and the Netherlands. In Ireland the inegalitarian structure of pay differentials plays a major role, while in the Netherlands the major cause of the large gender gap is likely to be the high share of part-time work among women.

Information on the extent and concentration of low pay in general and by sex is patchy and is found in different sources for the different countries, but nevertheless a consistent story emerges. For Denmark the only information available is for both sexes combined, but this shows nevertheless that Denmark has a relatively narrow earnings distribution by international standards (narrower than all except the Nordic countries included in the 1993 OECD study (OECD: *Employment Outlook*, 1993)), although there was some widening of the distribution in line with changes towards more decentralized bargaining in the 1980s. For the Netherlands and Ireland the only information

Table 4.13 Level and concentration of low earnings

	United Kingdom	Ireland	Netherlands	Belgium
% full-timers with earnings[a] below 66% of median:				
All	20	18	11	5
Women	40	29	28	10
Under-25, all	41	45	40	30
% of all low-paid full-timers:				
Women	63	51	53	62
Under-25, all	49	62	89	37
% of part-timers with less than 66% of full-time median hourly earnings (% full-timers in brackets)	60 (17)	33 (19)	23 (11)	9 (5)

[a] Earnings are gross weekly earnings for the United Kingdom, normal gross weekly earnings for Ireland, annual earnings for the Netherlands and gross daily earnings for Belgium.
Source: Gregory and Sandoval, 1994.

available on income distribution by sex is found in a 1991 study of low pay (CERC, 1991; see table 4.13 – Belgium and the United Kingdom are included for comparison as the countries with the lowest and the highest risk of low pay respectively). This showed Ireland to have an overall higher level of low pay than the Netherlands, but the risk of women being low paid was 160 per cent higher than that for men in the Netherlands, though only 60 per cent higher in Ireland, so that the end result was a similar share of full-time women workers classified as low paid (28 per cent and 29 per cent, respectively). Moreover, the share of low-paid full-timers potentially understates the full extent of low pay for women, particularly in the Netherlands, because of the high share of part-timers who are excluded from these data and are often expected to face a particularly high risk of low pay. Evidence from the same study but based on hourly wages to some extent confirms this. While 11 per cent of full-timers in the Netherlands received low hourly earnings, 23 per cent of part-timers were in the low-wage category. However, this rate of low payment of part-timers was much lower than that found in the United Kingdom, where no less than 60 per cent of part-timers were on low hourly wages, compared to 17 per cent of full-timers. In Ireland the calculation of low pay on an hourly pay basis raises the share of full-timers, who are low paid compared to the Netherlands, to 19 per cent compared to 11 per cent in the latter country; and the risk of low pay among part-timers is in turn higher, at 33 per cent.

Thus in comparative terms the Netherlands has a relatively low risk of low pay for part-timers, and the apparent similarity between the Netherlands and Ireland disappears once hourly wages are considered. One factor increasing the relative risk of low pay among full-timers in the Netherlands may be the tendency for most full-timers to be young, with almost all prime-age women working part time. It must, however, be remembered that, as a consequence, most female prime-age workers will be low paid in annual terms and certainly will receive substantially lower income over the life cycle. If we take labour force participation rates, earnings differentials and working-time patterns into account, it is clear that women in Denmark enjoy much greater equality in lifetime earnings from employment than is the case in Ireland or the Netherlands. Moreover, as Ireland is catching up with the Netherlands in participation rates, but based upon a higher full-time employment share, in the future there may be greater gender equality in lifetime income in Ireland than the Netherlands. Austria has wide earnings dispersion, approaching the high levels of inequality found in North America and the United Kingdom and above the range found in most other European countries (OECD: *Employment Outlook,* 1996). It also has a high incidence of low pay among women compared to men. This high incidence of low pay for women arises out of institutionally determined wage differentials by sector, occupation and seniority, and not, as is perhaps the case in the United Kingdom and the United States, out of the concentration of women in deregulated sectors.

Employment contracts, flexibility and working time

The greater equality between women and men in Denmark in terms of their labour market integration is evident again from data on length of job tenure (table 4.14). In Denmark there is only a gender difference of 0.8 years, compared to gaps of 2.4 to 3 years in the other countries. Women in Denmark do not, however, have the longest average tenure; average tenure is 7.5 years in Denmark and 8.6 years in Austria, but Austrian men have higher average tenure, at 11 years compared to 8.3 years for Danish men. The relatively low tenure rate in Denmark probably reflects the high share of small firms and

Table 4.14 Average job tenure by sex, age and education

	Austria	Denmark	Ireland	Netherlands
All	10.0	7.9	8.7	8.7
Men	11.0	8.3	9.8	9.9
Women	8.6	7.5	7.2	6.9
Gender gap	2.4	0.8	2.6	3.0
Age: 15–24	2.8	1.5	2.2	1.8
25–44	8.8	6.3	8.5	7.6
45+	17.8	14.5	15.4	16.0
Education:				
Primary/lower secondary	9.3	9.3	9.5	8.2
Upper secondary	10.1	8.2	8.0	8.9
Tertiary	10.7	7.8	8.6	8.5

Source: OECD: *Employment Outlook*, 1997, table 5.6.

Table 4.15 Share of temporary-contract workers aged under 30 (percentages)

	Men	Women
Austria	73.8	70.8
Denmark	66.9	60.5
Ireland	53.9	56.0
Netherlands	73.8	49.6

Source: European Labour Force Survey, 1994; Rubery, et al., 1999.

the emphasis on inter-employer mobility, cushioned by generous benefit levels, a model that applies to women as well as men (Kongshoj Madsen, 1998).

When we look at another dimension of flexibility, namely employment on temporary contracts, we find that the use of such contracts is approximately equal to the average European incidence in the case of Denmark and the Netherlands, but below average in Ireland and particularly in Austria. Although women's involvement in temporary work tends to be higher than that of men, a sizeable gender gap emerges only in Ireland and particularly in the Netherlands. For all four countries temporary work is primarily concentrated among the younger age groups (see table 4.15), but that is particularly the case for men in the Netherlands and for both sexes in Austria where the share of temporary contracts for workers aged 30 or under exceeds 70 per cent. The lowest share concentrated in the under-30 range is for women on temporary contracts in the Netherlands, but even here the share is around 50 per cent. The share of temporary workers among prime-age women is greatest in the Netherlands, and there is also evidence that it is in those jobs that wage inequality is highest; hourly wages for part-time and full-time workers are on average roughly equal and it is flexible workers who are the worst paid (Fagan et al., 1995; Rubery et al.,1999).

The use of part-time work is more clearly gender determined, and more subject to variation between countries than the use of temporary contracts. However, although women account for the majority of all part-time jobs in all four countries, these four countries include two of the three European States – the third being the United Kingdom – where male part-time work is becoming significant. Thus the share of women among part-timers drops to under 65 per cent in Denmark and the Netherlands, compared to 74 per cent in Ireland and 89 per cent in Austria (OECD: *Employment Outlook*, 1998, table E). However, most of this part-time work is found among the younger age ranges and is associated to a large extent with combining work and studying. Another major difference arises from the fact that while in three of the countries studied the role of part-time work has been expanding, in Denmark it has been contracting, particularly for that group most often associated with part-time work, namely prime-age women of childbearing age. Danish women are thus no longer tending to leave the labour market when they have children or to return to reduced-hours jobs. In contrast, only a very tiny share of prime-age women in the Netherlands works full time, and virtually no mothers of young children (see table 4.18 on activity patterns of mothers in the EU). In Austria and Ireland part-time work has been expanding but the majority of women still work full time. Moreover, in Ireland the recent expansion of employment has been relatively evenly split between full and part time. These differences in the use of part-time work cannot be explained mainly by differences in the available work but relate, on the one hand, to systems of regulation and labour market organization and, on the other, to patterns of gender relations and societal values. In the Netherlands it appears to be societal values more than the system of regulation which is leading to the growth of part-time work, as many of the advantages of part-time work, from the point of view of employers, have been removed in the Netherlands through the inclusion of widespread pro rata rights and benefits in collective agreements and in legal entitlements.

The other main way in which the role of part-time work may differ between countries – apart from the issue of low pay, dealt with earlier – is whether part-time work is only found in lower-level occupations or reaches up into higher-level occupations; this will determine whether women who wish to work part time are faced with having to accept a lower-level job because of the shortage of part-time work opportunities in higher-level jobs. In this context the Netherlands offers proportionately more opportunities to work in managerial, professional and technical occupations (see table 4.10). However, full-timers also have a higher share of these occupations in the Netherlands than in the other countries and there is thus still a tendency for more part-time jobs to be found in service and elementary jobs relative to full-time work.

Gender, and labour market and social policy

To consider fully the gender equality issue in recent employment performance, we need to look not only at conventional measures of labour market equality, but also at how far the set of policies pursued in the fields of labour market and social policy are compatible, or otherwise, with the promotion of greater gender equality. We also need to consider the potential costs, and the distribution of these costs, of policy approaches that fail to live up to these criteria. In undertaking this assessment we will take the position that the absence of measures is as much a policy as the presence of measures. Nor will we assume that policies need be consistent across all areas of activity; thus one issue to be considered is whether a coherent policy for equal opportunity can be identified within each of these four countries.

Representation of gender interests within policy-making

The first issue to be considered, before a detailed evaluation of specific policy areas, is the effectiveness of representation of women's interests within the policy-making apparatus. All four countries analysed fall into the corporatist or neo-corporatist spectrum of governance systems, so that the representation of women's interests is important not only within government, but also among the social partners. The evidence, such as is available, suggests very different patterns of inclusion of gender interests, although in all cases except Denmark there appears to be only limited recognition of gender interests within, in particular, industrial relations forums.

In the Netherlands we find that there is a strong tradition of consensus building, which has been continued into current policy-making, but nevertheless information on policy debates within the Netherlands suggests that these debates do not take into account the specific interests of women (Plantenga et al., 1996). For example, the debate over whether to allow the creation of minimum-wage and low-wage jobs was conducted without reference to the gendered nature of low-paid jobs and the concentration of women at the bottom end of the labour market.

In Austria, collective bargaining institutions have traditionally been dominated by men, and the corporatist system in Austria, it has been argued, depends upon acceptance of the current distribution of income (Pichelman and Hofer, 1998), which has the effect of creating large wage differentials between male- and female-dominated sectors, even compared to average standards in Europe. There is more evidence of action to promote women's interests at the level of the State, with equal opportunities issues being given some prominence in the Austrian Government's National Action Plan on employment in accordance with the EU employment guidelines. However, there would need to be more change within the social partners for a coherent policy of equal opportunities to develop.

Ireland is another country where there is a clear gender imbalance in the representation of interests within collective bargaining. However, one of the main examples cited of the neglect of gender issues has been the failure to enact minimum-wage legislation, except in a piecemeal fashion (Barry and Roche, 1993); however, the recent announcement of the introduction of a minimum wage could mark a stage in the development of greater concern over low pay and conditions in unregulated sectors. Moreover, within the national social partnership there has been an interesting inclusion of groups other than the traditional social partners, among them women's interest groups, and youth and community interest groups, along with farming organizations. These are not integrated on an equal footing, but it is highly unlikely that women's interest groups would have been allowed to play any role in the development of the national accord without the recent growth of female employment.

Denmark provides the only example of a country where there is evidence of the integration of women's interests in the policy formulation phase, largely through their active role within the trade union movement. Some of the major unions representing less-skilled workers, for example in the public sector, are dominated by women, and it is through the industrial relations institutions that at least some attention to gender issues, including the pay levels in female-dominated jobs, are articulated. This does not mean that women are fully and equally represented in all policy-making bodies, but there does appear to be a greater matching between women's labour market position and their position in policy-making in Denmark than in the other three countries. However, it should also be noted that the principles on which the Danish system is based, including citizenship rights and universal benefits, provide a framework in which women's interests are less likely to be ignored than under a system where rights and benefits are tied to labour market status and earnings, i.e. the system which predominates in Austria and Ireland, and to some extent in the Netherlands.

Family policy and family structure

Family policy has been increasingly recognized as part of the framework for employment policy, in a context in which increasing shares of women are now in the labour market and it cannot be assumed that most women, even when they have young children, will stay at home full time. However, it is also the case that not all, or even most, aspects of family policy are necessarily geared towards employment objectives. For example, paid leave, such as is found in Austria, may be interpreted as much as a means of providing a transfer to low-income households with children as a means of integrating women into the labour market. The recent requirement that men should participate in the leave for the full entitlement to be available has been widely interpreted as a means of reducing costs rather than as a genuine equal opportunities measure (see table 4.16). Only in 1998, when Austria assumed the European presidency, was there evidence of action to establish childcare provision in line with the European employment policy guidelines. Table 4.16 shows that although paid leave is relatively long in Austria, it is paid at a low and flat-rate level, and the share of children aged 3 years and under in public day-care in the early 1990s (table 4.17) was only 3 per cent.

Ireland also lacks childcare facilities, with only 2 per cent of children aged 3 and under in day care, and even the proposal to increase childcare provision under the new National Action Plan will only make a marginal difference to this level of provision (Barry, 1998). Ireland also did not have any form of parental leave (table 4.16) until the Parental Leave Directive was passed, only providing three months of maternity leave. In fact, the Government requested a six-month derogation in the implementation of the Directive, which was due in June 1998 (Barry, 1998). In its lack of a family policy, Ireland could be seen as regarding the care of children as primarily an issue for private households and in particular for women, and not an issue of either employment or social policy.

Policy in the Netherlands is not far from that prevailing in Ireland, as the Netherlands also lacks significant childcare provision, with only 8 per cent of

Table 4.16 Parental leave provisions in EU Member States, 1994–95

Country	Duration		Transferability	Benefits		Flexibility		Conditions
	Maximum	Boundaries		Rate	Period	Part-time	Fractioning[a]	
Paid leave								
Austria	24 months	Until child is 4 years	Family: last 6 months only available if partner takes at least 3 months leave	Flat-rate[b]	104 weeks	Yes[c]	No	No
Denmark[d]	10 weeks +3–9 months[c]	Until child is 9 years	Family Individual	Flat-rate: 80% of unemployment benefit	10 weeks 20 weeks	No No	No Yes	No
Part-time leave								
Netherlands	6 months part-time (new provision to allow 13 weeks full-time as alternative)	Until child is 4 years	Individual	Unpaid		Only	No	12 months of service
No parental leave								
Ireland	None							

[a] The possibility of taking the leave in more than one instalment. [b] Higher for single-parents or low-income families. [c] Only with employer's agreement.
[d] Leave can also be used for other reasons, such as training: workers taking leave are not guaranteed their jobs.
Source: CEC, 1997.

Table 4.17 Services for young children, school age and length of school day

	Year	Proportion in publicly funded[a] services for children (%)		Compulsory school age	Length of school day in hours	Proportion in publicly funded services for children 6–10 years[b]
		0–3 years	3–6 years			
Austria	1994	3	75	6	4–5	6%
Denmark	1995	48	82	7	3–52[c]	62% + all 6-year-olds in pre-primary education
Ireland	1993	2	55	6	4.40–5.40[c]	<5% (estimate)
Netherlands	1993	8	71	5	7	<5% (estimate)

[a] "Publicly funded" means that more than half of the total costs of a service are paid from public sources, and usually between 75 per cent and 100 per cent. [b] This figure does not include children in compulsory schooling; it is confined to services providing care and recreation. [c] School hours increase as child grows older.
Source: CEC, 1997.

children aged 3 and under in day care, and instead has chosen to promote part-time work. Moreover, until very recently parental leave was only available in the form of reduced hours, thereby further promoting part-time work. Thus the Netherlands differs from Ireland in acting to promote women's partial integration into employment even when they are mothers, but the main emphasis is on care in the home, with women effectively being encouraged to take only very limited part-time jobs.

Denmark stands out as having the most developed family policy in terms of both childcare provision and paid leave. No less than 48 per cent of children aged 3 and under were in public day care in the early 1990s, and both parents are entitled to paid leave, although it represents only 60 per cent of unemployment benefit, reduced from 80 per cent when the leave schemes were first introduced. The recent development of job-rotation schemes raised concerns that they would undermine the position of women in the labour force by encouraging them to take leave and, at the same time, perhaps allow the provision of childcare places to be reduced. Women have been the main takers of parental leave schemes under the job-rotation scheme, but the commitment of women to full-time work for most of the time when their children are young seems nevertheless to have remained strong. It is not clear whether the fears relating to childcare provision have been realized.

So far we have considered the policies enacted by government to encourage or discourage participation of mothers. Table 4.18 provides more detailed information on the actual practices of women with respect to labour market participation according to their family situation. It shows the economic activity of mothers with a child under 10 for all 15 EU Member States, with eastern and western Germany listed separately. On that basis Denmark had the second highest activity rate for mothers after eastern Germany, although Sweden has

Table 4.18 Activity patterns of mothers[a] in EU Member States

	Labour market activity rate	Part-time employment	Unemployed	Full-time employment
Germany (eastern)	88.0	14.0	19.0	55.0
Denmark	84.0	25.0	10.0	49.0
Sweden	82.0	40.0	7.0	35.0
Finland	77.0	8.0	12.0	57.0
Portugal	75.0	7.0	5.0	63.0
Belgium	71.0	24.0	9.0	38.0
France	70.0	19.0	11.0	40.0
Austria	67.9	24.0	3.9[b]	40.0
United Kingdom	59.0	35.0	6.0	18.0
Netherlands	52.0	41.0	5.0	6.0
Germany (western)	50.0	28.0	4.0	18.0
Greece	50.0	3.0	7.0	40.0
Italy	49.0	6.0	6.0	37.0
Spain	49.0	6.0	14.0	29.0
Luxembourg	54.0	13.0	3.0	29.0
Ireland	42.0	10.0	8.0	24.0

[a] The definition of a mother is having a child aged 10 or under, but for Austria a child under 15 and for Sweden a child under 7. [b] The unemployment rate for Austrian mothers is taken here as the average unemployment rate for all women, as the data were not available for mothers alone.
Source: European Childcare Network, 1996.

a slightly higher and eastern Germany a lower overall (full-time and part-time) employment rate. Austria has a middle-level economic activity rate for mothers, but actually a relatively high employment rate, only lower than the three Scandinavian countries, eastern Germany and Portugal. The Netherlands has a much lower employment rate of mothers, only just higher than western Germany and not much above the rates found in the three southern countries, Luxembourg and Ireland; the latter has both the lowest activity rate for mothers and, along with Spain, the lowest employment rate. Table 4.18 also reveals the major differences between the four countries in terms of the tendency for mothers to work full or part time. Between 40 and 50 per cent of all mothers in Denmark and Austria are in full-time work, while the share drops to 24 per cent in Ireland and 6 per cent in the Netherlands. The share of mothers working part time varies from 10 per cent in Ireland to 41 per cent in the Netherlands.

We have reviewed the impact of family policy on the activity rates of mothers but we also need to consider the different family and social environments prevailing in the four countries, as well as the activity and employment rates for mothers who are not in standard nuclear families. The changes that have been taking place in women's position in society are related not solely to labour market change, but also to changes in patterns of household and family formation, in the stability of family and household relationships, and

Table 4.19 Trends in childbearing

	Austria	Denmark	Ireland	Netherlands
Share of live births outside marriage				
1960	13.0	7.8	1.6	1.4
1989	22.6	46.1	12.8	10.7
1990	26.3	46.8	19.5	13.1
Crude fertility rate (/1,000 pop.)				
1960	2.7	2.5	3.8	3.1
1989	1.4	1.6	2.1	1.6
1993	1.5	1.8	1.9	1.6
Completed fertility women aged 35				
1970	2.45	2.38	3.44	2.50
1980	1.93	2.06	3.27	1.99
1990	1.77	1.83	2.68	1.87
1992	1.72	1.84	2.54	1.86
1995	1.68	1.84	2.39	1.83

Source: Eurostat, 1995, tables E4, E9, E10.

in social attitudes, expectations and behaviour. However, these social changes have taken different forms and different degrees within European countries. Table 4.19 outlines the variations in fertility rates and the share of children born outside marriage in the four countries studied (see also table 4.21 on lone-parent families). In Denmark close to half the children are born outside marriage, reflecting the high rate of both cohabitation and single-parent families (at 15 per cent of private households with a child under 15). In Austria over a quarter of births are outside marriage and 8 per cent of families are single-parent households. The Netherlands and Ireland have lower rates of children born outside marriage and lower shares of single-parent households. Perhaps surprisingly, the proportion of children born outside marriage is higher in Ireland than the Netherlands, at nearly 20 per cent compared to 13 per cent, but possibly reflecting the absence of divorce in Ireland. Single parents account for around 6 per cent of families in each case.

If we look at fertility rates (table 4.19) we find that Ireland has a relatively high rate by European standards using both the crude fertility rate figure and particularly the completed fertility estimates. These data also reveal the dramatic decline in fertility rates over the post-war period, underlining the rather late transition of Ireland to the smaller family sizes found in most European countries. The Netherlands and Denmark have around average fertility rates by European standards, with Denmark showing higher rates in the crude fertility statistics. Both have experienced significant declines in fertility through the 1970s and 1980s, but there is no evidence of the dramatic declines in fertility found more recently in some of the southern European countries, particularly Italy and Spain. Austria has the lowest fertility rate of the four countries, at close to the average by the crude rate but below average according to completed fertility statistics. However, the fertility rate in Austria exceeds that in Germany, the country often regarded as having the closest relationship to Austria, despite or perhaps because of a higher employment rate among mothers and women in general. Overall there is no relationship between fertility rates and employment rates; fertility is high in Ireland with low employment rates, but equally Spain and Italy have low fertility rates and low employment rates, while Scandinavian countries, including Denmark, tend to have relatively high fertility combined with high employment rates. There is also no relationship between opportunities for part-time work and fertility, as the Netherlands has only an average level of fertility despite very widespread opportunities, apparently, for reconciling work and family life.

In Denmark fertility is no longer linked to marriage, and there are much higher proportions of single-parent households. This change in household arrangements thus mirrors and reinforces the position of women in the labour market, where continuous participation on a full-time basis and for equal wages has become the social norm, reinforced by state provision of childcare and a relatively equal distribution of wage income. In the Netherlands there is a much stronger link between marriage and fertility. Again there is a close relationship between labour market patterns and social norms; mothers are primarily found in marital relationships where financial support is provided by the father to the mother, who either does not work or works part time. Ireland is similar to the Netherlands except that there are somewhat more births outside marriage and a greater tendency for mothers – when they do work – to work full time, especially if they are more highly educated. This suggests that in Ireland there may be more diversity around the social norm and also more of a tendency for the social norm to break down when women have realistic opportunities of earning a reasonable wage. Austria occupies a middle position, with a relatively high but still minority share of births outside marriage and a higher share of single-parent families than in Ireland and the Netherlands. It also has a lower birth rate, perhaps suggesting that more women may be choosing not to have children or to have fewer children.

Table 4.20 collates the available information, by no means complete, on activity patterns by type of household in Austria, Ireland and the Netherlands. (There are no data for Denmark.) Taking dual-adult households first, we find that in all three countries there is a very low share of female "breadwinners" and that the major variations are between dual-earner and male breadwinner households. If we consider only those households with at least one earner (Part B of table 4.20), we find over 60 per cent of two-person households to be dual-earner households in Austria and the Netherlands, but only 47 per cent in Ireland; the share of male breadwinner households thus varies from 30 per cent in Austria to 48 per cent in Ireland. It is clear that if Denmark were included, the share of male breadwinner households would be even

Table 4.20 Labour market activity patterns of households

	All two-adult households (households with children in brackets)		
	Austria	Ireland	Netherlands
A. *Share of all two-adult households*:			
All dual earners	59.5 (60.6)	41.3 (39.0)	56.4 (52.4)
Dual earners/both full time	37.0 (33.0)	29.5 (25.9)	13.4 (3.9)
Dual earners/male full time/female part time	20.5 (25.7)	10.7 (12.1)	37.6 (43.5)
Dual earners/male part time/female full time	1.1 (1.1)	0.6 (0.6)	1.3 (0.8)
Dual earners/both part time	0.8 (0.8)	0.4 (0.4)	4.1 (4.2)
Single earners (men)	28.2 (32.0)	42.6 (45.4)	32.3 (39.8)
Single earners (women)	6.1 (4.8)	4.4 (4.1)	4.5 (2.6)
No earners	6.2 (2.7)	11.7 (11.6)	6.8 (5.2)
B. *Two-adult households with at least one adult in work:*			
Share of dual earners	63.4	46.6	60.6
Single earners (men)	30.1	48.3	34.6
Single earners (women)	6.5	5.0	4.7

Source: European Labour Force Survey, 1996, special tabulations.

lower than the 30 per cent in Austria. Thus for two of the countries dual breadwinner households are the norm, while in Ireland the male breadwinner household is equal in importance to the dual breadwinner household.

However, so far we have only looked at whether both partners are in work; when we look at the patterns of full- and part-time work as well as numbers of earners (table 4.20, Part A) we find, as we might expect, that only 13 per cent of Dutch households have both partners in full-time work. The norm in the Netherlands is for the man to be in full-time and the woman in part-time work, accounting for 37.6 per cent of all households. In contrast, the most frequent form of dual-earner household in Austria and Ireland is one in which both are in full-time work, at 37 per cent and 30 per cent of all households respectively. In fact Ireland has a relatively low share of households with the man in full-time work and the woman in part-time work (11 per cent), while Austria has over 20 per cent in this category. The Netherlands is also the only country to record a significant share of households where both partners are in part-time work (4.1 per cent). When we divide the sample into parents and non-parents, the share of dual earners within households with children falls by two percentage points compared with the average in the Netherlands and Ireland, but actually rises in Austria. The patterns of working-time arrangements within dual-earner households with children are also similar to the patterns found for all households. There is in fact a larger fall in the share of full-time workers for households with children as against all households in the Netherlands than for Austria and Ireland.

Table 4.21 Activity patterns of lone-parent families, 1994

	Lone-parent families as share of all families with children[a]	Male lone-parent activity rates	Female lone-parent activity rates
Austria[b]	8.3	(98.8)	88.1
Denmark[c]	15.0	96.9	78.1
Ireland	5.8		40.4
Netherlands	6.6	84.1	50.1

[a] Private households with children aged under 15. [b] 1995. [c] 1993.
Source: Eurostat.

Table 4.21 looks at activity rates for lone-parent households by sex. In all the countries for which activity rates for men are available, these are uniformly high for lone fathers; for women who are lone parents, however, the activity rates vary from 88 per cent and 78 per cent in Austria and Denmark to 50 per cent and 40 per cent in the Netherlands and Ireland. These variations are greater than might be expected with reference to overall employment rates, and may reflect benefit arrangements and access to childcare, as well as women's orientation towards paid work. However, while the aim of giving options to lone parents requires the provision of childcare facilities and the avoidance of penal marginal tax rates on benefits, it is still necessary to ensure that preferences by single parents to care for their children are recognized. In some countries, including the United Kingdom and also the Netherlands, there have been moves to restrict the rights of lone parents to claim benefits, thereby placing pressure on them to enter the labour market (Plantenga et al., 1996). This type of policy may be presented as a policy of improving the life chances of lone parents compared to long-term welfare dependency, but it also tends to obscure the unpaid work undertaken by such lone parents and the limited job opportunities often open to lone women with children. Thus, an equal opportunities family policy must involve the recognition of unpaid care work and the opportunity to undertake care work, as well as providing opportunities to reconcile unpaid care work with wage work.

Taxation and benefits

Taxation and benefit systems have been subject to increasing scrutiny from an employment policy perspective, in order to identify ways in which the welfare State system may create welfare traps or disincentives to employment. For example, there have been concerns to remove obstacles to integration by providing in-work benefits or increased opportunities to work in part-time jobs when unemployed. However, unfortunately the analyses of tax and welfare State systems pay relatively little regard to issues of gender, from the perspective of analysing both the equity aspects of the systems and the incentive and disincentive dimensions. Many taxation and welfare systems have a household – and not simply an individual – dimension to them, and it thus becomes essential to identify the impact on other members of the household. For example, an in-work benefit may help an unemployed man move off benefits into work, but may create major obstacles to the spouse entering employment on his or her own account (see OECD: *Employment Outlook*, 1997, for an analysis which is aware of these household dimensions). This review of tax and benefit policies will therefore focus on both gender equality dimensions and labour market incentive dimensions from a household as well as an individual perspective.

Taxation

Three of the countries have individualized taxation systems, while Ireland has retained the system of aggregating married couples' income. However, all three countries with individualized taxation have in fact not adopted a "pure" model of individualization. In the Netherlands and Denmark unused allowances can be transferred to spouses and in Austria there is an additional, although small, allowance for a dependent partner. All of these features maintain some disincentives for the second person to enter the labour market (Dingledey, 1998). In principle these non-individualized aspects of the systems should provide greater disincentives for second-income earners. However, the size of these incentives depends both on the system and on the rates of taxation, while their impact on actual labour market participation also depends on the institutional and social context in which the tax system operates (Gustafsson, 1996). Denmark, in line with other Scandinavian countries, has relatively high rates of income tax, which tend to provide greater incentives for two earners under individualized taxation, despite the transfer system. Although the taxation system in Denmark may have played some role in establishing the dual-earner system, it is no longer the case that women's participation is highly sensitive to tax incentives. This probably also applies to the other three countries, although individual taxation may yet do something to stimulate female participation in Ireland. What is clear is that the aggregation principle leads to married women receiving lower net take-home pay than their equivalent single counterparts on the same income, although the overall income received by the household will be higher than that for two single people. In general, taxation is now regarded as more an issue of gender equality within a partnership than a major disincentive to participation, but it is notable that Austria has a much higher female employment rate than Germany, where the taxation system is based on the income-splitting principle and perhaps provides a significant disincentive to female participation.

Unemployment benefits

There are various ways in which the system of unemployment benefit can discriminate against access for women. First, there may be stiff eligibility requirements in terms of continuity of employment or minimum hours or earnings thresholds; second, there may be either short duration of non-means-tested benefits or low benefits topped up with means-tested or family-conditional allowances; third, there may be requirements for recipients to be available for full-time work; fourth, either access to or the level of benefits may be linked to the household; and, fifth, there may be tight restrictions on the earnings of spouses married to unemployed people. Before looking at these dimensions of discrimination, how far they apply within the specific countries in question and how they can be considered discriminatory, we look first at the outcome of the systems in terms of equity of access. Table 4.22 shows that, of the four countries under study, only Denmark has a similar proportion of female unemployed (according to the ILO measure) in receipt of unemployment benefits as male unemployed, and only in Denmark could the share of unemployed women receiving benefits be considered high, at 70 per cent. Austria has the next highest share (at 57 per cent), but well below the male share of 75 per cent. In Ireland 82 per cent of men unemployed by the ILO definition were receiving benefits but only 43 per cent of women, and in the Netherlands the male share was lower, at only 62 per cent, but matched by an even lower share for women of just one-third. These figures suggest that there is some discrimination against women in the unemployment benefit system in at least three of the countries.

Stiff continuity requirements for unemployment benefit discriminate against women because of their more intermittent participation. However, Denmark – with the greatest continuity of female labour force participation – has the lowest continuity requirements, while the other three countries have eligibility requirements classified as "medium" according to comparative criteria. Perhaps most important for this assessment of recent employment performance, several European countries, including the Netherlands, have tightened eligibility without apparently seriously considering the gender implications of this move. In terms of eligibility requirements for part-timers, on the other hand, it is the Netherlands and Austria where the thresholds for the inclusion of part-timers are lowest; but access to benefits for part-timers in Austria may not be very meaningful as the benefits are earnings related with no minimum floor. Denmark sets up medium barriers, but in practice has few part-timers working below these thresholds, while Ireland has the stiffest eligibility rules for part-timers. Non-means-tested benefits tend to favour women as they are more likely than men, when unemployed, to be in households where there is another person in work. The long duration of non-means-tested benefits in Denmark and the Netherlands thus favours women, while the short duration of non-means-tested benefits in Austria and Ireland works to their disadvantage. Moreover, in Ireland there is a very low replacement rate for single people (or those married to an employed person) and much higher replacement rates for couples, and particularly families with children (OECD: *Employment Outlook*, 1996, table 2.1). This type of benefit system reduces the cost to the government of unemployment for those who are not single breadwinners. None of the

Table 4.22 Unemployment benefit systems in EU Member States

	A Share of unemployed (ILO) receiving unemployment benefits or assistance, 1994		B Continuity requirements for unemployment benefits	C Requirements affecting access of part-timers to unemployment benefits	D Duration of non-means-tested benefits
	Male	Female			
High share					
Finland	90.4	91.6	Low	High	Medium
Belgium	84.0	85.8	Medium	High	Long
Sweden	78.7	76.8[a]	Low	High	Short
Denmark	68.2	70.4	Low	Medium	Long
Germany	77.5	69.2	Low	High	Medium
Medium share					
Austria	74.6	56.5[b]	Medium	Low[c]	Short
France	53.5	43.8	Medium	Low	Medium
Ireland	82.0	42.9	High	High	Short
United Kingdom	71.0	36.8[d]	Medium	High	Short
Netherlands	62.2	33.9	Medium	Low	Long
Low share					
Luxembourg	26.6	30.7[e]	Medium	Medium	Medium
Portugal	25.5	23.5	High	–	Medium
Spain	37.4	19.2	Low	Low	Medium
Italy	8.5	7.1	Medium[f]	–	Short
Greece	10.2	5.2	Low	–	Short
EU 12	38.1	33.0	–	–	–

[a] 1990 data.
[b] Data for share in receipt of benefits are for 1995.
[c] Benefits are earnings related with no minimum level for part-timers.
[d] Data are missing from the Eurostat data and are therefore derived from LFS quarterly data, winter 1995/96.
[e] Data are missing, and therefore figures refer to 1991 data based on the annual ILO Labour Force Survey (Plasman, 1995).
[f] Details refer to "ordinary unemployment benefits".

Column B: Continuity requirements

Low	Less than 6 months employment in past year or equivalent.
Medium	Approximately equal to 6 months in past year or equivalent.
High	Greater than 6 months in past year.

Column C: Requirement affecting access of part-timers to unemployment benefits

Low	Minimum hours threshold of 12 hours or less; no requirement to be available for full-time work.
Medium	Minimum hours threshold more than 12 hours but less than 17; no requirement to be available for full-time work.
High	Minimum hours threshold of 17 hours or more, or minimum earnings requirement or requirement to be available for full-time work.

Column D: Duration of non-means-tested benefits.

Short	15 months maximum or less.
Medium	More than 15 months maximum but less than 3 years maximum.
Long	More than 3 years maximum.

Source: European Labour Force Survey (LFS), 1994; 1995; Grimshaw and Rubery, 1997.

countries requires recipients to be available for full-time work, in contrast to, for example, Germany and the United Kingdom. In Ireland, however, only one person in a household can be registered as unemployed and this may reduce the number of women registering and receiving benefit, thereby serving to hide much of the unemployment among women in Ireland (Barry, 1995).

The Danish system, given the long duration of non-means-tested benefits, should not, in principle, provide disincentives for the partners of the unemployed to work. Means-tested housing benefits do provide some disincentive effects for spouses, but the impact on actual working patterns appears to be minimal, thereby confirming women's commitment to full-time work in Denmark.

The tax and benefit system may have more impact on women's participation in the other three countries, where the dual-earner household is less firmly embedded. In Ireland and the Netherlands – with no information for Austria – there are disincentives for the spouses of the unemployed to work, with relatively low entitlements for retention. A woman in the Netherlands cannot improve net family income when her partner is unemployed unless her earnings exceed 70 per cent of the average production wage (Doudeijns, 1998). Such benefit systems are associated with the tendency for unemployment to be concentrated within households. However, this concentration is also linked to problems of low employment opportunities for those in similar areas or with similar educational backgrounds.

For all four countries there is a greater tendency for unemployed women to have an unemployed spouse, and indeed for unemployed men to have an unemployed spouse, except in Denmark. However these concentration effects are greatest in Ireland and may be related at least in part to the benefit system, where low disregards on entitlement to social assistance benefits reduce incentives for spouses of the long-term unemployed to work part time (Doudeijns, 1998). Similar disincentive structures apply in Austria, but more of the unemployed may receive non-means-tested benefits than in Ireland. The concentration of unemployment by household is also relatively high in Denmark, certainly from the perspective of unemployed women, but these effects may reflect not only the use of means testing for household benefits but other factors associated with a concentration of risk of unemployment, for example among the lower educated. In Ireland there are possibilities for those on benefits to enter part-time work and to retain access to benefits. Although part of a policy to encourage movement between the labour market and the welfare system, the low share of women who have access to benefits in their own right means that such policies will primarily affect men. Thus to the extent that men begin to compete in the part-time labour market in Ireland, they are likely to do so while in receipt of subsidies from the State.

Pensions

Gender equality in the labour market depends not only on access to current wage income but also on the income women are likely to enjoy in old age, relative to that of men. Gender equality also carries with it the notion of independent income, and not simply income as a dependant of men, but, as we will see, that principle is particularly difficult to apply with respect to pensions. The pension schemes most likely to provide gender equality according to both principles are those that treat entitlements as a citizenship right, independent of employment history. Denmark and the Netherlands have elements of this type of pension and therefore provide a better basis for gender equality than other systems. The universal systems coexist with supplementary pensions where employment history and earnings determine benefits, thereby reducing women's average entitlements relative to men's, but in the case of Denmark the supplementary pension is relatively low, reaching a maximum of 15,000 kroner per year, compared to a basic pension of over 45,000 kroner per year. In the Netherlands, too, the basic pension is more than twice the supplementary pension, at least at low income levels (Jepsen et al., 1997, p. 17).

In Austria, by contrast, pensions are treated as a form of insurance and women have access to the pensions of their husbands as dependants. This form of provision for old age creates major problems in terms of dependency; the pensions of women who are not in nuclear families with relatively high-earning husbands are based solely on their own employment earnings, which in Austria tend to be low. Austria has recently given some "credits" for the time women spend in childcare, but these are given only at the lowest rate. In Ireland, as in the United Kingdom, the state pension only provides a residual safety net that needs to be backed up by means-tested benefits. Additional pensions depend upon private provision and, again, women are less likely to have access to these, although they may still benefit from derived rights within private occupational schemes, assuming the schemes take similar forms to those in the United Kingdom.

Given the more complex and varied systems of family formation emerging in all countries, these arrangements where women are dependent primarily on their partners' employment record for access to a reasonable pension are becoming anachronistic but, in the context of government attempts to reduce expenditure on pensions, a policy of individualizing pensions, without prior equality within the labour market, could well lead to a reduction in lifetime income for many women. It is interesting to note that the Netherlands, despite the low share of births outside marriage, and thus the continuation of the significance of marriage within the society, is the first country to establish rights to a survivor's pension to either partner in a couple, irrespective of whether the couple was married or not (Jepsen et al., 1997, p. 34).

Wage policies

Wage policies can be regarded as including the overall systems and structures of wage differentials, on the one hand, and policies related to recent variations in wages, on the other. The first dimension has been discussed when analysing the size and form of the gender pay gap, so that here we concentrate on recent pay trends and policies related to them.

The four countries have been engaged in a policy of wage moderation, but the form that it takes will often be of significance for gender pay differentials. One part of a wage-moderation policy is to restrict the growth of minimum wages. This policy has been followed in the Netherlands over the long term (Eurostat, 1998). It has reduced the share of workers, both male and female, on the minimum wage but more women are still concentrated at this level and therefore the policy will have had a greater impact on women. Moreover, although part-timers were recently brought into the minimum wage net, this was at a time when the minimum provided less protection against low pay. In Ireland only certain specific sectors are currently covered by minimum wages and, although the scope of these sectors has been increased, many still remain outside the wage-protection system. Austria and Denmark rely on collectively agreed minima, with only a narrow range of minimum rates in Denmark but a wide range, depending on the sector, in Austria. Since 1977 minimum wage rates in Denmark have fallen from around 80 per cent to 70 per cent of the average wage, but there has been little change since 1990 (European Community Labour Market Studies – *Denmark*, 1997). In Austria sectoral differentials have widened over recent decades, but in the 1990s there has been some effort to raise minimum wage rates faster than the average, a policy which should benefit women (Eurostat, 1998).

Another area of wage policy of particular importance to women is that of public sector wages. Here the Netherlands and Denmark have followed a policy of reducing the relative value of public sector wages (Hartog, 1998; Kongshoj Madsen, 1998; Boje, 1996), with clear negative implications for the women concentrated in these areas, whereas there has been some improvement in relative wages in the public sector in both Ireland and Austria (O'Connell, 1998). The squeezing of public sector wages is often seen as part of macro-economic stabilization policy, and the gender-specific impact of such polices is rarely identified and debated within economic policy circles.

Labour market policies

All the countries under consideration have been increasingly "activating" their labour market policies, and some have been developing innovative policies – for example, the job-rotation schemes in Denmark – for ensuring integration into the labour market even at times of job shortage. The objective here is to identify the gender equality dimensions of active labour market policies in general, and of any new schemes and measures in particular.

One problem for gender equality with respect to active labour market policies has been the criteria for access to such schemes; where such criteria are confined to those registered as unemployed, then women returning to the labour market after having children, or who are unable to claim benefit for other reasons, may be excluded. Ireland had a particular problem in this respect because of the underrepresentation of women on the unemployment register, owing to the rule about only one family member registering. However, over recent years steps have been taken to establish access for returners in at least some schemes, and even to set up specific schemes for women returners (Barry, 1995). Austria has also identified a tendency for women to be underrepresented and has set gender-specific targets for the inclusion of women in active labour market policies in its 1998 National Action Plan (Pastner, 1998). Such quantitative targets may prove increasingly important to counter the impact of the quantitative targets vis-à-vis young and long-term unemployed included in the European employment policy guidelines, which could have the effect of crowding out efforts to include more women in such schemes (Rubery and Fagan, 1998).

Other gender-specific problems relate to the types of schemes women are allocated to. In Ireland research has shown that not only do men and women both benefit most from market-related job and training schemes, but women benefit even more proportionately than do men. The importance of market-oriented active labour market programmes for employment opportunities has recently been confirmed in a study of participants in programmes in Ireland. Not only are specific skills-training programmes more effective than general training, and employment subsidy schemes more effective than direct employment schemes, but these effects are markedly stronger for women than for men (O'Connell and McGinnity, 1997). Thus any tendency for women to be excluded from these near-market schemes would have a particularly disadvantageous impact on their employment chances. It is also worth noting that the same study revealed the greater importance of completing secondary education for women's employment chances compared to men's. These findings suggest that there are differences in the ways in which education and training facilitate entry into employment for men and women, and that both education and access to near-market vocational training may be vitally important for women to overcome their current higher rates of unemployment.

Another type of concern related to active labour market policies is that they may, either intentionally or by default, encourage or reinforce the development of labour market conditions which have proved disadvantageous to women. For example, schemes such as job pools in the Netherlands may stimulate the growth of low-wage jobs, which may undermine the conditions in competing job segments, primarily occupied by women. In Denmark there may be concerns that the job-rotation schemes could encourage a more contingent approach to women's participation, thereby reversing some of the progress women have made in moving towards continuous participation in the labour market.

A further concern related to the current widespread adoption of active labour market policies as the only appropriate welfare policy applies to the treatment of those people who are dependent upon benefits, but may have genuine reasons for not seeking to enter the active labour market. This applies to the genuinely sick or disabled but also, particularly within the context of gender equality, to lone parents. The Netherlands has reduced the rights of lone parents to automatic benefits once their children reach the age of 5 (Plantenga et al., 1996). This policy approach may be presented as promoting women's employment, but runs the very real risk of denying the importance of care work, particularly in households where children are especially vulnerable and the single parent has to provide all the care, instead of sharing it with partners.

Overall assessment

An assessment of gender equality within the four countries depends not only on current labour market statistics, but also on the extent to which the societal system has adjusted to the new conditions for gender relations, both inside and outside the labour market (Ellingsæter and Rubery, 1997). This adjustment process involves meeting the needs of a society composed of dual-earner – and not simply single-earner – couples, and single adult households, and not only those with couples or multi-adult households; providing a labour market framework which ensures that the integration of women is based on greater equality and not greater differentiation; the mainstreaming of gender interests into representative bodies and recognition of gender interests in policy formation; and consideration of whether current patterns of gender relations are sustainable, or whether action needs to be taken in advance to recognize the likelihood of further change in the future.

On this basis it is clear that the four countries display varying strengths and weaknesses. Denmark has made the most concerted adjustments to the dual-earner system, particularly through its policy of relatively narrow wage differentials, which reduces the likelihood that the move to dual earning will greatly increase household income inequality. It has also supported women's greater involvement in the labour market with rights to individual benefits, which reduces the tendency for women to become dependants at various stages over the life cycle. The Netherlands has also developed more appropriate welfare policies for dual earners than Austria or Ireland, but only Denmark provides the childcare support that could be expected to be a critical part of a society where the notion of a housewife is becoming outdated. The need for this level of adjustment could be argued to be less intense in both Ireland and the Netherlands, as fewer dual-earner households exist. Yet it is here that the issue of the sustainability of current patterns needs to be confronted. There is more actual evidence in Ireland of women rejecting the dependent wife model and becoming full-time earners even when they have children. However, even the Netherlands needs to pay attention to what has happened in Denmark, where women have begun to reject the notion of part-time work as the appropriate form of work for mothers of young children. Austria has already moved much further towards a dual-earner society than either Ireland or the Netherlands, but here again there has been little evidence of policy adjustment, with labour market inequality by sex remaining high and the welfare State still based primarily on the derived rights model.

In all four countries the integration of women has been based on gender differentiation rather than gender equality within the labour market, but the form taken by the differentiation varies between countries. In Denmark it is primarily based on segregation, while in Ireland, Austria and the Netherlands there is greater differentiation by pay. Yet, with respect to pay, gender differentiation itself takes different forms. In the Netherlands the problems of low hourly earnings for part-timers, at least relative to female full-timers, has been avoided, but the low hours worked by women result in very low annual earnings for women relative to men. In Austria and Ireland, where women do work their contribution to household income may be greater because they work longer hours. There is scope therefore in all four countries for steps to reduce gender differentiation, whether related to segregation, pay or employment contracts and hours. The sheer variety of forms of differentiation found even within these four countries does suggest that there is nothing inevitable about current patterns of gender differentiation and that there is scope for taking policy actions to reshape the labour market according to more egalitarian principles. The possibility of adopting such an approach to employment policy of course in part depends upon whether there is any evidence of effective mainstreaming of gender issues within policy-making bodies and the social partners. Denmark appears to be the country where most progress has been made in this respect, but we also need to take into account the different starting points for the four countries. In this respect, the interest by the former Austrian Government in equal opportunities issues and the increasing recognition of gender issues within the new social partnership arrangements in Ireland are worthy of note, although there is still much progress to be made before either representation of women's interests or indeed mainstreaming of gender issues could be said to be a reality.

4.4 EQUAL OPPORTUNITIES BY AGE AND EDUCATION

A successful employment policy should provide employment opportunities for all age brackets and education levels. There are different expectations with respect to employment opportunities by age, related in part to the prevailing societal system. We thus need to discuss, for each age bracket, what standards or principles should be used as criteria for assessing equality of opportunity by age. Young people might reasonably expect not to have to wait for a very long period of time before gaining access to the labour market; such delays may create long-term problems of social exclusion and lack of self-esteem, as well as preventing young people planning their lives, forming independent families and the like. Nevertheless, the impact of a long transition into work will depend on other characteristics of a societal system: in some societies it may be considered relatively normal for young people to be supported into adulthood by the family, whereas in others a long period without a steady job may lead to stigmatization in the labour market. For prime-age workers there is still a widespread consensus that prime-age men should almost all be within the active labour market unless severely disabled, and that those who are unemployed should be reintegrated into the labour market within a reasonably short space of time. Clearly, there are more problems in deciding on the criteria for assessing the level of integration of women in prime age; many of these problems have been discussed in section 4.3 and will not be repeated here. As far as older workers are concerned, it is clear that early retirement has become socially more acceptable in Austria and the Netherlands than in Denmark and Ireland, and it is not clear whether those in the early retirement age brackets would see the curtailment of early retirement opportunities – even if backed up by better employment opportunities for older workers – as an improvement or a deterioration in their life chances.

While part of an employment policy may involve the upgrading of the skill and educational level for those at the bottom of the labour market, it must be recognized that some groups, more or less by definition, will not succeed within the education system. The labour market needs to be able to accommodate these workers without confining them to a lifetime of unstable and casual jobs or benefit dependency. Yet, education affects prospects and patterns within each age bracket, so that the issue of equal opportunities by age and educational level are best considered together rather than separately.

Equality of opportunity for young people

A detailed picture of the diverse situations facing young people in Europe has been painted by the 1997 Eurostat publication, *Youth in the European Union*. It provides statistical information backing up, to a large extent, the differences we might expect to find between the four countries resulting from their respective societal systems of education and training and employment organization, as outlined in section 4.2.

The employment rates of young people aged 15 to 24 vary from only around 33 per cent to 38 per cent in Ireland, to around 53 to 58 per cent in Austria and the Netherlands, and to well over 60 per cent – and approaching 70 per cent of men – in Denmark (see table 4.1). However, a somewhat different ranking emerges if we look at full-time and part-time employment rates; the Netherlands has the lowest full-time employment rates and Austria the highest. Calculating the employment rates on a full-time equivalent basis still leaves Ireland at the bottom, but the gap with the Netherlands is much reduced to 5 to 7 percentage points, while Denmark and Austria are closer, but with Austria now having the highest employment rates (table 4.2). These differences in employment patterns are explained mainly by three factors:

- differences in education and training systems;
- differences in the share of young people combining education and training with part-time employment;
- differences in unemployment rates for young people between the four countries.

The widespread use of a dual system of apprenticeship training in Austria lies behind the higher rate of integration of young people into employment on a full-time basis. In contrast, the employment rates in Denmark and the Netherlands are boosted by the share of young people who combine part-time work with education, particularly in Denmark. In Ireland, however, most education and training are conducted separately from employment, involving neither workplace-based training nor part-time work to fund education and training. Ireland also has a very underdeveloped vocational training system with the result that young people tend either to progress to higher education or attempt to enter the labour market directly without access to training. Denmark and the Netherlands provide a wider spectrum of options from higher education to vocational education and training, but have a lower share entering vocational education than Austria.

These different training and education systems create very different conditions for young people entering the labour force. However, while these differences in paths into employment still exist, each country has been experiencing pressure on its existing system or has been attempting to introduce reforms to improve and develop its transition routes for young people. Thus in assessing the effectiveness of these systems we need to take a dynamic perspective and look at the sustainability of the current system, the effectiveness of recent policy changes, and the continuing or emerging problems of youth transition.

Ireland has an underdeveloped system of integration of young people into employment. In the past this has been combined with too low levels of educational attainment, calling into question the ability of Ireland to compete as a high-productivity economy. Most of the effort in recent years has been directed at overcoming the problems of low average educational attainment, with clear success. Ireland still has the lowest shares completing upper secondary education, but the gap with the other countries has been significantly narrowed. However, less has been done to provide satisfactory routes into employment for the inevitable minority that are unsuccessful within the education system. This group is still unacceptably large (O'Connell, 1998) and likely to become the future long-term unemployed. The impact of lack of education on employment is even greater in Ireland than in the other three countries, with unemployment rates for the low-educated 25–29 year-olds four times as high as for those with higher education (table 4.23).

Table 4.23 Characteristics of the youth labour market

	Austria		Denmark		Ireland		Netherlands	
Youth unemployment								
Unemployment rate, aged 15–24	5.6		10.1		19.5		11.6	
As % aged 15–24	3.4		7.4		8.9		7.0	
Long-term unemployment as % of aged <25	14.1		9.3		48.1		32.6	
Unemployed seeking first job as % all aged <25 unemployed	22.8		13.4		45.2		56.7	
Unemployment aged 25–29 by level of education								
Low (0–2)	6.0		10.4		16.9		10.7	
Medium (3)	3.7		6.0		7.5		5.8	
High (5–7)	2.4		4.9		4.2		4.7	
% on fixed-term contracts								
aged <25	19		32		19		29	
All	6		12		10		11	
% involuntary part-time								
aged 15–29	13		13		46		12	
aged 30–59	7		21		31		6	
Sectors where concentration aged 15–29 is higher than that for aged 30–59								
% total employment aged	*15–29*	*30–59*	*15–29*	*30–59*	*15–29*	*30–59*	*15–29*	*30–59*
Manufacturing	24.4	21.4	21.5	19.8	25.4	16.5	n.a.	n.a.
Construction	10.2	8.2	n.a.	n.a.	n.a.	n.a.	n.a.	n.a.
Wholesale/retail	19.1	14.3	22.3	10.5	17.6	12.2	22.9	13.3
Hotels	6.4	4.4	4.8	1.5	8.1	4.3	5.9	2.4
Business services	n.a.	n.a.	n.a.	n.a.	7.4	5.9	n.a.	n.a.

n.a. = not available.
Source: Eurostat, 1997.

Austria faces a very different problem, that of adapting its well-established vocational training system to meet new needs and conditions (Pichelman and Hofer, 1998). First it has to adjust to a rising desire of young people to enter higher education. Austria has a below-average share of the working-age population with higher education and it is highly probable that there will be further demands from young people to catch up with their counterparts in the rest of Europe. The second problem is a lack of willingness by employers to provide apprenticeship places. The third is that apprenticeship training is proving less helpful in providing access to employment than was the case in the past. The fourth is that although the apprenticeship training system does include service sector jobs, the range of occupations covered is rather traditional and there is also strong evidence of gender segregation. There is evidence that Austria has begun to tackle some of these problems, notably by providing new incentives for employers to offer training places. However, more may need to be done to rethink the apprenticeship system in order to modernize it in line with the changing educational desires of young people and the changing nature of labour markets. A closer integration between further and higher education and the apprenticeship system may be required.

In Denmark there has been significant progress in reducing the share of young people without educational or vocational qualifications. Indeed, a major part of the active labour market programme has been the commitment to ensure that any long-term unemployed youngsters without educational or vocational qualifications first of all have to obtain such qualifications. It is also worth noting that in Denmark there is close integration between the training and education made available to those on active labour market programmes and the normal types of training and qualifications available for the whole workforce. This helps to avoid the problems of stigmatization which may attach to training programmes designed specifically for the unemployed – problems that have been noted, for example, with active labour market policies in Ireland, as the main forms of training available there are in fact only for the unemployed. Denmark thus appears to have developed a relatively successful system of education and training provision for the young. Labour market mobility tends to be horizontal between employers, but linked to the employee's particular education and training qualifications. Mobility up the labour market ladder requires the acquisition of further education and training qualifications, and this linkage could help explain the popularity of the training and educational leave measures, particularly as such training tends not to be provided within Danish firms because of their small size (Kongshoj Madsen, 1998).

The Netherlands also appears to have developed a relatively successful form of education and training. It has an apprenticeship system, but not as extensive as that found in Germany and Austria. Moreover there is an increasing emphasis on formal education, and even within vocational training systems the focus is on broad-based education which may promote the adaptability of the workforce. One of the key features of the training and education system, according to Hartog (1998), is that there are multiple chances available for young people to move between the different strands of education and training. Thus the process of stratification by education and training may be less rigid than in Ireland, and mobility patterns more fluid than perhaps under the Danish or the Austrian systems. However, the Netherlands has the second highest share of long-term unemployed among young people, and also the highest share of young unemployed who are seeking their first job. So although there are opportunities to move between educational and training systems, it still seems as if a relatively high share of young people face long-term unemployment and possible social exclusion.

Ireland appears to have the greatest problem of failing to provide an adequate route into stable employment for its least-educated workforce. This problem is exacerbated by the high levels of unemployment among prime-age and older workers without educational qualifications (see below) and by the low wages accruing to the less educated in Ireland (see table 4.12). There is

Table 4.24 Earnings by age and education

	Earnings aged 45–54/aged 25–29				
	Less than upper secondary	Upper secondary	Tertiary, non-university	University	Overall
Denmark	1.21	1.23	1.29	1.60	1.29
Ireland	1.24	1.59	1.59	2.25	1.41
Netherlands	1.19	1.41	–	1.73	1.43

Source: OECD: *Employment Outlook,* 1998, table 4.4.

also a steeper progression by age among the higher-educated groups in Ireland than in other countries, indicating the greater lifetime loss of income for those who lack education (see table 4.24).

Despite the differences in the education and training systems, the shares of young people who are unemployed, expressed as a share of the youth population, are in fact fairly similar in three of the countries, with Austria the exception, recording a much lower rate of youth unemployment (table 4.23). The differences are more marked, however, in the shares of long-term unemployment for young people: they account for nearly half of all youth unemployment in Ireland and almost a third in the Netherlands, but for much lower proportions in Denmark and Austria. Young unemployed are also more likely to be seeking their first job in both Ireland and the Netherlands.

Young people suffer not only from unemployment but also from precarious employment in all four countries. They are much more likely to be on temporary contracts than older workers, although the ratios are particularly high in Denmark and the Netherlands, where many young people combine education with employment. Recent OECD data (OECD: *Employment Outlook*, 1998) on the jobs occupied by young people one year after leaving education again suggest a very high level of temporary employment, but while in Austria the majority of temporary jobs are described as training posts and are taken voluntarily, there is a much higher level of involuntary temporary work in the other three countries, and in the Netherlands in particular, where very few temporary jobs are training positions. The incidence of part-time work is also much higher than for "all-in employment" in all four countries, but the ratios are particularly high in Denmark and the Netherlands. Most part-time jobs are described as training jobs, but it is not clear if this means jobs taken while studying or jobs where training is provided, the former being the more likely. Most part-time work is voluntary, but there is a higher level of involuntary part-time work in Ireland than elsewhere.

There are some differences between the countries in the sectors into which young people make the transition to work. All four countries reveal an

Table 4.25 Risk of living in households with no other person in employment

	All non-employed				Unemployed				Inactives			
	Youth	Prime-age men	Prime-age women	Older	Youth	Prime-Age men	Prime-age women	Older	Youth	Prime-Age men	Prime-age women	Older
Austria	14.2	47.4	22.3	58.4	20.5	45.9	41.5	50.6	13.5	48.5	19.5	58.6
Ireland	26.9	61.0	26.9	50.6	42.4	61.2	42.9	61.9	24.7	60.7	24.6	50.0
Netherlands	23.2	64.1	23.8	70.3	30.7	65.2	31.3	64.3	21.8	63.6	22.6	70.4
European Union	20.0	55.3	26.4	62.1	31.7	57.8	38.2	59.5	19.1	54.2	24.0	62.3
OECD	18.2	50.5	24.6	56.3	27.5	51.9	35.0	53.6	17.2	49.8	22.7	56.5

Source: OECD: *Employment Outlook*, 1998, table 1.5.

over-concentration of young people in the distribution and catering sectors, although with a higher rate of over-representation in Denmark. Only Ireland and, to a lesser extent, Austria reveal an over-concentration in manufacturing. For Ireland this may be evidence of the tendency for new investment in manufacturing to draw upon educated but lower-paid young labour. In Austria the over-concentration is likely to be related to the high share of manufacturing within the apprenticeship systems. Similar reasons account for a slight over-representation in construction, while in Ireland young people are under-represented in this sector.

Table 4.25 reveals that youth unemployment is more associated with a pattern of non-employment for the whole household in Ireland than is the case in Austria and the Netherlands (no data for Denmark). Thus 42 per cent of young unemployed people in Ireland are in households with nobody else in employment, compared to just over 20 per cent of young unemployed people in Austria and around 31 per cent in the Netherlands. These findings reinforce the picture, already revealed by the high shares of long-term unemployed in Ireland, of youth unemployment not being a transitory or frictional form, but related to a more entrenched process of disadvantage and social exclusion.

Equality of opportunity for those in prime age

The goal of achieving close to 100 per cent activity rates for prime-age men has been achieved in all four countries; the activity rates of men aged 25–54 ranged from 90.5 per cent to 93.5 per cent in 1997. The similarity in activity levels masks a rather wider range of employment rates, with three of the countries recording employment rates between 88 per cent and 90 per cent, while Ireland has a rate of only 81.7 per cent (OECD: *Employment Outlook*, 1998, table C). Thus there is a much greater problem of unemployment for prime-age men in Ireland, while

Table 4.26 Relative hiring intensity by age group[a]

	Aged 15–24	Aged 25–44	Aged 45–64
Austria	2.3	0.9	0.4
Denmark	2.1	1.0	0.4
Ireland	2.3	0.7	0.4
Netherlands	2.5	0.8	0.3

[a] Share of new contracts relative to share in labour force.
Source: OECD: *Employment Outlook*, 1998, table 4.10.

the levels of inactivity among this group remain roughly comparable across the four countries. Many of the unemployed prime-age men in Ireland are long-term unemployed. There are legitimate concerns that the current focus within European employment policy, as reflected in the recent Irish National Action Plan, on preventing entry into long-term unemployment may divert funds and attention from solving the problems of those who are already in long-term unemployment, but who have too many years of active life ahead for them simply to be written off. In Ireland there does appear to be a problem that the less well- educated prime-age workers have not been able to participate in the current boom as the new jobs are being made available to younger, more educated people. Moreover, the current employment boom is also associated with Irish women catching up in terms of employment opportunities, both with Irish men and with women in other European countries. Some evidence in support of lower employment opportunities for prime-age workers (aged 25–44) may be found in the OECD data, which reveal Ireland as having a lower hiring intensity among prime-age workers than in the other three countries (table 4.26).

Equality of opportunity for older workers

The Netherlands and Austria have relatively low participation rates for older workers. The offer of early retirement schemes and other benefits such as the Dutch disability benefits, which have allowed early exit from the labour market, have been responsible at least to some extent for the increase in early retirement in both societies. In contrast Denmark has relatively high participation rates for both men and women, while Ireland has low participation rates for women, reflecting the tendency for this group to quit the labour market when they have children and not return; and relatively high participation rates for older men. However, Ireland also has a severe problem of long-term unemployment among its older workers, a problem which early retirement and disability pension systems may keep hidden. It is also the case that such systems may be regarded as more humane policies for helping displaced older workers than keeping them on the unemployment register.

In comparing countries with respect to older workers it makes more sense to consider employment rates than participation rates, as unemployment rates are affected by differences in the benefit regulations and perhaps give rise to misleading pictures of differences between countries. For instance, the employment rate for older workers in Austria is some 5 percentage points below the EU average, but their activity rates are some 10 percentage points below. If all those who have taken early retirement were classified as unemployed, in Austria unemployment would have been 50 per cent higher in 1996 (Pichelman and Hofer, 1998). This example outlines the greater similarity of the problems facing the four countries than a straight comparison of activity rates would suggest.

All countries face problems in reintegrating older workers and there is little to suggest that any of the four countries under study are better than the others in terms of rehiring older workers. Indeed, recent OECD evidence shows a very similar hiring rate for older workers in all four countries. This rate, calculated as the share of new employment contracts by age group, is only around 40 per cent of the rate which could be expected if the share of new hires were proportional to the share of older workers in the labour force (see table 4.26). Thus to some extent the main way in which employment rates of older workers are likely to be maintained or improved is by taking measures to reduce the likelihood of older workers being displaced from employment, or providing specific incentives for firms to hire them.

Austria appears to have taken the most active recent measures in this respect, although starting from a situation of very low employment rates and very high rates of early retirement. Most of the entries into early retirement came from workers who were already not in jobs, but on unemployment or disability registers. Nearly two-thirds of early retirements were associated with disability or ill health, yet the rate of early retirements was high enough to bring down the average retirement age from 65 to 57 years. In 1997 only 14 per cent of new pensions were granted to people at the statutory retirement ages, with 26 per cent awarded to those with long service contributions before statutory age, 25 per cent invalidity pensions, 4 per cent pre-retirement benefits due to unemployment and 31 per cent survivors' pensions (Hörndler and Wörister, 1998, p. 43). One reason perhaps for the high levels of early retirement on grounds of reduced capacity is that the criterion for incapacity is inability to carry on doing the same kind of work – and not incapacity for any kind of work – the principle adopted in, for example, the United Kingdom welfare system. This approach fits with the insurance principle, whereby protection is not provided at the same level for all, but is expected to maintain individual occupational status and income. Such an approach is considered by some as in conflict with the new emphasis on maximizing involvement in work; others see linking benefits to established standards of living and occupational status as part of a fair and just employment system. Although the age of retirement for men has stabilized, that of women has fallen, partly as a consequence of more favourable treatment for the years spent raising children. Moreover, with the ageing of the population the number moving into early retirement has risen. Thus the new measures – which discourage firms from making older workers redundant, provide incentives to firms to hire older workers and reduce opportunities to retire within the state pension system – could be regarded as useful measures, but perhaps they come too late to reverse the expectation of retirement at below age 60 (European Community Labour Market Studies – *Austria*, 1997, pp. 125–126).

The situation in the Netherlands has similarities to that in Austria, particularly with respect to disability pensions. As in Austria, rights to disability pensions were linked to not being able to continue to work in the same field, or to earn an income of the level expected by someone of that age or education. Since 1993 eligibility has been linked more directly to evidence of physical disability and previous earnings are no longer relevant (Hartog, 1998). Entitlements are also restricted often to partial disability and in any case are no longer given until retirement. Early retirement schemes in the Netherlands are popular even for the non-disabled, but these are negotiated through collective agreements and are more difficult for the State to influence or control.

Denmark and Ireland face much less of a problem of reversing expectations of early retirement. In Denmark early retirement is largely confined to the period over age 60, the scheme for those between 55 and 59 having been discontinued. Even for those above age 60, early retirement does not appear to be very frequent. Employment rates for older workers have been declining – from very high levels by international standards. Ireland has high activity rates but a relatively large problem of unemployment for older men which has been growing in quantitative terms, while the numbers unemployed in other age and sex categories has been declining. Ireland also has a problem in that the long-term unemployed has very low educational qualifications, so that one issue must be whether there can be realistic prospects for the current cohort of older workers to expect re-entry into work. This problem might diminish as the more educated groups move through the age structure. Ireland may also need to pay attention to its very high levels of earnings inequality by age, particularly for more educated groups, as this could continue to militate against a high employment rate for older workers (table 4.24).

4.5 SOCIAL INEQUALITY AND SOCIAL EXCLUSION

According to European Community Household Panel data, Denmark has the lowest level of social inequality of the four countries, as measured by both distribution of household income and share of poor households. The bottom quintile received nearly 11 per cent of household income, compared to only 7 per cent in Ireland, under 8 per cent in Austria and 9 per cent in the Netherlands. Similarly, the top quintile received under 34 per cent in Denmark, compared to 35 per cent in the Netherlands, 38 per cent in Austria and 43 per cent in Ireland (Eurostat,

Table 4.27 Household net income distribution and poverty rates (base year: 1994)

	Austria	Denmark	Ireland	Netherlands	EU 13
Bottom quintile 1	7.7	10.7	7.2	9.0	7.1
2	13.6	15.3	11.0	15.3	12.7
3	17.9	18.3	15.9	18.0	17.5
4	23.3	22.1	23.3	23.2	23.4
Top quintile 5	37.5	33.6	42.6	34.5	39.3
Gini coefficient	30	23	36	25	32
Poverty rate (below 60% of the national median equivalized income)	18	10	22	10	21

Source: Eurostat: *Statistics in Focus*, 1998, p. 11.

1998). The tendency for Ireland, and to some extent Austria, to have much higher poverty rates emerges more starkly when the share of the population living in poverty is calculated, based on the definition of below 60 per cent of the national median equivalized income. On this basis 22 per cent of the population in Ireland and 18 per cent of the Austrian population is living in poverty, compared to only 10 per cent in both Denmark and the Netherlands (table 4.27).

These data are based on the 1995 European Community Household panel, with 1994 the base year for income. Earlier data on income distribution and poverty were computed using the 1993 wave of the panel that did not include Austria. The positions of Denmark and Ireland in this earlier study were similar, but the Netherlands was found to have higher levels of income inequality and poverty than in the 1995 wave. No explanation is provided by Eurostat for these differences. The 1993 data gave more detailed information on the composition of poverty. For example, Ireland had the second highest share of children living in poverty among the EU12 Member States at 28 per cent, with only the rate in the United Kingdom exceeding the Irish rate at 32 per cent. There were also differences in the rates of poverty between types of household. For example, single-parent households were particularly likely to be poor in Ireland, at 65 per cent of all such households, compared to only 8 per cent in Denmark (no information for the Netherlands or Austria). Ireland also had a high share of poverty among elderly one-person households (42 per cent compared to only 16 per cent in the Netherlands). However, for young single people poverty was higher in the Netherlands at 42 per cent, but only 13 per cent in Ireland.

These differences in the composition of poverty reflect differences both in social organization and in welfare systems. In the Netherlands the integration of large numbers of young people into part-time work could explain the high share of young single people living below the poverty line, while in Ireland more young people either work full time or remain fully dependent upon the family. The impact of a universal citizenship pension system in the Netherlands may be evident in the low share of elderly one-person households in poverty, compared to the situation in Ireland. These figures suggest that the Netherlands has a pension system more compatible with providing basic income security, even for those who do not participate on a continuous basis in full-time employment, than is the case in Ireland. Similar conclusions are likely to apply to Denmark, although data are not available on poverty in elderly one-person households.

The differences in poverty among single parents between Denmark and Ireland are likely to reflect both differences in wage levels available to this largely female group, and also differences in the benefit system. Ireland, like the United Kingdom, had a low participation rate among single mothers, presumably fuelled by a means-tested benefit systems which discourages participation.

There is also evidence that Ireland has a higher level of social exclusion than the other three countries, measured by the tendency both for non-employment to be concentrated in specific households, and for the unemployed to be long-term unemployed. Table 4.25 shows the higher tendency for young unemployed persons and for prime-age unemployed men to be in households where no one else is in work than is the case in Austria or the Netherlands (no information for Denmark). Being in a multi-adult household with children also seems to provide a higher degree of protection against non-employment in Austria and the Netherlands than is the case in Ireland. However, the Netherlands, along with Ireland, has a high risk of non-employment among single-parent households, even though there has in both cases been a substantial decrease in this risk since the mid-1980s. Austria has a much lower risk of non-employment among single-parent households, a characteristic likely to be shared with Denmark, given the high participation rates of single parents there.

Further information on risk of low income associated with different types of households is provided in table 4.28. The data differentiate between households with and without work and, for those without work, between households with and without children. They give us information on how adequately the benefit system protects against low income for those without work, but this needs to be combined with the above information on the risk of non-employment for a full picture of social inequality. Unfortunately, data for Austria are not available for this Household Panel data, while data for Denmark are lacking on the risk of non-employment by household (table 4.25). From these data we can see that households with children but without work in Denmark, whether single- or two-person households, are much better protected against low income than is the case in Ireland or the Netherlands.

All four countries have adopted policies over recent years to "activate" their labour market policies, thereby supposedly taking steps to reduce the risk of social exclusion. However, active labour market policies can exacerbate social exclusion if they serve to penalize the unemployed through enforced forms of

Table 4.28 Risk of low income for members of different types of households

	Denmark	Ireland	Netherlands
Households without work			
Single adults	52.4	76.9	52.2
Without children	3.0	70.7	47.9
With children	44.5	86.8	78.6
Two or more adults	31.8	43.4	28.0
Without children	29.9	21.9	19.3
With children	40.1	55.9	59.6
Households with some work	9.5	6.6	10.9
Single	21.6	10.2	18.3
Two or morc adults	6.9	6.4	10.1

Note: Income adjusted for equivalent income. Risk of low income is defined as being in the bottom quintile of household income.
Source: OECD: *Employment Outlook*, 1998, table 1.10.

workfare or training programmes which stigmatize rather than provide opportunities to reintegrate. By and large the four countries appear to have avoided these problems, although Ireland does have a number of labour market programmes that have limited impact on reintegration, and has failed to use active labour market policies to improve the skill base of the workforce, or to counter the lack of education and training among many of the unemployed (O'Connell, 1998). The Netherlands has adopted some controversial programmes to stimulate low-wage employment opportunities, with possibly damaging impacts on those concentrated at the bottom of the labour market if these experiments encourage a downgrading of wage levels in these segments. Denmark has tended to avoid stigmatization by integrating active labour market training policies with its general education and training programmes. Moreover, benefit recipients are allowed two years to find a job before being required to participate in these measures. Austria has faced a more limited problem of long-term unemployment than Ireland or the Netherlands, but has moved relatively rapidly towards developing active labour market programmes following its integration into the European Union and the emerging problem of higher unemployment.

4.6 EQUALITY, EMPLOYMENT PERFORMANCE AND EMPLOYMENT REGIMES: AN ASSESSMENT

Having considered the equality dimensions of the four employment regimes with respect to sex, age, education and social exclusion, we will attempt to assess the performance of the four employment regimes according to the criteria outlined in section 4.2.

Labour market regulation and industrial relations

The equality dimension of the labour market regulatory regime is primarily concerned with the ability of the system to protect against low pay and poor labour standards, and to represent the interests of potentially excluded and disadvantaged groups. Here we found major differences between the four regimes. The Danish regime provides the best protection against low wages for disadvantaged groups through a system of voluntary regulation and low income differentials. Austria has an equally strong system of regulation, but one which legitimates much wider wage differentials. The Netherlands stands in a middle position, offering better protection against low hourly earnings, but generating high inequality in annual income due to the high share of part-time work. Ireland has the least regulated labour market and the greatest risk of low pay. Indeed, some of the recent success of the Irish economy may be built on the low wage levels in some segments, but this may not be either a sustainable or a desirable basis for comparative economic success. We need to take into account not only the cross-sectional patterns of wage inequality, but also the relationship between various parts of the employment regime which may modify or reinforce these patterns on a lifetime basis. Examples of how different elements of the employment regime need to be considered include the pension system in the Netherlands and Denmark, which reduces the impact of labour market inequality and low wages on lifetime inequality, in contrast to the picture in Austria and, particularly, Ireland. The low level of legal employment regulation in Denmark also has to be considered alongside the high level of unemployment benefits which increases the effective protection offered to those vulnerable to job loss.

Any assessment of the system of labour market regulation must also take into account the direction of change and the extent to which the system is being adapted and modified to meet changing labour market conditions and to represent effectively the interests of all groups. There are three main challenges facing labour market regulation systems in this respect. The first is how far the systems have adjusted to the new types of sectors and jobs; the second is how far they are providing protection for flexible workers; and the third is how far they are adjusting to the changing position of women and the growth of dual-earner households.

Three of the countries have relatively well-developed representative and regulatory systems covering the growing service sectors of the economy. Ireland has more patchy regulatory coverage, concentrated more in traditional industries. Trade unions in both Denmark and the Netherlands have not been entirely successful in protecting workers within the public sector from the erosion of wage standards.

The countries started with very different levels of regulation covering atypical and flexible workers, but the direction of change has been towards extending rights. For example, Ireland has been extending its legal regulation of the labour market and offering better employment rights to workers in atypical jobs. The Netherlands has also extended minimum wage protection and granted more pro rata rights to part-timers. However, this has occurred in a context where the level of minimum rights has been eroded through reductions in the relative and real level of the minimum wage.

Adjustments to the changing position of women and to dual-earner households require not only the implementation of policies which are compatible with objectives, but also the inclusion of women's interests within the policy-making bodies and social partners. These policies may have benefits for society more generally: for example, a low dispersion of earnings may, in addition to reducing the gender pay gap, allow societies to move towards a dual-earner household system without encountering rapidly increasing patterns of household income inequality. Narrower earnings dispersion could also be considered a positive factor in reducing labour costs in the high-skill areas where countries arguably could expect to achieve comparative advantage (Ellingsæter and Rubery, 1997)

According to these criteria, there are very different patterns and levels of success across the four countries. Ireland is now committed to implementing a minimum wage, although the level has yet to be decided. Moreover, the links between the minimum wage and lifetime equality and protection against poverty have still not been fully recognized in Ireland, where the debate about poverty focuses on the share of current low-wage workers within households with at least one earner (EC Labour Market Studies – *Ireland*). However, the evidence on the share of elderly single people in poverty does suggest that moves towards a more dual-earner society would be an effective means of fighting poverty and social exclusion in the longer term. Up to now the policy on wages has focused on wage moderation rather than modernizing the wage structure to reduce the high levels of inequality by sex and over the life cycle. Austria has begun to improve the level of its minimum wages relative to the average wage, but from a low basis, and it still has made very limited progress towards reducing the gender pay gap. At the same time earnings dispersion has remained high. The Netherlands has been reducing minimum wage levels, but the share of employees at this wage level has lessened, as many are protected by the higher minima set in collective agreements. However, public sector workers, many of whom are women, have been required to take a disproportionate cut in their relative living standards. The degree of wage equality between full- and part-timers has remained relatively high in the Netherlands, and the danger of dual-earner households giving rise to high household income inequality is being contained by the very high shares of women who work part time only.

Denmark – through its wage solidarity policy and extensive collective bargaining coverage – has positioned itself best to provide effective protection for women in the labour market and to make the transition to a dual-earner society without major increases in household income inequality. Recent trends have been towards greater wage inequality, and there are particular problems for public sector workers, but the trend towards decentralization of wage determination has not had a major deteriorating effect on women's wages in all sectors. Denmark also has the best record of representing women's interests among the social partners and in wage policy, largely through women's involvement in trade unions in the public and private service sectors. In contrast, the remaining three countries have done relatively little to ensure that women's interests are represented within social partnership frameworks and in the overall debate on employment policy. Ireland has just begun to listen to the organizations representing women's interests outside the collective bargaining system, but more needs to be done to integrate such interests within the social partnership frameworks, if these are to be sustainable as bodies representing the interests of the majority of people in the labour market.

Education and training systems

Education and training are critical for both the sustainability of the high employment performance of the four economies and for distributional objectives, including providing routes into reasonably well-paid employment. Under both criteria Ireland appears to have the most severe problem. It has done little to establish a vocational training system to upgrade and improve the skills of its workforce and, although a much higher share of the labour force now has higher educational qualifications, there must be doubts about the sustainability of high employment performance once wage levels in Ireland begin to catch up with other European countries. To capitalize on its success and to overcome its severe problem of social exclusion, for both young and old, it needs to establish a broader-based system providing vocational skills. In contrast, Denmark and the Netherlands appear to have established a broad-based access to vocational education and training which has high status and high credibility with employers, contributing to both access to employment and overall competitiveness. Denmark also seems to have done most to promote lifelong learning, through its job-rotation scheme. However, such schemes might not work in other countries where there is less emphasis on external training and credentials. Austria has perhaps the most well-established initial vocational training system, but appears to need to do more to adjust to the greater participation of young people in higher education and to reduce the gender segregation and occupational traditionalism that characterize its apprenticeship schemes. Moreover, its system of further training is less developed than that in Denmark, for example.

Flexibility and labour market regimes

The four countries have different models of labour market organization and different systems of flexibility, with Austria having longer average tenure, and

Denmark combining high flexibility with high benefit levels. However, in no case have we identified any major employment problem related to lack of labour market flexibility. Where there is a high and persistent problem of social exclusion, as in Ireland, the problem cannot be attributed to labour market rigidity. The large number of new jobs within the Irish labour market have made little impact on the long-term unemployed, in part because of their perceived inappropriateness for the new positions. None of the countries seems to have effectively resolved the problem of age discrimination, as all have low hiring rates for older workers. The higher employment rate of older workers in Denmark appears to be due primarily to a higher retention rate of older workers, suggesting that policies to encourage retention may be more effective for maintaining high employment rates among older workers than policies to enhance the employability of older workers already displaced from their established employment positions.

The extent of flexible employment forms and their implications for cross-sectional and lifetime earnings opportunities vary significantly between the four countries. The Netherlands offers the best opportunities for part-timers to be employed in higher-level jobs. However, when lifetime prospects are taken into account the Netherlands appears in a less favourable light, as most women remain in part-time work, thereby severely reducing their shares of wage income. The part-time earnings economy of the Netherlands is thus based on a continued economic dependency of women, a pattern which may prove not to be fully sustainable in the longer term. Nevertheless, there is as yet little evidence in the Netherlands of women joining their Danish counterparts in rejecting part-time in favour of full-time work even when their children are small. The extent of low pay among part-timers is greater in Ireland than the Netherlands, and although in Austria part-time earnings may be pro rata with full-time earnings, these can be very low within some service and female-dominated segments.

Welfare regimes and gender relations

We have not been able to consider all aspects of the welfare systems and labour market equality here. This chapter has focused on three main questions: the extent of adjustment to the dual-earner society; the extent of adjustment to the new forms of flexible employment; and the extent to which the welfare system provides support at reasonable levels for all those without work. To take the last point first, it is clear that Ireland provides much lower levels of benefits for the unemployed, particularly those who are not breadwinners, and also excludes many women from access to benefits, in part through a rule whereby only one person in the household can register (Barry, 1995). These lower levels of benefits have been shown in a recent study of European Union unemployment and social exclusion to constitute a much higher level of material deprivation than in Austria, Denmark or the Netherlands (Gallie, 1999).

Similarly, despite some improvements to the rights of part-timers in Ireland, they still face more barriers in gaining access to unemployment benefits than is the case in the other three countries. The universal-type benefit systems characteristic of pension schemes in Denmark and the Netherlands are probably best suited to giving effective social protection to those with either intermittent employment records or largely part-time employment histories. Little has been done in Ireland or Austria to reform the welfare system towards a more individual rights model, or in particular towards a citizenship-based model which tends to provide the best protection for workers with low-paid, intermittent or predominantly part-time employment patterns. Austria has maintained a full insurance system, so that part-timers have no basic floor of rights, but instead receive benefits proportional to earnings, while Ireland has maintained more of a residual welfare State system, where access to benefits above the minimum floor depends on household means-testing.

With respect to the issue of adjustment to the dual-earner society, it is clear that Denmark has gone further than the other three countries, not only in providing support for the family in the form of childcare, but also in establishing a wage structure that reinforces the dual-earner model. The Netherlands could be considered to have made a different transition to a dual-earner society, with a new pattern of part-time work established as the norm. However, this still embeds a high level of gender inequality within the society, and it should not simply be assumed that the basic problems and tensions between the desires for involvement in both wage and care work have been resolved through this approach. On the other hand, the strength of the social norms in favour of part-time work are also quite evident in the Netherlands and, to this extent, there is a greater degree of compatibility between the social and employment system than is the case in the two remaining countries, Ireland and Austria. Here women's increasing participation in the labour market, often on a full-time basis, has not yet led to any major adjustment or rethink of the welfare system, although some signs of a new approach may be beginning to be evident in the recent National Action Plan for Austria. Even in Ireland, which perhaps lags furthest behind, the social partnership system is beginning to raise the profile of gender issues within national economic and employment policy-making. Nevertheless, there is little evidence of the level of action needed to ensure that Ireland is even beginning to catch up with other European countries on issues such as access to childcare or parental leave.

4.7 CONCLUSIONS

Adopting an equality perspective has provided a method of analysing the comparatively good employment performance of these four countries from a more analytical perspective than that of quantitative accounts of changes in employment and unemployment rates. The questions posed have related to the distribution and the quality of employment, as well as its quantity.

Moreover, we have considered both the sustainability of current employment growth trends and current employment forms, and the compatibility between labour market developments and the broader social and economic context in which these are taking place. The need to see employment policy as part of a broader framework of modernizing the social and economic system to meet current and future needs and aspirations has been stressed. The focus has been more on the longer-term prospects than on the short-term evolution. The frequent focus on the short term in employment policy can perhaps be explained by the long-term consequences for individuals of even relatively brief spells in unemployment. Thus the success of employment policies in getting people back to work quickly should not be belittled as a goal. However, the employment policy agenda nevertheless tends to adopt too narrow and too short term a framework: major trends in employment patterns tend not to be foreseen or understood until they are already with us.

It has taken Europe until the late 1990s to take the integration of women into the labour market seriously, with the inclusion of equal opportunities as one of the pillars of European employment policy in 1998. Yet we still have not addressed many of the major questions which emerge from the changing patterns of labour force participation of women and men, and from the changing composition of labour demand, which is calling into question the sustainability of many traditional career trajectories. Assessment of short-term employment policy success has its part to play in the European employment debate, but this should not deflect attention from the wider and longer-term issue of the type of labour markets and social systems we need to create to meet the needs of competitiveness, combined with employment and income security for the majority of citizens in the global economy.

Acknowledgements

In preparing this chapter, I have drawn upon previous work undertaken within the European Work and Employment Research Centre (EWERC) at the Manchester School of Management, UMIST. This has been collaborative work, and I am grateful to all the EWERC team for their contributions, particularly to Mark Smith who has taken prime responsibility for the statistical analyses which have been drawn on here. My understanding of the four countries under review was developed during the 1990s as a consequence of my work as coordinator between 1991 and 1996 of the European Commission's Network of Experts on Women's Employment, a network to which I still belong as the United Kingdom expert. I would also like to acknowledge the work of the national experts for these four countries, which over the years has provided me with the insights into the societal systems in these countries on which this comparative report is based (for the Netherlands, Janneke Plantenga; Ireland, Ursula Barry; Austria, Ulrike Pastner; Denmark, Thomas Boje and Karin Sjørup). I am also grateful for detailed comments on the first draft from

Peter Auer and from the other participants at the ILO seminar on the Country Employment Policy Reviews in October 1998.

Bibliography

Anker, R. 1998. *Gender and jobs: Sex segregation of occupations in the world* (Geneva, ILO).

Anotonnen, A.; Sipilä, J. 1996. "European social care services: Is it possible to identify models?", in *Journal of European Social Policy*, Vol. 6, No. 2, pp. 87–100.

Barry, U. 1995. *Women and the European employment rate: The causes and consequences of variations in female activity and employment patterns of Irish women*, report for the network of experts on women's employment, Equal Opportunities Unit, DGV, European Commission, Brussels (available as a working paper, Manchester, Manchester School of Management – (UMIST)).

——. 1998. *Equal opportunities and the Irish employment action plan*, report for the expert group, Gender and Employment, Equal Opportunities Unit, DGV, European Commission, Brussels.

——; Roche, A. 1993. *Pay determination and women's pay in Ireland*, report to the European Commission for the network of experts on the situation of women in the labour market (available as a working paper, Manchester, UMIST).

Blau, F.D.; Kahn, L.M. 1992. "The gender earnings gap: Learning from international comparisons", in *American Economic Review*, Papers and Proceedings, Vol. 82, No. 2, pp. 533–538.

Boje, T.P. 1993. *Women between work and family – Employment patterns for female workers in different welfare state systems (the US and Denmark)*, paper presented at the Comparative Research on Welfare States in Transition Conference, ISA Research Committee 19, Oxford, 9–12 Sep.

——. 1994. *Occupational segregation, mobility patterns and gender*, paper presented at the 18th World Congress of Sociology, Bielefeld, Germany, July.

——. 1996. *Trends and prospects for women's employment in Denmark in the 1990s*, report for the network of experts on women's employment, Equal Opportunities Unit, DGV, European Commission, Brussels (available as a working paper, Manchester, UMIST).

CEC (Commission of the European Communities). 1997. *Equal opportunities for women and men in the European Union: Annual report 1996* (Luxembourg).

CERC (Centre d'études du revenu et des coûts). 1991. *Les bas salaires dans les pays de la CEE*. V/20024/91 – FR (Brussels, Commission of the European Communities).

Daly, M. 1996. *Social security, gender and equality in the European Union*, working paper (Dublin, Economic Research Institute).

Doudeijns, M. 1998. "Are unemployment and related welfare benefits a disincentive to take up part-time employment?", in J. O'Reilly and C. Fagan (eds.): *Part-time prospects: Part-time work in Europe, North America and the Pacific Rim* (London, Routledge).

Dingledey, I. 1998. *Work, the family and the tax and social security system: The rewards and penalties of various patterns of household economic activity and working time*, report prepared for the Equal Opportunities Unit, DGV, European Commission, Brussels (Gelsenkirchen, Institut Arbeit und Technik).

EC Labour Market Studies, European Commission. 1997. Series No. 1. European Commission Employment and Social Affairs: *Austria* (L&R Sozialforschung and ECOTEC Research and Consulting Ltd.); *Denmark* (PLS Consult. – Haahr, Ørsted and Hansen, and Peter Jensen); *Ireland* (Sexton and O'Connell, ESRI, with Fitzgerald, Nolan and Malley, ESRI, and Geary and Lalor, UCD); *Netherlands* (Netherlands Economic Institute).

Elias, P. 1995. *European labour force survey: Cross-tabulations, frequency distributions of employment by NACE (Rev. 1) and ISCO-88 (COM), males and females by country* (Warwick, University of Warwick, Institute for Employment Research, Oct.).

Ellingsæter, A.; Rubery, J. 1997. "Gender relations and the Norwegian labour market model", in J. E. Dølvik, and A.H. Steen (eds.): *Making solidarity work?* (Oslo, Scandinavian University Press).

Esping-Andersen, G. 1990. *The three worlds of welfare capitalism* (Oxford, Polity Press).

European Childcare Network. 1996. *Review of children's services*, report prepared for the Equal Opportunities Unit, DGV, European Commission, Brussels.

Eurostat. 1993. *Unemployed women in the EC* (Luxembourg, Office for Official Publications of the European Communities).

——. 1995. *Demographic Statistics 1995* (Luxembourg, Office for Official Publications of the European Communities).

——. 1997. *Youth in the European Union* (Luxembourg, Office for Official Publications of the European Communities).

——. 1998. *Statistics in Focus* (Luxembourg, Office for Official Publications of the European Communities).

Fagan, C.; Plantenga, J.; Rubery, J. 1995. "Part-time work and inequality? Lessons from the Netherlands and the UK", in J. Lapeyre and R. Hoffman (eds.): *A time for working - A time for living* (Brussels, European Trade Union Institute/Labour Research Department).

Gallie, D. 1999. "Unemployment and social exclusion in the European Union", in *European Societies*, Vol. 1, No. 2, pp. 139–167.

Gregory, M.; Sandoval, V. 1994. "Low pay and minimum wage protection in Britain and the EC", in R. Barrell (ed.): *The UK labour market: Comparative aspects and institutional developments* (Cambridge, United Kingdom, Cambridge University Press).

Grimshaw, D.; Rubery, J. 1997. "Workforce heterogeneity and unemployment benefits: The need for policy reassessment in the European Union", in *Journal of European Social Policy*, Vol. 7, No. 4, pp. 291–315.

Gustaffson, S. 1996. "Tax regimes and labour market performance", in G. Schmid, J. O'Reilly and K. Schömann (eds.): *International handbook of labour market policy and evaluation* (Cheltenham, Edward Elgar).

Hartog, J. 1998. *ILO Country Employment Policy Review: Netherlands* (Geneva, ILO).

Hörndler, M.; Wörnister, K. 1998. *The Austrian welfare system: A survey of social security systems* (Vienna, Austrian Presidency of the European Council of Ministers, Federal Ministry of Labour, Health and Social Affairs).

Humphries, J.; Rubery, J. 1984. "The reconstitution of the supply side of the labour market: The relative autonomy of social reproduction", in *Cambridge Journal of Economics*, Vol. 8, No. 4, pp. 331–346.

IFO (Institut für Oekonomische Forschung). 1994. *Long term labour force scenarios for the European Free Trade Association* (Munich).

——. 1995. *Long term labour force scenarios for the European Union* (Munich).

Jepsen, M., et al. 1997. *Individualization of the social and fiscal rights and the equal opportunities between women and men* (Brussels, DULBEA Université Libre de Bruxelles).

Kongshoj Madsen, P. 1998. *ILO Country Employment Policy Review: Denmark* (Geneva, ILO).

Lewis, J. 1992. "Gender and the development of welfare regimes", in *Journal of European Social Policy*, Vol. 2, No. 3, pp. 159–173.

Maurice, M.; Sellier, F.; Silvestre, J.J. 1986. *The social foundations of industrial power* (Cambridge, MA, MIT Press).

O'Connell, P. 1998. *ILO Country Employment Policy Review: Ireland* (Geneva, ILO).

——.; McGinnity, F. 1997. *Active labour market policies, market orientation and gender*, paper prepared for a project conference of the TSER TRANSLAM Training and Human Capital Group, Spain.

OECD (Organisation for Economic Co-operation and Development). 1994a. *The jobs study* (Paris).

——. 1994b. *Women and structural change* (Paris).

——. 1996. *Education at a Glance* (Paris).

——. Various years. *Employment Outlook* (Paris).

Pastner, U. 1996. *Trends and prospects for women's employment in the 1990s in Austria*, report to the European Commission for the network of experts on the situation of women in the labour market (available as a working paper, Manchester, UMIST).

——. 1998. *The gender aspects of the Austrian National Action Plan*, report for the expert group, Gender and Employment, Equal Opportunities Unit, DGV, European Commission, Brussels.

Pichelman, K.; Hofer, H. 1998. *ILO Country Employment Policy Review: Austria* (Geneva, ILO).

Plantenga, J.; Kochand, E.; Sloep, M. 1996. *Trends and prospects for women's employment in the Netherlands in the 1990s*, report for the network of experts on women's employment, Equal Opportunities Unit, DGV, European Commission (available as a working paper, Manchester, UMIST).

Plasman, R. 1995. *Women and the European employment rate: The causes and consequences of variations in female activity and employment patterns in Luxembourg*, report to the European Commission for the network of experts on the situation of women in the labour market (available as a working paper, Manchester, UMIST).

Rubery, J. 1997. "What do women want from full employment?", in J. Philpott (ed.): *Working for full employment* (London, Routledge).

——.; Fagan, C. 1993. "Occupational segregation of women and men in the European Community", in *Social Europe*, Suppl. 3/93 (Luxembourg, Office for Official Publications of the European Community).

——.; ——. (in collaboration with D. Grimshaw). 1994. "Wage determination and sex segregation in the EC", in *Social Europe*, Suppl. 4/94 (European Commission, Directorate General for Employment, Industrial Relations and Social Affairs).

——.; ——. 1995. "Gender segregation in societal context", in *Work, Employment and Society*, Vol. 9, No. 2, pp. 213–240.

——.; ——. 1998. *Equal opportunities and employment in Europe* (Vienna, Austrian Federal Ministry of Labour, Health and Social Affairs).

——.; Smith, M. 1999. *The future European labour supply*, research paper for Employment and Social Affairs, European Commission, Directorate V/A1.

——.; ——.; Fagan, C. 1999. *Women's employment in Europe: Trends and prospects* (London, Routledge).

Rubery, J. et al. 1998. *Women and European employment* (London, Routledge).

Sengenberger, W.; Campbell, D. 1994. *Creating economic opportunities: The role of labour standards in industrial restructuring* (Geneva, International Institute for Labour Studies).

Whitehouse, G. 1992. "Legislation and labour market gender inequality: An analysis of OECD countries", in *Work, Employment and Society*, Vol. 6, No. 1, pp. 65–88.

INDUSTRIAL RELATIONS AND SOCIAL DIALOGUE 5

Jelle Visser[*]

5.1 INTRODUCTION

This chapter considers industrial relations and social dialogue in Austria, Denmark, Ireland and the Netherlands, placed in a wider European context. We understand industrial relations in a broad sense, encompassing not only the relations between unions and management and the regulation of wages and employment conditions, but also the public policies towards labour markets and labour market organizations, and the legal and institutional framework within which these organizations interact. The emphasis of this chapter is on the implications of social dialogue and collective bargaining for employment performance.

In these four countries, perhaps least in Denmark, "concertation" or social dialogue at the national level has continued (Austria) or has been revitalized (Ireland, the Netherlands) in recent times. Extending the definition of Konzertierte Aktion put forward by Lehmbruch (1984), we define concertation as a process in which actors inform each other of their intentions and capacities, elaborate information provided to them by experts, and clarify and explain their assumptions and expectations (Visser, 1998a). Concertation or social dialogue is not the same as bargaining, but provides a setting for more efficient bargaining by helping to separate bargaining over "the state of the world" from bargaining over the division of costs and benefits.

Those negotiating changes in the welfare State, labour market regulation or wage-setting practices face two problems which are difficult to solve at the same time. First, they must identify, and then agree about, a course of action that is superior to the status quo. Second, they must reach agreement over the distribution of costs and benefits of any specific measure or solution they choose. Concertation can contribute to easing the dilemma by helping to solve the first problem, spelling out "win/win" solutions before engaging in hard

* Centre for the Study of European Societies and Labour Relations (CESAR), University of Amsterdam, Amsterdam, the Netherlands.

bargaining over distributional aspects (Scharpf, 1997). In a cooperative system oriented towards problem-solving, the negotiators may develop a "joint utility function". In a decision-making style based on bargaining, by contrast, each side tries to maximize what it sees as its own "fair share". Scharpf (1989) distinguishes a third style, called "confrontation", in which actors deny each other the right of play. The promise of social dialogue and concertation clearly lies in the possibility of a "problem-solving" style of decision-making. We will return to this issue in section 5.6.

We begin by placing the industrial relations systems of the four countries in the context of the diverse systems that coexist within Western Europe, subsequently going on to discuss the various aspects of such systems in turn – collective actors, collective bargaining patterns, the role of bipartite and tripartite organizations – with reference to the four countries. The concluding evaluation in section 5.6 assesses these findings and looks at their relevance for employment policy.

5.2 THE EUROPEAN MOSAIC OF PERSISTENT DIVERSITY

In spite of the many similar pressures to which they are exposed – the increase in firms' cross-border activities and the influence of European integration – industrial relations, labour markets and social policies are characterized by persistent diversity (Crouch, 1993; Esping-Anderson, 1990; van Ruysseveldt and Visser, 1996). Table 5.1 distinguishes four "ideal types" of industrial relations (based on Ebbinghaus and Visser, 1997).

In the *confrontational* model capital and labour "are alienated, their relationship is unformed, interaction is likely to be thin on the ground and to take the form of conflict" (Crouch, 1993, p. 31). Recognition is limited or absent, parties dispute each other's claim to legitimacy, relations are highly conflictual and frequently require the intervention of the State. In this model labour law has an important role in defining individual rights in substantive (rather than procedural) terms, but this is often merely on paper, since the State's capacity of implementation is weak or contested.

In the *pluralist* model capital and labour have developed a bargaining relationship; both entertain an adversarial value system, though they may agree on procedures and accept defeat, provided that the winner plays by the rules. The structure of interest organization is fragmented and coordination structures are weak. The State tends to abstain and to rely on the self-regulatory capacity of markets to produce fair contracts. Industrial relations are characterized by "voluntarism"; trade union action is not protected by a system of rights, but granted freedoms by parliament through so-called immunities; collective agreements "bind in honour" and do not constitute a legal and enforceable constraint. The welfare State takes on a role as compensator of last resort.

In the *corporatist* model collective bargaining tends be conducted or supervised by encompassing organizations representing capital and labour, and to be

Table 5.1 Models of industrial relations in Western Europe

	Northern corporatism	Central social partnership	Anglo-Saxon pluralism	Latin confrontation
Organized interests (unions and employers)	Cohesive Disciplined Comprehensive	Segmented Disciplined Partial/stable	Fragmented Volatile Variable	Rivalry Volatile Variable
Relationship	Labour-led/ balanced	Balanced/employer-led	Alternating/ unstable	Weakness both sides/large role for the State
Wage bargaining				
. dominant level	Sector	Sector	Company	Alternating
. coverage	High	Medium to high	Small to moderate	Medium to high
. depth	Significant	Moderate	Significant	Limited
. style	Integrative	Integrative	Adversarial	Contestational
. pattern	Stable	Stable	Unstable	Unstable
Coordination	Considerable	Considerable	Absent	Variable
Conflict	Medium to low Highly organized	Low Highly organized	Medium to high Dispersed	High Spasmodic
Role of the State	Facilitating	Facilitating and regulating	Abstaining	Intervening
	Collective labour rights	Individual and collective labour rights	Voluntarism	Individual and collective labour rights
Welfare State	Comprehensive Right of work	Fragmented Right of income	Residual –	Rudimentary Right of work and welfare proclaimed
	State is employer of first resort	State is compensator of first resort	State is enforcer of work in marketplace	–
Countries	Sweden Finland Denmark Norway	Austria Germany Switzerland Belgium Netherlands	United Kingdom Ireland	France Italy Spain Portugal Greece

based on integrative, partly overlapping value systems. Bargaining tends to be supported by consultation, in national policy institutions and also on the ground, in works councils or joint committees of workers and management. The role of the State tends to be facilitating, for instance by recognizing general or industrial union federations, granting privileged access to policy forums and discouraging rival organizations and "enterprise unions". Within this model one may distinguish between a Nordic or Scandinavian and a Central or continental European variant. The position of trade unions tends to be much stronger in the Nordic group; labour law tends to establish collective rather than individual rights; and the collective bargaining method as provider of rights has historically played a larger role than state provision. Consultation and participation in the workplace have been developed through collective bargaining and "single" union representation, rather than through a "dual" works council system based upon public law that exists alongside union representation, as is typical in the continental corporatist States (Rogers and Streeck, 1995). Esping-Andersen (1990) has stressed the differences in welfare State development, class structure, labour market participation and the role of women in employment between these variants of corporatism and the pluralist (Anglo-Saxon model); these themes are taken up in Chapter 4 of this book.

In the Nordic group the State backs up the right to work by a concept of social citizenship and has acted as employer of first resort and compensator of last resort. The entry of women into the employment system has been supported through a vast development of state-supported collective services, especially in education, health and social welfare services. In the Bismarckian or Central group, the State tends to act as compensator of first and employer of last resort, and welfare entitlements tend to be institutionalized in different regimes for different categories. Here, the State has supported the exit of various groups from the labour market since the 1970s, particularly older and unskilled workers. In the Nordic group the labour movement has remained united and has played a dominant role in shaping a universalistic welfare State. In the Central group visions of the social market economy, social partnership and the welfare State were shaped by the competition between Christian and Social Democratic forces within a federal democratic polity.

The application of these "ideal types" to individual countries is not unproblematic. We have placed Ireland in the pluralist (Anglo-Saxon) group, but, as we will see later, Irish industrial relations are moving away from the United Kingdom model. Ireland may still have aspects of a rudimentary welfare State, as in some of the Southern European countries, with a larger traditional agricultural sector than the other countries in this comparison and a post-war history that was marked by high unemployment and emigration. But Ireland has made enormous strides forward since it became a member of the European Community in 1973. Its British origins are still visible in trade union structures and traditions, in wage bargaining behaviour and in labour law, but there is now a well-established trend to seek corporatist solutions to social and economic problems, rather similar to Austria or the Netherlands. The Irish industrial relations system may appear to be a case of "aspiring corporatism" (Crouch, 1996), yet it lacks the consultation and participation structures at the enterprise level and the institutionalized "stake-holder concept of the business firm" which is typical of the Rhineland version of corporatism (Albert, 1991; Lane, 1989).

There are other – structural – aspects in which these countries differ. Foreign capital, especially from North America, Japan and the United Kingdom, has been playing an increasingly important role in the Irish economy. In 1990, just under half of all employees in the manufacturing sector (93,000 of 200,000) were employed by foreign-owned firms. Attracted by favourable tax incentives and substantial capital grants, many multinational enterprises (MNEs) have established subsidiaries in pharmaceuticals, electronics and the food industry, as well as in advanced industries such as consumer electronics. Many of these firms employed sophisticated personnel management tactics combined with a preference for a non-union environment (Gunnigle et al., 1997; Roche and Geary, 1996). In the past, these firms were less easily subjected to national pay policies (Hardiman, 1992).

The Netherlands is the only one of these four countries with an important "indigenous" MNE sector. In all, MNEs employ about one million people or one-sixth of total employment (and around two-fifths of manufacturing employment, around two-thirds of them for MNEs with their headquarters in the Netherlands). Many of these firms, the most important of which include Philips, Shell, Unilever, AKZO-Nobel and Heineken, negotiate their own company agreements, but are at the same time prominent members of sectoral and peak-level employers' associations.

Like the Netherlands, Denmark is a small open economy dominated by export-oriented firms in relatively mature industries, and a large service sector. But there is a noticeable absence of large firms and MNEs in the Danish economy. During the past decades there was even a de-concentration of employment; by the early 1990s only around one-fifth of the Danish industrial workforce was employed in firms with 500 or more employees, compared with one-quarter in the late 1970s. Eighty per cent of all firms, employing 23 per cent of the workforce, had fewer than 10 employees; one-quarter of the workforce is in firms of between 10 and 50 employees (according to the Danish Statistical Office, in Scheuer, 1997b, p. 147; Boje and Kongshoj Madsen, 1994, p. 97). This structural aspect of the Danish economy is combined with low levels of job security: high staff turnover between firms; occupational labour markets, vocational training in the public educational system and outside the firm; and a relatively flexible employment system which can quickly compensate for the short-run effects of world market changes by rapid changes in level of activity (Kristensen and Sabel, 1993; Nielsen and Pedersen, 1991). Boje and Kongshoj Madsen (1994) also note a high degree of "numerical flexibility" with respect to working hours, in particular among women, but a lesser degree of "functional flexibility". Numerical flexibility, through part-time employment and the increased use of temporary job agencies, had also characterized the Dutch labour market of late, and appears to have compensated for the much higher degree of job security, organized around internal labour markets, in the Netherlands (Visser and Hemerijck, 1997).

The relative weakness and fragmentation of domestic private capital in Austria is underscored by the fact that none of the major MNEs has its home base in Austria. Austrian firms are relatively small. Among the 15 current EU Member States, in the early 1980s the contribution of large enterprises (with more than 500 employees) to employment in the manufacturing sector was smaller only in Denmark and Ireland (OECD, 1985). This fragmentation and relative weakness of capital are to an extent compensated for by a unique degree of unity and concentration of business interest organization in Austria. The Austrian Economic Chamber (Wirtschaftskammer Österreichs, WKÖ) is probably Europe's most comprehensive, well-resourced and politically influential association (see below).

Tálos (1993) has characterized the Austrian social model as a concerted, multi-dimensional network of institutionalized formal and informal interaction between the large umbrella organizations, but also between them and the Government. These relationships and interconnections are complemented by those between the interest groups and the parties, in particular the Christian Peoples Party and the Social Democratic Party, which since the mid-1980s have maintained a solid coalition. Interconnections on the personal level with respect to functions in the interest associations, social partnership organizations, political parties, Parliament and the Cabinet further solidify social partnership.

The Danish business community is, despite its apparent fragmentation, well organized in a multitude of associations; the State has traditionally played a restricted role in economic governance and industrial relations. As in Austria, the trade unions are both a very powerful opposition force and an important partner in national corporatist regulation (for Austria: Traxler, 1993; 1997; for Denmark: Due et al., 1994; Scheuer, 1992; 1997b). Some authors have dubbed Denmark a "negotiated economy" (Jessop, Nielsen and Pedersen, 1993; Nielsen and Pedersen, 1991). Five aspects of the Danish version of "associative corporatism" can be distinguished (Amin and Thomas, 1996): a high level of interest representation of both capital and labour; a considerable dispersion of decisional authority and autonomy across organizations and to local levels; a limited role for the State as arbitrator and facilitator of agreements between autonomous interest organizations; a dense network of vertical and horizontal channels of representation and communication as the basis for decision making; and reliance on iterative dialogue for conflict resolution and policy consensus. These characteristics also apply to Austria (but with a more pronounced role for social and labour legislation) and to the Netherlands (but with a weaker role for organized labour and a more pronounced role of (large) companies within the employers' associations).

In a negotiated economy (but where "negotiation" takes the form of "dialogue" rather than "bargaining"), the "mobilization of voice", and the preference of "voice" over "exit" (Hirschmann, 1970), are characteristic elements. In the words of Nielsen and Pedersen (1991, p. 151):

> In the negotiated economy decisions are made through institutionalized negotiations between the appointing agents who reach binding decisions based on discursive, political and moral imperatives rather than formal contracts and legal sanctions. The behaviour of the agents is regulated not by authoritative means but rather

through normative forms of regulation, through incentives broader and more indirect than economic gains, and through measures intended to influence the preferences of the counterpart.

There are many similarities to what the Dutch today call their "*poldermodel*", but used to call "*overlegeconomie*", where the word "*overleg*" means "consultation" rather than "negotiation" and denotes the preparedness to "talk it over" in case of conflict. "*Overlegeconomie*" can be defined as "the propensity to let organized consultation have every possible chance of resolving conflicts, avoiding contention, and compromising differences" (Windmuller, 1969, p. 438). As in Denmark, it involves a dense associational network in which it is easy – socially and informally – to communicate across the boundaries of interests and Weltanschauung (or world view). In both the Netherlands and Denmark, the ideology, if not practice, of equality is pervasive. In terms of these "cultural" aspects there are probably more similarities between these two countries than with Austria and Ireland (see also Hofstede, 1989). But as previously noted, in the Netherlands the role of large firms is more pronounced than in any of these countries and the power of the unions rather more limited. And the influence of the State in industrial relations and wage setting, at least up to the 1980s, was more pervasive.

In the following section we consider the organizations representing labour and capital in the four countries in more detail.

5.3 COLLECTIVE REPRESENTATION: TRADE UNIONS AND EMPLOYERS' ASSOCIATIONS

Austria, Denmark and Ireland are highly unionized economies (see table 5.2). More recent figures show density rates varying between 41 per cent in Austria, 52 per cent in Ireland and 77 per cent in Denmark – far above the European (weighted) average of 32 per cent (or the unweighted average of 40 per cent), and far above the current unionization rate for France (10 per cent or lower), Germany (29 per cent), the United Kingdom (36 per cent) or the United States (14 per cent) (Ebbinghaus and Visser, 2000; table WE 13/14, data for 1995). At only 24 per cent (or 28 per cent if very small part-time jobs of less than 12 hours per week are excluded), union density is much lower in the Netherlands than in the other three countries. But through their participation in the statutory works councils, covering approximately 70 per cent of all employees (Visser, 1995), and their institutionalized presence in national policy forums, the influence of Dutch trade union influence counts far beyond their modest membership numbers.

Bargaining coverage in the three countries ranges from 70 per cent in Denmark to 85 per cent in the Netherlands and a high 98 per cent in Austria (Ebbinghaus and Visser, 2000). The exact figure for Ireland is unknown, but recent central agreements do in theory cover most workers even though, on

Table 5.2 Unionization, employer organization and bargaining coverage in the market sector, selected countries, mid-1990s

Country	Union density rate (%)	Workers in firms belonging to the main employers' organizations (%)	Workers covered by collective agreements (%)	Extension of agreements through public law	National minimum wage
Sweden	77	60	72	Absent	Agreement
Finland	65	58	67	Limited	Agreement
Denmark	68	48	52	Absent	Agreement
Norway	45	54	62	Negligible	Agreement
Belgium	40	80	82	Significant	Statutory (69%)
Austria	37	96	97	Significant	Agreement
Germany	25	76	80	Limited	Agreement
Switzerland	18	37	50	Limited	Agreement
Netherlands	19	80	79	Limited	Statutory (60%)
Ireland	37	44	...	Negligible	(Industry councils)
Great Britain	21	57	40	Absent	No
Italy	32	40	...	Absent	Agreement
France	<7	71	75	Significant	Statutory (73%)
Spain	<15	70	67	Limited	Statutory (40%)
Portugal	<20	...	...	Limited	Statutory (70%)
Greece	<15	...	...	Significant	Statutory (57%)
Average[a]	36	62	69		

[a] Unweighted average; unionization rate and employers' organizations = average based on 14 countries (without Portugal and Greece); bargaining coverage = average based on 12 countries (without Portugal, Greece, Ireland and Italy). All rates are standardized (see Traxler, 1994; Visser, 1991).
Source: Visser, 1998c.

the ground, implementation through locally negotiated terms of employment may be somewhat less pervasive. In the private sector the figures are 52 per cent in the case of Denmark (Scheuer, 1997a), 79 per cent in the Netherlands (Venema et al., 1996; and Visser and van der Meer, 1998), and 96 per cent in Austria (Traxler, 1997). All this points in the direction of the enduring importance of collective wage setting, of the collective agreement as an instrument of regulation of employment relations, and of the trade unions as co-managers of the terms of employment for workers in these four countries. Table 5.2 shows that these four countries are no outliers in the European context. Only when a comparison is made with the United States and Japan, possibly also with the United Kingdom, do we find considerable differences, especially in the level of employer organization and in bargaining coverage.

Figure 5.1 shows the trends in trade union density – downwards in Austria, Ireland and the Netherlands, upwards and stable in Denmark and at a much higher level than in the other countries. It is not possible to draw a similar graph for employers' organizations. Data on membership of employers' organizations are much harder to come by and less easy to evaluate against a common

Figure 5.1 Union density rates, 1970–96

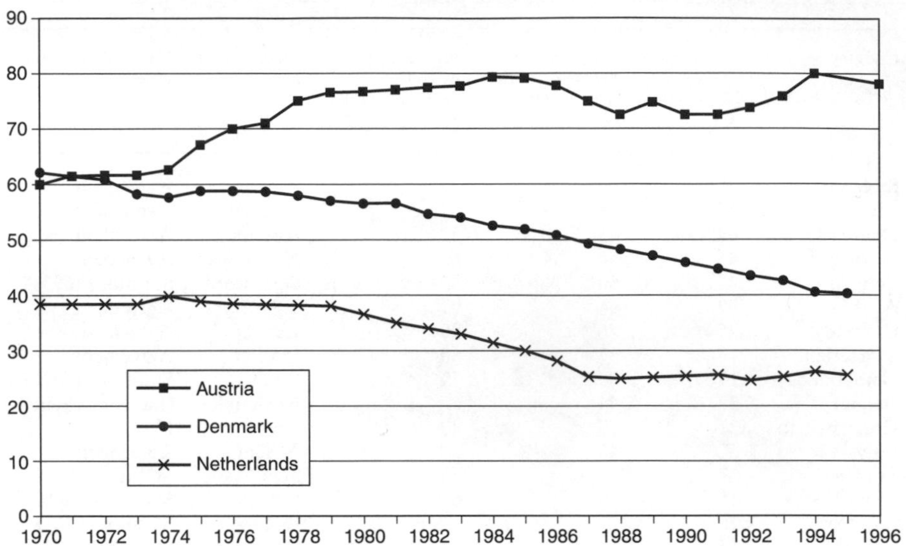

yardstick. But some data are available and comparison with the Organization of Business Interests (OBI) data of the early 1980s, published by Traxler (1993) and van Waarden (1995), does not suggest a decline in employers' organizations in Western Europe (Britain being the main exception). In two of the four countries, Austria and the Netherlands, the level of employers' organizations – as well as of their staff and financial resources – is significantly higher than the level of unionization. Tables 5.3 and 5.4 summarize the main characteristics of the central organizations of trade unions and employers in the four countries.

Austria

According to the law on collective agreements (ArbVG), the right to make collective agreements in Austria is granted to both corporations under public law (chambers) and associations with voluntary membership. In practice the Austrian Economic Chamber (WKÖ) makes use of this right, while the Chambers of Labour (BAK, Bundesarbeiterkammer) relinquishes it for the benefit of the Austrian Federation of Trade Unions (ÖGB, Österreichischer Gewerkschaftsbund). It is noteworthy that the ÖGB's de facto monopoly in collective bargaining derives from the Chambers of Labour, which can opt to waive their right or not. Since the Chambers and the ÖGB are strongly linked by personal ties and party interests, there is virtually no scope for additional, competing unions. There is nothing in the law that prevents their

Table 5.3 Major trade union confederations, 1995

	Confederation (1)	Orientation (2)	Domain (3)	Affiliates (4)	Membership (end 1996) (5)	Confederal monopoly (6)	Density, private sector (7)	Density, total economy (8)
Austria	ÖGB	All	All	14	1 583 356	1.0	37	41
Denmark	LO-DK	Socialist	Manual +	24	1 502 400	0.69	68	77
	FTF	–	Non-manual	44	338 400	0.16		
	AC	–	Professional	19	143 400	0.07		
Ireland	ICTU	All	All	41[a]	482 800[a]	0.97	37	52
Netherlands	FNV	[Socialist]	All	17	1 152 900	0.64	19	24
	CNV	Christian	All	15	347 800	0.19		
	MHP	Liberal	Staff	3[b]	161 600	0.09		

[a] Excludes affiliates with 198,980 members in Northern Ireland. [b] Of these, two federations have a total of about 100 affiliated company and staff unions.

Columns:
1. Major peak association of trade unions. Abbreviations: See list on p. xx for full names.
2. Political, ideological or religious orientation (in [ ] brackets: weak or fading).
3. Part of working population which the association claims to represent: manual (only blue-collar workers); manual + (including lower-graded clerical and technical staff); non-manual (only white-collar workers); professional (only employees with higher education); staff (only managerial and supervisory staff); or all (no groups excluded).
4. Number of member organizations (national unions or federations only, local unions are not counted).
5. Total number of members of affiliates (including those who are direct members of the confederation, and including retired, unemployed and self-employed workers, students, conscripted soldiers, etc.).
6. Membership of the confederation as a ratio of total union membership in the country.
7. Standardized density rates (see below), excluding public or semi-public sector (for definition, see Visser, 1991).
8. Density, total economy: Standardized density rate: employed members as a proportion of wage and salary earners in employment.

Sources: Ebbinghaus and Visser, 2000; Visser, 1998c.

establishment, but the ArbVG sets high entry barriers for any competing union, requiring that it must represent a broad domain of workers and encompass both several sectors and several territorial regions before it is entitled to take part in bargaining and concertation.

Chambers are self-governing bodies established under law, with mandatory membership, and which to some extent fulfil governmental functions under government control; they are a defining element of Austria's specific type of corporatism or social partnership (table 5.5). The ÖGB and the WKÖ are responsible for collective bargaining; the BAK provides expert know-how for the unions. Industrial enterprises form one of the six divisions of the WKÖ, but are at the same time represented in their own association, the Association of Austrian Industrialists (VÖI), with many officials holding functions in both organizations. However, the VÖI is not usually directly present in social partnership negotiations, but represented by the WKÖ. The strong position

Table 5.4 Major employers' confederations, 1995

	Confederation	Domain	Type	Affiliates	Members		Density	
					Firms	Workers	Private sector	Total economy
	(1)	(2)	(3)	(4)	(5)	(6)	(7)	(8)
Austria	WKÖ[a]	All	M	[136]	320 000	2 600 000	96	100
	VÖI	Industry	T	0	2 000	420 000	...	
Denmark	DA	Industry +	M	30	17 000	550 000	48	72
	DI[b]	Industry	T	59	4 300	300 000	...	.
Ireland	IBEC	All	M	53	3 700	300 000	44	55
Netherlands	VNO-NCW	All	M	150	80 000	4 000 000	80	82

[a]Not an association but a chamber, with compulsory membership (see main text). [b]Member of DA.
Columns:
1. Central general employers' (and trade) associations in the private sector, without agriculture, retail trade, SMEs and the public or subsidized sector. Abbreviations: See list on pp. xv–xvii for full names.
2. Part of the economy which the association claims to represent: industry; industry + (= including parts of trade and private transport, but not financial and business services); or all (= private sector, including commercial and financial services).
3. Complexity of tasks; E = employers' association only; T = trade association; M = mixed, i.e. employers' and trade association.
4. Number of member associations, organized on the basis of sectors (branches of the economy). In brackets: subdivisions rather than independent member associations.
5. Number of firms organized, directly and/or through affiliates.
6. Total employment in member firms.
7. Employment in member firms as a proportion of total employment in the private sector.
8. Weighted sum of density of all employers' associations in private-sector (including minor associations in banking and other services) and public-sector employment. (It is assumed that employers' density in the public sector is 100 per cent; agricultural organizations are ignored.)
Source: Visser, 1998c.

of the chambers is further enhanced by the fact that they are responsible for the autonomous administration of the social insurance institutions. Moreover, they have a comprehensive right to present expert opinions on laws and decrees (this applies to all bills, not only to those in the areas of labour legislation and social policy).

According to recent figures, the WKÖ employs 5,400 officials and 12,000 support staff (BWS, 1997, p. 9). The high degree of associational concentration and centralization compensates at the political level for the low degree of economic concentration; small firms, more than large ones, need the collective interest representation and the individual consultancy provided by associations (Traxler, 1993). The WKÖ has public status in so far as it was established by a special law that regulates its coverage, organizational structure and functions. All firms in the WKÖ's domain are legally required to be members. Thus it

Table 5.5 The main actors in the Austrian social partnership

Austrian Economic Chamber (WKÖ) 9 state chambers 320,000 member-firms	*Federal Chamber of Labour (BAK)* 9 state chambers 2.6 million members
Association of Austrian Industrialists (VÖI) 9 state sections 2,000 member-firms with 420,000 employees	*Austrian Federation of Trade Unions (ÖGB)* 9 state sections, 14 unions 1.6 million members

Source: Austrian Economic Chamber.

embraces all privately and publicly owned firms in industry, the craft sector, commerce, banking and insurance, transport and tourism. Recent figures provided by the WKÖ put the number of member firms at 320,000. The WKÖ comes close to having a representational monopoly in collective bargaining. About 95 per cent of all collective agreements are signed on behalf of business under the umbrella of the WKÖ. Only about 4 to 5 per cent of all members remain outside these agreements, and for these members the chambers act only as a trade association (Traxler, 1997). Historically, their labour market interests have been represented by specialized employers' associations based on voluntary membership (especially in printing and in banking). These associations tend to base their policies on the collective agreements concluded by the WKÖ.

The Austrian union movement is the most centralized in Western Europe. Uniquely, in terms of unity, the ÖGB encompasses all 14 unions existing in the country, covering the whole of the economy (table 5.6). In the private sector, blue-collar workers are organized separately from white-collar workers; whereas the former are represented by eight unions demarcated by industry, the latter are in one "catch-all" union. The four unions in the public sector and the union in arts and media organize blue- and white-collar employees. Union density stood in 1995 at just over 41 per cent, well above

Table 5.6 The main trade unions in Austria

Austrian Federation of Trade Unions	Members[a]	% Female
Gew. der Privatangestellten (GPA, white-collar employees, private sector)	326 552	43.7
Gew. des öffentlichen Dienstes (GÖD, public sector, all grades)	231 968	44.9
Gew. Metall-Bergbau-Energie (GMBE, workers in metal, mining, energy)	219 462	16.4
Gew. der Gemeindebediensteten (GGB, municipal employees, all grades)	179 621	48.6
Gew. der Bau- und Holzarbeiter (GBH, construction and wood workers)	184 257	4.3

[a] As of 1995.
Source: Ebbinghaus and Visser, 2000, p. 109.

the European average, but much lower than in the past. The decline in unionization may be due, in part, to the structural changes of a contracting industrial base and public sector in which, traditionally, density is high. Union density in manufacturing industry was 57 per cent (with peaks among the larger companies), against only 16 per cent in commercial and 17 per cent in financial services; in the public sector 70 per cent of workers are union members, almost double the rate (37 per cent) in the private sector. Among male employees union density is 51 per cent, against 33 per cent among females (figures for 1995).

Since 1974 the GPA has been the single largest union, assuming the position from the metalworkers' union (GMBE), which, however, has retained its role as wage leader. In recent years the public sector union has moved into second place. Attempts to restructure Austrian unions by further reducing their number, based on the principle of "industrial unions" or "one firm, one union" (as in Germany), have so far failed because it would mean that the GPA would have to be carved up. It is more likely that the smaller blue-collar unions will seek mergers across industry borders (as has happened in Germany and the Netherlands for example; see Streeck and Visser, 1998).

Intra-associational centralization is broadly determined by three variables: control over finances (and strike funds), control over full-time officials, and allocation of representative functions (Visser, 1984). On each of these dimensions, the Austrian union movement is without parallel in Europe. Formally, the ÖGB is a unitary organization rather than a federation; its 14 member unions are subdivisions rather than organizations in their own right. According to the ÖGB constitution, these unions are not entitled to make binding agreements with third parties (i.e. employers); this is a prerogative of the federation. Yet, in practice the unions do sign agreements, on the basis of a devolved right. However, the powers of the federation to influence the timing and content of these agreements remain formidable. The ÖGB enjoys "*Finanzhoheit*" (literally, financial sovereignty): membership contributions are collected by the unions (and works councils members) for the federation, which then withholds 27.6 per cent on average (for the years 1990–94; Traxler, 1997, p. 247). This percentage is twice as high as in the next most centralized federations, the LO (Landesorganisation) in Sweden or the FNV – Netherlands Trade Union Confederation (Visser, 1990). The ÖGB also sets the level of subscription (at 1 per cent of gross earnings), although some variation does occur. Control over personnel is regulated in a similar fashion; the federation appoints not only its own officials but also those of the unions. In total, the ÖGB employs around 1,600 staff (around one-quarter at central office). These numbers and proportions are very much larger than in other European trade union federations (Visser, 1990). The close (personal) integration between union and chamber (which employs many more staff of its own) gives the Austrian unions additional resources, in particular expertise. Finally, all appointments to representative and consultative bodies are made through the ÖGB.

Denmark

In Denmark, recognition and bargaining rights are matters for the social partners themselves. Some 17,000 firms, employing about half the unionized workforce, are affiliated with the Dansk Arbejdsgiverforening (DA, the Danish Employers' Confederation), directly or through membership in trade associations. The DA still has the authority to order a general lockout with the approval of three-quarters of its affiliates and to restrain individual members from negotiating independently on certain issues. Other, smaller employers are affiliated with other organizations. The DA covers the private sector (except agriculture, construction and financial services) (figure 5.2). Its member firms employ around half the Danish workforce in the private sector, some 70 per cent in manufacturing industry but much lower proportions in private services. The so-called LO-DA area corresponds only to some 25 per cent of all unionized employees in the national labour force. The public sector covers 33 per cent, while SALA (agriculture) and financial services cover around 3 per cent each. The remaining one-third is employed in firms which are perhaps members of smaller, unaffiliated associations, or in firms that have remained unorganized. In this area unions have had some success with so-called "adhesion agreements".

Within the DA power has shifted to Dansk Industri (DI, Confederation of Danish Industry) and within the Danish Confederation of Trade Unions (LO-DK), the main union confederation, to CO-Industri (CO-I). Rather than their peak associations, DI and CO-I have taken over the role of conducting "aggregate bargaining", as do similar cartels in other sectors. CO-I is a cartel of 12 trade unions with approximately 330,000 members: the cartels of Metal with 116,976 members and SiD with 100,075 are the most important. In the public sector there are two cartels: the (central) state sector (CFU) and municipal employees (KTO). State employees once had civil servant status, but employment on the basis of collective agreements became more common in the 1970s; today collective bargaining is conducted on behalf of all employees, irrespective of formal status. Disputes are settled by applying the same principles as in the LO-DA area, but in the early 1980s a special industrial court was introduced for the public sector.

According to Due, Madsen and Jensen (1997, p. 127) "the late 1980s and the early 1990s will in all probability be regarded by historians as a crucial period in the development of the Danish system of labour market organizations and collective bargaining". Yet, "the structural changes which are now under way can be perceived as an attempt to maintain the main features of the system" (ibid.). They refer to this process as "centralized decentralization", "because it simultaneously embodies (a) the merger – at the national level – of a large number of local trade unions and employers' associations, forming a few all-inclusive aggregations, and (b) a decentralization of the competence to take decisions on pay and working conditions from the DA to local level, that is,

Figure 5.2 Main bargaining areas in Denmark

Private sector (LO-DA area)

Unions	Employers
CO-Industri: Cartel of unions in industry, Metal, SiD and others	DI: Confederation of Danish Industry
HTS: Cartel of unions in trade, transport and services, HK and others	BKA: Danish Employers' Federation for Office and Trade
BAT: Cartel of unions in building and woodworking, SiD and others	BYG: Danish Masterbuilders' Organization, and Danish Contractors' Association

Other private sector (outside DA)

Unions	Employers
LO (agriculture) and FTF (finance) unions	SALA (agriculture), financial sector employers
	Independent employers' association in construction

Public sector

Unions	Employers
CFU: cartel of LO, FTF and AC unions among state employees	Ministry of Finance
KTO: cartel of LO, FTF and AC unions among municipal employees	Local Government Employers

Note: Abbreviations: see list on pp. xv-xvii for full names.

Source: Danish Ministry of Labour.

the single workplace" (ibid.). The DA took the initiative in 1989, pressured by its affiliates (especially in metal engineering), who at first went ahead without the blessing of the DA leadership. The 1991 and 1993 wage bargaining rounds reflected the organizational changes in the employers' camp, leading to "comprehensive framework agreements", the details of which are subsequently filled in at workplace level. According to Due, Madsen and Jensen (1997, p. 141) the DA leadership had tried to persuade LO, without success, to maintain a kind of central bargaining, but with more room to manoeuvre for unions and employers' associations below central level. The unions – especially the SiD – saw this as an attack on solidaristic bargaining. The LO found it impossible to restructure its affiliates and the DA was unable to control its members. After a series of mergers, the industrial employers, led by the firms in metal engineering (JA or Jernets Arbejdsgivere) formed a new bloc (DI: Dansk Industri), which acts both as a separate confederation, for trade interests, at home and in Brussels (where it is a member of UNICE, the European Employers' Federation) and as an employers' association and affiliate to DA (which is also affiliated with UNICE). Within the DA, the new combination represents about 50 per cent of the aggregate wages of all DA members.

The outcome of the power struggle within the employers' camp was a decisive decentralization, but one based on greater employer concentration. In the course of a few years, the 150 or so member federations that had existed prior to 1990 became less than 30. Other changes in the DA statutes abolished the overrepresentation of small firms, grouped the remaining federations in four main aggregates (manufacturing, construction, retail and services, and wholesale and transport), reduced membership dues and generally scaled down activities. Staff were reduced from 230 to 180 (which makes the DA much smaller than, for instance, the Dutch central employers' organization). One DA aim was the reduction of the number of collective agreements from about 650 to 20 or 25 when the process is completed. Until late 1980 it was not uncommon for a firm to cover different aspects of employment relations through different collective agreements, concluded not only with different unions, but also through different employers' organizations. The new aim is "one firm, one contract", and "one firm, one representation". The DA's power has decreased, and the federation may turn from a bargaining into a lobbying organization. But under its present statutes it has still some important functions: approval of collective agreements of member organizations; handling of the basic agreement with the LO (the main "Peace Treaty" between the two sides); the regulation of the voting system after proposals by the conciliator (as well as the appointments to the labour court); and the joint industrial action fund to be applied in strikes or lockouts.

In Denmark, as in Britain or Ireland, but unlike the rest of Scandinavia and the European continent (including Austria and the Netherlands), the union movement has developed along craft and general union lines, rather than in the form of industrial unionism. General unions, once established as a response of unskilled workers to craft unions that had little to offer them, stood in the way of later attempts to create industrial unions on the basis of the "one industry – one union" basis. By straddling the boundaries of industry, general unions in Denmark grew very large. Excluded from what became the Specialarbejderforbundet (SiD), unskilled female workers formed their own union, the Kvindeligt Arbejderforbundet (KAD). Largest among the general unions is now the Handels- of Kontorfunktionærernes Forbund (HK), the union of commercial and clerical (salaried) employees. HK organizes in both the private and public sectors. Among the skilled ("craft-like") unions, the Metalarbejderforbund (Metal) is the most important one (see table 5.7).

Danish workers are among the most heavily unionized in the world, ranking directly after Sweden and Finland (see table 5.2 above). One factor here is that they have retained their involvement in the administration and adjudication of unemployment insurance, a selective benefit which in the 1970s was extended to early retirement (Ebbinghaus and Visser, 1999; Rothstein, 1992; Scheuer, 1992). Other contributory factors lie in the strong workplace basis of Danish

Table 5.7 Danish trade unions, 1995

Organization	Unions	Members	% female
Danish Federation of Trade Unions (LO)	24	1 502 400	48.4
5 general unions (65% of all members),			
of which: HK (salaried staff in clerical and commercial services)		361 000	74.8
SiD (unskilled workers)		306 773	14.5
FOA (municipal employees)		202 500	88.0
KAD (female workers)		92 500	100
8 craft unions (15% of all members),			
of which: Metal		143 800	1.4
5 industrial unions (13% of all members),			
of which: Wood and building		71 600	12.2
6 other unions (6% of all members)			
Confederation of Salaried Employees (FTF),	44	338 400	64.9
of which:			
Teachers' union		59 688	62.6
Nurses' union		50 579	96.6
Banking union		44 470	57.0
Confederation of Professional Associations (AC)	19	137 200	33.4
Central Organization of Supervisors' Unions	3	75 900	15.0
Other unions,	40	106 800	41.6
of which:			
Christian workers' and employees' organizations (2)		52 011	54.7
Total	**117**	**2 160 700**	**48.3**

Source: Ebbinghaus and Visser, 2000, data as of 1 January 1997.

unionism, and an industrial tribunal system which presupposes representation through the union. According to recent survey data (Scheuer, 1997, p. 158), there are hardly any differences in the extent of unionization between manual and non-manual workers, or between men and women; in each group four out of five Danish workers are members of a union. Our figures for the late 1980s indicated that in manufacturing union density was well over 90 per cent, against 53 per cent in commercial and financial services; our estimate for the public sector was 87 per cent, compared to 68 per cent for the private sector (Visser, 1991).

There has been a steady fall in the number of affiliates to the LO from 35 in 1980 to 24 in 1996, as a result of mergers and takeovers of smaller unions. The proposal to form nine industrial unions, approved at the 1971 LO congress, was never implemented. Neither Metal nor SiD was prepared to compromise. In the mid-1980s five cartels were proposed; this was accepted at the LO's 1989 congress, six months after the DA had made its changes (Scheuer, 1992). But the schism between SiD and Metal remained, both fearing loss of influence; SiD because its members would be parcelled out over various cartels, Metal because it would become a minority within its own cartel. This led to the collapse of the proposal at the 1991 LO congress. Ongoing changes on the employer side and shifts in collective bargaining could not be ignored, however, and the LO unions were forced to come up with new proposals for coalition building. The CO-Industri cartel was formed in 1992 as a coalition of virtually all skilled and unskilled workers' unions, including SiD and Metal. This shifted the problem to internal discord within SiD, the leadership of which was unsuccessful in preventing the transfer of bargaining competence to CO-I. The 1989 proposal was revitalized and slightly changed (from five to six cartels). It has now more or less been implemented as a counterpart to the changes in the employers' camp. This means, equally, a shift in bargaining responsibilities and competence away from the peak association. The LO, too, scaled down its operations somewhat (including 50 redundancies) (Scheuer, 1997). The separation from FTF and AC is also a problem (cooperation has been slow; on the other hand, the LO in Denmark has defended its share much better than its sister organizations in Sweden, Norway or Finland, mainly because that it organizes salaried employees in the lower ranks).

Ireland

Irish employers are well organized (O'Brien, 1989), although representation is less extensive than in Austria and the Netherlands. Sectoral organization is not very well developed, and neither is sectoral (multi-employer) bargaining, except in construction and a few small domestic sectors; the most influential of these is the Construction Industry Federation. When legislation was passed in 1941 requiring all organizations engaged in collective bargaining to have "trade union status" with so-called "negotiation licences" (an aspect of the move to corporatist structures at the time), a large number of employers set up the Federated Union of Employers (FUE). Conceived initially as a private sector association, the FUE eventually admitted various public sector employers. In 1989 it changed its name to the Federation of Irish Employers (FIE), largely in response to the changing patterns of industrial relations, and the growing number of MNEs for whom the designation "union" was suspect. In 1993 the FIE merged with the Confederation of Irish Industry (a pressure group lobbying for member companies in all matters other than industrial relations) to become the Irish Business and Employers' Confederation (IBEC). IBEC is a so-called mixed organization and represents both the social and trade interests of business. IBEC organizes firms with a total workforce of approximately 300,000.

The key feature which differentiates Ireland from the other countries in this comparison is the rapid development, since the 1970s, of the foreign-owned sector of manufacturing (see above). These firms are generally more profitable, and concentrated in the modernized, export-oriented segment of the Irish economy. Hardiman (1992) reports data showing that these firms were as likely to be organized in employers' associations as were domestic firms, but their interests often diverged and they were rather reluctant to accept any outside interference in their in-house employment relations. Their ability to pay higher wages had a destabilizing impact on the national pay policies of the 1970s and 1980s.

The umbrella organization for Irish trade unions is the Irish Congress of Trade Unions (ICTU). In recent years, well over 95 per cent of all union members have been in organizations affiliated to the ICTU, making it the sole voice for workers both in Ireland and Northern Ireland. In Northern Ireland a separate committee provides a forum for local negotiations. Most of the unions in Northern Ireland have their headquarters in Great Britain but are affiliated to the ICTU (as well as to the Trades Union Congress in Great Britain). Some of these unions also have members in Ireland (table 5.8). In 1996 there were 12 unions with members in Ireland which had their head office outside the country, with a total membership of 63,700 (13 per cent of all union members in Ireland). Historically their role has been controversial and their presence contributed to a split in the Irish trade union movement (McCarthy, 1977), but currently they have a secure place in Irish industrial relations.

In 1980, 94 trade unions organized a total membership of 4,545,200, a figure which represented about half of the national workforce. Of these trade unions, 72 were affiliated to the ICTU, representing a total of 496,100 members. By 1995 the number of trade unions had decreased to 54 (mainly as a result of mergers), with a total membership of 517,900; of these, 41 were ICTU affiliates, with a total membership of 504,600. Hardiman (1992) cites figures showing that all but 15 of these unions had members in the public sector, and about half of all union members were employed in the public sector. During the 1980s there

Table 5.8 The main trade unions in Ireland, location of headquarters and membership

Organization	HQ	Members	Ireland	Northern Ireland
Irish Congress of Trade Unions (ICTU)	Ireland	699 190	499 560	199 630
Services, Industrial, Professional and Technical Union (SIPTU)	Ireland	197 502	190 501	7 001
Amalg. Transport and General Workers Union (ATGWU)	UK	53 536	17 506	36 530
Northern Ireland Public Services Alliance	UK	35 500	–	35 500
UNISON (health service and public sector)	UK	31 700	–	31 700
Manufacturing, Science and Finance (MSF)	UK	31 000	21 000	10 000
MANDATE (retail and distribution)	Ireland	31 308	31 308	–
Irish Municipal, Public and Civil Trade Union (IMPACT)	Ireland	31 000	31 000	–
Amalg. Engineering and Electrical Union (AEEU)	UK	27 010	8 000	19 010
Irish National Teachers Association (INTA)	Ireland	25 939	20 580	5 359
Technical, Engineering and Electrical Union (TEEU)	Ireland	24 200	24 200	–

Source: Irish Congress of Trade Unions, data as of 31 December 1996.

was a considerable drop in membership (Roche and Larregy, 1990), but this was perhaps to be expected in a decade of recession, massive unemployment, growing employer militancy, and political ambivalence towards trade unions. In the 1990s membership levels have picked up again. In December 1998, according to ICTU figures, its affiliates organized 520,900 members in Ireland (up from 459,300 in 1990). In Northern Ireland the ICTU represents 204,900 members (organized in 32 unions). Union density stood at 52 per cent in 1995, well above the European average, varying from 73 per cent in public administration, 71 per cent in transport and communication, 60 per cent in professional services, including health and education, 55 per cent in manufacturing, 49 per cent in construction, 34 per cent in commerce and finance, and 26 in other private services. Among male workers 58 per cent were unionized, against 42 per cent of female workers (National Labour Survey data).

It is possible that the status of the ICTU, in centralized negotiations with employers and the Government, as well as its involvement in conflict resolution, have cushioned the organization from the downward membership trends visible elsewhere, especially in Great Britain. Irish unions have not had to cope with a government and a programme of legislation bent on diminishing their role (Freeman and Pelletier, 1990). There appears to be greater willingness by multinational employers investing in Ireland to recognize trade unions than in the United States and the United Kingdom, where they have a record of refusing to do so.

Trade unionism in Ireland has been marked, since almost the beginning of the century, by the dominant position of large general unions (Cassells, 1989). As in Great Britain and Denmark, this reflects in part the strongly entrenched position of craft unionism in the formative stages of modern Irish trade unionism, which effectively precluded the continental pattern of industrial unionism. But it may also be attributed to the powerful impact, in the early decades of this century, of the idea of "One Big Union" as a vehicle for working-class and nationalist interests. From the foundation of an independent Irish State, trade unionism was dominated by the Irish Transport and General Workers' Union (ITGWU), later to become the Services, Industrial, Professional and Technical Union (SIPTU), by far the largest union in the country and claiming 197,502 members in 1996, or around 40 per cent of the total membership of unions affiliated to the ICTU (Nevin, 1997). The next largest Irish unions are much smaller – the Irish Municipal, Public and Civil Trade Union (IMPACT), formed by amalgamation in 1991, had some 31,000 members in 1996, as did MANDATE (the retail and distribution workers' union), UNISON (health service and public sector) and the MSF (Manufacturing, Science and Finance). At the other extreme are numerous small organizations: in 1996, almost three-quarters of the Irish unions had fewer than 3,000 members and 20 had fewer than 1,000 members in Ireland. The law requires unions and employers' associations to register in order to obtain a "bargaining licence" and qualify for immunities from certain legal effects that otherwise apply. Irish unions must prove their financial independence and have a minimum of 1,000 members. There are state supports for union mergers.

The ICTU's capacity for coordination and authoritative policy-making used to be inhibited by the fragmented character of Irish unions (Hardiman, 1992). British-based unions were deeply attached to a workplace focus on collective bargaining and opposed to incomes policies (Roche, 1992). In the light of the limited authority and comprehensiveness of the peak associations in Ireland, it is not the move away from national pay bargaining in the 1980s, but the return to centralized bargaining in later years, that is surprising and in need of further explanation (see below).

The Netherlands

Since the recent merger between the Christian and general employers' organizations, the VNO-NCW is the one and only peak organization for large and middle-sized firms in industry and services; MKB-Nederland represents SMEs; and LTO-Nederland organizes agricultural interests. Each represents the employer and trade interests of its members. VNO-NCW has about 150 affiliates representing entire sectors such as metal engineering, textiles, construction or banking, and has a tradition of direct involvement of the major multinational firms in its governing body. One of the largest affiliates, the General Employers' Association (AWVN), organizes throughout industry and services and, in an advisory role, is involved in three-quarters of the 800 company agreements (applying to some 12–14 per cent of the employed). Until 1993 the VNO maintained a central joint resistance fund in order to bolster internal discipline, and employers have jointly upheld a veto against general rounds of working-time reduction. Overall, VNO organizes around 80,000 firms, covering 80 per cent of total employment. Among the large firms, including the MNE sector, the organization rate is near complete.

In collective bargaining terms the sector has remained the dominant level: 200 multi-employer agreements applying in most manufacturing industries (except chemicals), and in construction, road haulage, commerce, banking, insurance, hospitals and in the public sector, cover 65–67 per cent of all workers (Visser and van der Meer, 1998). Regional agreements are rare. This distribution has hardly changed in the past 15 years. MNEs (Philips, Shell, Unilever, AKZO-Nobel and Heineken) have traditionally negotiated their own collective agreements, many of which are as large as sectoral agreements and have a multi-establishment character.

In the Netherlands any group of workers can found a trade union and try to gain a place at the bargaining table. There is no exclusive jurisdiction and in nearly all bargaining units (firms, sectors) there are two or more unions. Union pluralism – historically based on religious and ideological differences – is a defining characteristic of Dutch unionism. The 1927 Collective Bargaining Act leaves employers free to decide whether and with whom they bargain; if they conclude an agreement with any particular union, its direct terms apply to members of other unions and non-members in the same domain. Any one union can be excluded, something which happens just often enough to be a real phenomenon. In the absence of a legal right of union recognition, and given the threat of exclusion, coalition building – what in the United Kingdom is called "single table bargaining" – is their best strategy. Since only unions which sign the contract are bound by its peace clause, employers are normally keen to involve all unions with significant membership. Unions prefer not to stand aside, because only signatory unions gain the union representation rights established through collective bargaining, and only they receive the annual employers' fee in compensation for the *erga omnes* application of agreements.

Low membership levels and a split between the three main federations are the weak points of Dutch trade unions (see table 5.9). Together, Dutch unions lost about one-sixth of their members in the early 1980s, but had made a strong recovery by the end of the decade. Union density dropped from over 35 per cent before 1980 to 23 per cent later in the decade, but has edged up one or two percentage points since (see figure 5.1). About one-fifth of all union members are retired from the labour force. Union density rates vary across sectors; the highest rates are in public administration, police and defence (45 per cent), education and research (43 per cent), construction (41 per cent), and transport and communication (39 per cent), falling to 31 per

Table 5.9 The main trade unions in the Netherlands

Organization	Members	% Women
FNV: Netherlands Trade Union Confederation (15 unions)	1 227 336	25.6
1. Bondgenoten (manufactruing, transport, services, agriculture)	495 903	
2. AbvaKabo (central and local government, health, universities)	330 808	
3. Bouw en Houtbond (construction and wood)	162 071	
4. Algemene Onderwijsbond (teachers)	71 593	
5. KIEM (arts, information, media and printing)	49 295	
6–15: Police, military, hairdressers, soccer players, etc.	117 666	
CNV: Christian-National Union Federation (13 unions)	355 407	23.7
1. CFO (central and local government, health, universities)	86 518	
2. Bedrijvenbond (manufacturing, services, agriculture)	64 389	
3. Onderwijsbond CNV (teachers)	57 800	
4. Hout- en Bouwbond (wood and construction)	49 227	
5. Dienstenbond (private services)	33 054	
6–13: Police, military, transport, arts, churches, etc.	64 419	
MHP: Federation of Staff and Managerial Personnel (3)	151 972	17.9
Independent unions	ca. 200 000	31.3
Total	**1 914 000**	**25.1**

Source: Central Statistical Office (CBS) and Dues database, data as of 1998.

cent in manufacturing, 25 in medical, cultural and social services, 19 per cent in banking and insurance, 17 per cent in hotels and restaurants, and 14 per cent in business services. The male-female difference has narrowed, but at 20 per cent the female density rate is still much lower than the male rate of 33 per cent. Among part-time workers (20–34 hours) density is 25 per cent, compared to 13 per cent of those working between 12 and 19 hours per week, 3 per cent of those working less than 12 hours, and 31 per cent of full-time workers (survey data for 1997).

There are three main peak federations, of which the FNV, with 1.2 million members, or 62 per cent of all union members in the country in 1996, is the most important. The FNV was formed between 1976 and 1982 through a merger of the Social Democratic and Catholic unions. Its largest affiliate in the private sector, FNV-Bondgenoten, organizes almost all manufacturing industries and private services, and negotiates around 700 of the 1,000 collective agreements in existence. The coordinating abilities of this union are helped by the fact that it maintains a strong central strike fund which is used to prevent large wage differences across sectors and firms. The second largest FNV affiliate is the public employees' union, AbvaKabo, which negotiates the eight sectoral agreements in the government sector, the major national agreements in the health service, and numerous company agreements in privatized firms, such as the PTT or utilities. This union is currently preparing a cartel, possibly followed by a merger, with other public sector unions (teachers, police). The

Christian-National Union Confederation (CNV) has around 350,000 members. Its structure mirrors that of the FNV of which it is nearly always the junior partner. The majority of its membership is in the public sector. The Federation of White-Collar and Senior Staff (VHP) organizes occupational and company unions in most large firms and in the public sector. This organization has recently attracted a number of independent unions and is in a process of restructuring and growth. Around 10 per cent of all union members are organized in unaffiliated unions, mainly in public services, nursing, teaching, transport and construction. The FNV and CNV are comparatively strong peak federations, with an entrenched position in national policy forums and a well-established capacity to influence the behaviour of affiliates. In the 1970s this capacity was severely tested by the rivalry between unions in the public and private sectors.

5.4 PATTERNS OF COLLECTIVE BARGAINING AND COORDINATION

For workers, collective bargaining has a protective function (ensuring adequate pay and working conditions), a voice function (allowing the expression of grievances and aspirations), and a distributive function (providing a share in economic progress and the fruits of training, technology and productivity). For employers, the most important function of collective bargaining is probably the aspect of conflict regulation. Management control is more effective when legitimized through joint rules (Flanders, 1975). A "peace rule" may ensure continuous production while the agreement is in force. Collective bargaining relieves the State and politicians from the complex task of setting standards in an area with high conflict potential and a high risk of implementation failures.

Under single-employer bargaining each employer negotiates independently; under multi-employer bargaining employers combine in associations which have received a mandate to conduct negotiations and reach binding decisions. In Western Europe – unlike Japan and the United States – multi-employer bargaining has been the dominant mode of wage setting since the Great Depression of the 1930s. The major exception in Europe is Great Britain, where multi-employer bargaining disappeared in nearly all sectors in the course of the 1980s (Brown, 1993). In Austria, Denmark, Ireland and the Netherlands, multi-employer bargaining constitutes the dominant pattern, although in the Netherlands multinational and large firms tend to negotiate their own agreements. Ireland is the exception in that central rather than sectoral bargaining is the dominant form of multi-employer bargaining; in the other three countries sectoral bargaining replaced central bargaining in the early 1980s.

Multi-employer bargaining may be advantageous for workers to the extent that it generalizes the three above-mentioned (protective, voice, and distributive) functions across sectors, occupations and firms. Moreover, multi-employer bargaining tends to make the trade unions into a political force and may become an instrument for solidarity-based goals such as the achievement of full employment, or for pursuing egalitarian wage policies. There are also conditions under which employers find common bargaining to their advantage. First, multi-employer bargaining has a "cartelizing" effect by taking wages out of competition. In recessions it may help employers to avoid "cut-throat" competition; under conditions of tight labour markets it may protect them against "whip-sawing" union tactics. This aspect matters most for employers in labour-intensive industries. Second, multi-employer bargaining takes place far away from the workplace and may help to keep distributional conflicts out of the workplace. Sisson (1987) has shown that in many continental European countries the desire to insulate workplace management from union influence has been a major motive for employers to create or go along with centralized bargaining. Third, multi-employer bargaining may constitute a saving on bargaining or transaction costs, especially in homogeneous industries and in the case of SMEs. Finally, multi-employer bargaining may be used by governments as a means of macroeconomic governance aimed at keeping inflation low (Blyth, 1979; Headey, 1970; Traxler, 1996) or may assist in producing goods with positive external factors, such as high industrial training standards, apprenticeship systems, industrial peace, and so on (Soskice, 1990; Streeck, 1992).

There are strong intra-class differences in the balance of advantages and disadvantages of multi-employer bargaining (Svensen, 1989; Iversen, 1996). Multi-employer bargaining does restrict the freedom of individual companies and local unions to do as they like, and they may have deep ideological reasons to prefer autonomy ("self-government"), even at the expense of economic rewards. Air traffic controllers or medical doctors generally prefer single-employer as well as single-occupation bargaining as the best strategy to realise their demands. Unskilled workers generally do better through industry-wide or even economy-wide bargaining. From the point of view of workers, multi-employer bargaining has advantages as well as disadvantages.

The decentralization of collective bargaining can be observed in nearly all countries and is mainly driven by employers in the exposed sector of the economy who seek more room to manoeuvre in response to international competition and technological change (Streeck, 1996). It also feeds on growing worker diversity (Locke et al., 1995). However, workers may also gain advantages: the voice function is probably more intense when bargaining is conducted "on site", because workers will have more control over their representatives. New issues and developments are more swiftly recognized and it seems easier to monitor what management does. Single-level bargaining is exceptional; in nearly all countries unions and employers meet and negotiate at two or more levels. In the case of multi-level bargaining it is crucial that "the different levels are integrated so as to prevent them from mutually blocking their respective purpose" (Traxler, 1994, p. 174). The authority of central organizations of employers and national trade union centres over local bargaining and the strength of the mutual obligations enshrined in higher-level agreements (in particular the peace clause and procedures for conflict resolution) are critical conditions for the efficiency and effectiveness of such multi-level solutions. Internal coordination, contract compliance and conflict resolution mechanisms are also vitally important.

Let us consider the specific collective bargaining regime in place in each of these four countries in turn.

Austria: Wage leadership

According to Traxler (1997), there is some misunderstanding in the literature concerning the nature of Austria's collective bargaining system. Some authors have tried to explain why Austria, with its supposedly highly centralized system, is among the countries with the greatest wage dispersion (see OECD, 1996), in stark contrast to the Scandinavian countries (e.g. Rowthorn, 1992; see also figure 5.3). The puzzle can be resolved, however, by distinguishing

Figure 5.3 Centralization of wage bargaining and dispersion of earnings in 15 OECD countries, 1973–86

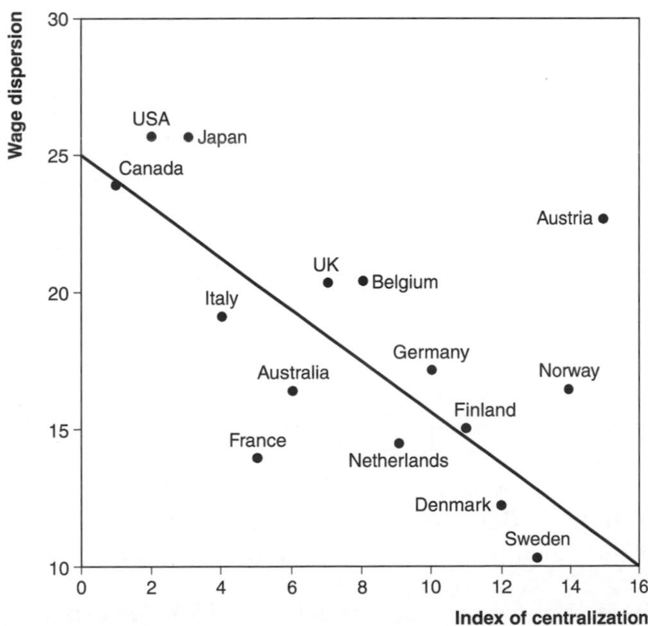

Note: Dispersion of earnings is the variance of the logarithm of hourly earnings by industry based on an average of United Nations, ILO, and United States Bureau of Labor Statistics (BLSA) data for the year 1973–83 (United Nations), 1975–84 (ILO), and 1975–86 (BLSA); a higher number means a higher level of centralization. There is no explicit period of reference for the centralization index, but it is reasonably applied to the 1970s and early 1980s.

Sources: Dispersion of earnings: Richard Freeman: "Labour market institutions and economic performance", in *Economic Policy* (1988), pp. 64–80; Centralization: Lars Calmorfs and John Driffill: "Centralization of wage bargaining", in *Economic Policy* (1988), pp. 14–61.

between centralization and coordination of bargaining (Traxler, Kittel, and Lengauer, 1996). In the early 1980s, collective bargaining switched from the central to the sectoral level in Austria. Since then, Austria has undergone, like the Netherlands and Denmark, but more slowly, a process of "organized" or "centralized" decentralization (Crouch, 1995; Due et al., 1995; Traxler, 1997; Visser, 1997): a step-wise shift to lower bargaining levels, while retaining coordination across bargaining tables through the development of a common bargaining agenda and – very strongly in Austria and the Netherlands – concertation of policy objectives and instruments between the social partners and the Government.

The high degree of coordination present in the Austrian system presupposes, firstly, that the representatives of the (umbrella) organizations of business and labour at the federal level are capable of making binding commitments on behalf of their associations and, secondly, that the representatives possess quite extensive negotiating powers in the political process. There is a high degree of centralization within each of the major interest federations. Unlike all other European countries, however, centralization in Austria has to be understood as monopoly of representation, meaning that there are neither competing trade unions nor competing employers' associations. Coordination across sectors has mainly been performed by the Parity Commission (PK, Paritätische Kommission) and was based on the bargaining parties' obligation to apply jointly for the Commission's approval before renegotiating agreements. Coordination was aimed at influencing the *timing* of bargaining rounds; no overt attempt was made to prescribe the outcome. Since the early 1980s, the metalworking industry has de facto gained the role of wage leader, and Parity Commission coordination has correspondingly declined in importance. A series of sectoral agreements in the 1980s represented a further step towards decentralization by combining a cut in working time with opening clauses allowing management and works council to negotiate over flexible working-time schedules. In 1993 an opening clause on wage flexibility was agreed for the metalworking industry, authorizing management to negotiate with the works council a pay increase below the rate stipulated by the collective agreement in order to facilitate joint measures to secure employment. It seems that this clause was not very widely used (Auer and Welte, 1994). The 1997 amendment to the working-time law, however, explicitly transfers the task of determining the conditions of working-time flexibilization to the sectoral social partners.

Wage leadership became the predominant bargaining mode during the 1980s (table 5.9) and remains so today. The annual sequence of collective agreements is always the same (with some minor exceptions such as the barbers, who have 18-month agreements). The Wage Committee (Lohnunterausschuss) of the Parity Commission opens the wage round, usually in October or November, by giving the go-ahead to the union of metalworkers (GMBE), followed by the union of salaried employees (GPA), then trade and commerce, financial services, and other industries producing for the home market. If the metalworkers start with high wage increases, the other sectors follow suit. If they start with low ones, the others do the same. However, more variation in effective wages is found than this procedure might suggest, reflecting differences in the economic situation of particular sectors. Since the early 1990s, the GMBE has cooperated closely with the GPA union of white-collar employees, and the two unions have conducted joint negotiations for blue- and white-collar employees in the metal industry. This in turn sets the pattern for GPA agreements for white-collar workers in the rest of the manufacturing industry. The agreements negotiated by the GMBE and the GPA (covering around 17 per cent of all employees subject to bargaining rights) define the framework for all other bargaining rounds, including negotiations in the public sector.

Pace-setting by the metal industry adopts a macro-level approach to wage coordination, since the GMBE bases its demands on overall productivity increases rather than the metalworking industry's (higher) productivity growth. According to Traxler (1997) there are two main reasons for this macro orientation. First, in response to the metal industry's exposure to the world market and its economic heterogeneity, the GMBE tends to tailor its demands to the situation of the industry's weaker subsectors and firms. This brings wage policy closer to overall productivity increases. Second, in 1983 the GMBE proposed that macroeconomic growth and inflation should be the main criteria for wage policy, and that the exposed sector be recognized as the pace-setter for the sheltered sector. This concept was subsequently accepted by all ÖGB affiliates.

For reasons of inter-union balance, the exposed sector – for which the GMBE is the most important union – can maintain its leading role in relation to public sector unions only if the union refrains from fully exploiting the metal industry's higher productivity increases. However, Austrian wage bargaining is known to produce considerable levels of wage drift, without this apparently being a source of great concern. In 1992, actual earnings for workers in manufacturing were on average 23 per cent above collectively agreed pay rates (Guger, 1993). Traxler (1997) suggests that the collective bargaining law exerts a downward ratchet effect on interest representation by the works council. On the one hand, the law confines works council activities to narrowly defined issues, which must be dealt with in a cooperative manner. On the other, the works council's ability to exploit its rights depends significantly on union strength, and particularly on a high union density in the enterprise. Additional pay and benefits are conceded either unilaterally by management, or settled in negotiations where an effective works council exists. In large enterprises, a second bargaining round often occurs, customarily resulting in a plant agreement. Since works councils are not formally authorized to negotiate wage increases, they can only conclude informal (i.e. legally unenforceable) plant agreements on issues of pay. This somewhat restricts pay drift and makes it reversible, allowing for a relatively flexible adaptation of wages to the business cycle and to company performance (for a slightly more sceptical view, see Walther, 1997).

An interesting feature of Austrian collective bargaining in manufacturing is that the unions negotiate not only annual changes in the minimum rate of pay (per job) but also so-called "Ist-Lohne" or "effective wage rates" which govern the actual pay increases. Such rates are also negotiated on a sectoral basis and cover around 25 per cent of all private sector employment; they are mainly found in the metalworking industry and among white-collar employees in industry. By negotiating the actual wage rises above the minimum rate of change, the Austrian metalworkers' union has been able to pursue its stability-oriented wage policy with even greater rigour (Guger and Polt, 1994). Often enough, the GMBE and GPA negotiate a lower increase in effective than in minimum pay scales. In 1997, for example, the rates of change were 2.1 per cent for the GMBE and 2.7 per cent for the GPA.

Distributional considerations do not appear to be a critical element of the ideology of Austrian trade unions. Solidaristic wage policy goals were never among the ÖGB's priorities. The choice for stability and employment was at the expense of a solidaristic wage policy of the type found in Denmark and the Netherlands before 1982. Over a period of three decades (1960–90), real wages increased at an annual rate of 3.3 per cent compared with average annual productivity growth of 3.1 per cent (Guger, 1993). The existing wage structure is generally accepted by the Austrian unions and, to the extent that changes in the functional distribution of income are desired, the legislative process is regarded as the appropriate instrument. Austria was the only country in the study by Flanagan, Soskice and Ulman (1983) of incomes policies in the 1970s (which also included Denmark and the Netherlands, but not Ireland) "in which union wage policy has been primarily directed at the securing of employment rather than at egalitarian or other objectives". It is against this background that inter-sectoral wage differentials in Austria are higher than in any other Western country with the exception of Canada, Japan, and the United States (Guger, 1993; OECD, 1996).

Denmark: Centralized decentralization

Until the early 1980s wage determination in Denmark was marked by two central institutional features – a more extensive system of indexation linking nominal wage changes to changes in consumer prices than was found in most other countries (though comparable with the Netherlands before 1982; see Braun, 1976), together with centralized collective bargaining over basic wage rates, and at the same time a persistent and significant wage drift. According to Flanagan, Soskice and Ulman (1983), the indexation system had contributed significantly to the momentum of Danish inflation in the 1970s and had built the effects of external price shocks – such as the 1973 oil price increases – into the domestic cost structure more rapidly than elsewhere. With accelerating inflation, indexation payments represented a growing proportion of wage increases during the 1970s, and the government's incomes policy came to be focused on possible alterations; finally, in the 1980s, the indexation arrangements were suspended, and then abolished in 1986 (Boje and Kongshoj Madsen, 1994, p. 103). After 1983 public sector employees could no longer expect automatic increases in their wages in parallel with the growth of private sector wages. All this is very comparable to the combination of policies (hard currency policy, tight fiscal policies, decoupling of public and private sector wages, wage moderation, and suspension of the indexation mechanism) that were adopted in the Netherlands in 1982–83, after a similarly troublesome period of crisis and frequent, but not very effective, state intervention in wage bargaining.

The Danish LO, like its Swedish sister organization, had a strong predilection towards an egalitarian or "solidaristic" wage policy. It had to implement its strategy under much less favourable organizational conditions, however (Elvander, 1990). The Danish union movement is much more fragmented than the Swedish one and reflects the stronger influence of its craft origins. LO bargaining objectives were dominated by consideration of distribution, as revealed by a tendency to negotiate equal absolute wage increases for all workers. During the 1970s this policy was extended to include a concerted effort to negotiate higher relative wages for women. This egalitarian wage policy, negotiated at the central level, suited the very large union of unskilled workers (SiD) and the women workers' union (KAD) more than many of the craft unions (Metal and others), but the latter were usually able to restore their relative pay through compensatory movements in non-collectively agreed wages and benefits (wage drift), frustrating the distributional objectives of the LO (Flanagan, Soskice and Ulman, 1983).

Throughout the 1970s, wage drift continued to contribute significantly to Danish wage inflation, accounting for more than 40 per cent of earnings growth. For the LO, the fact that a significant element of earnings emanated from uncontrolled as well as unauthorized local bargaining eroded the standing of the federation as a source of regulation. For employers, wage drift constituted an element of uncertainty in labour cost trends once a central agreement had been signed; as such, it was bound to lead to doubts whether they should continue negotiating (central) agreements that did not stick.

In Denmark, Parliament intervened to impose a settlement in the wage bargaining rounds of 1975, 1977, 1979, 1985 and 1998 (table 5.10). The positive side of such intervention and the rationale for it is that, in the short run, industrial peace is secured and major conflict avoided. There is a downside: the peace obligation in collective agreements has generally been justified on the grounds that agreements are subject to endorsement by the membership; this legitimacy is lost if settlements are repeatedly imposed by Parliament. Thus, from a long-term perspective, intervention by Parliament in collective bargaining must be minimal if the system is to work (Due et al., 1995, p. 122). In the 1970s and

Table 5.10 Patterns of bargaining and state involvement

Year	Austria	Denmark	Ireland	Netherlands
1970	Central wage bargaining *Wage Committee*, bipartite		*Price and Incomes Bill* Intervention threat	*Wage Act*: return to free wage bargaining, govt. retains some control
1971	"	Central agreement	NWA, bipartite	*Govt. intervention*
1972	"	"	NWA, bipartite	Central agreement, tripartite
1973	"	Central agreement	No agreement	Agreement fails, pattern bargaining
1974	"	"	NWA, bipartite	*Govt. intervention*
1975	"	*State intervention*	NWA, *govt. involvement*	Agreement fails, pattern bargaining
1976	"	"	NWA, *govt. involvement*	*Govt. intervention*
1977	"	*State intervention*	No agreement	Agreement fails, pattern bargaining
1978	"	"	NWA, *govt. involvement*	Agreement fails, pattern bargaining
1979	"	*State intervention*	National Understanding, tripartite	Agreement fails, *govt. intervention*
1980	"	"	National Understanding, tripartite	*Govt. intervention*
1981	"	**Some decentralization**	**Decentralized bargaining**	*Govt. intervention*
1982	**Wage leadership metal**, synchronization, Wage Committee/ÖGB	"	"	*Govt. intervention* **Central agreement, bipartite, some decentralization**
1983	"	Central agreement	"	"
1984	"	"	"	"
1985	"	*State intervention*	"	"
1986	"	"	"	1982 agreement prolonged
1987	"	**Declaration of intent (tripartite); agreement to decentralize (4 yrs.)**	**Central agreement (1987–91), govt. involvement**	"
1988	"	"		"
1989	"	"		Policy Memorandum tripartite, four years
1990	"	"		Employers withdraw from Policy Memorandum
1991	"	**Decentralized bargaining (shifting wage leaders)**	**Central agreement (1991–94), govt. involvement**	Decentralized bargaining

1992	"	"		"
1993	"	Idem		*Govt. threat*, **bipartite agreement (1994–96), decentralization**
1994	"	"	**Central agreement (1994–97), govt. involvement**	"
1995	"	Idem		"
1996	"	"		Agreement prolonged
1997	"	Idem, plus attempt central agreement working time	**Central agreement (1997–2000). Govt. involvement**	**Agreement renewed (Agenda 2002)**
1998	"	*State intervention*	"	"

early 1980s, wages rose faster than inflation, and increases in unit labour costs were larger than in partner countries, in particular Germany and Sweden. The limited authority and coverage of the DA was part of the problem; the rather fragmented union structure and the constant rivalry between unions representing unskilled and skilled workers, especially between SiD and Dansk Metalarbejderforbund, made the Danish LO much less effective than its Swedish counterpart (Visser, 1990; Wallerstein and Golden, 1997, p. 718). Like in Sweden, and in many other European union movements of the 1970s and 1980s, there was the impact of the rising influence of the public sector unions, in some cases challenging the wage leadership of the exposed sector. Danish employers drew the conclusion that something had to change.

According to Due, Kongshoj Madsen and Jensen (1997), the decision to seek a more decentralized approach to collective bargaining matured in the 1970s, although its implementation – together with the reorganization of the relevant employers' association and bargaining cartels – took place ten years later. First, the labour market had to change. In the slack labour markets of the 1980s, "the risk of handing over control of wage formation to the collective bargainers and market forces was limited, given the reduced bargaining position of the unions" (Boje and Kongshoj Madsen, 1994).

The suspension of the indexation system in Denmark led to "a striking recovery in the influence of union bargainers" (Scheuer, 1997b, p. 162). Self-restraint by means of central wage bargaining failed and necessitated intervention, yet again, by the Government in 1985. The final settlement allowed only small increases, but local unions did not feel particularly obliged to comply – it was not their agreement. Between 1984 and 1989 private sector wage growth varied between 4 and 10 per cent annually (but over the 1980s real wage growth was more moderate than in the 1970s). The problem of control and wage drift remained and could now be placed at the doorstep of the decentralized system, unable to prevent wage competition between different sectors and branches (Scheuer, 1997b). A fair proportion of local wage drift represented the continuing bottlenecks in the Danish labour market. The problem of drift was also a concern to the DA and LO. In 1987 they signed a so-called "declaration of intent", jointly with government, in which they undertook to keep Danish wage increases below the level of Denmark's main trading partners (Due et al., 1995; Meinertz, 1993, p. 81). (In 1998, following the strike over working time, the president of the LO declared the end of this "agreement", but called on the employers and government to start negotiations on a new "pact" – see Knudsen, 1998.)

That same year 1987 the employers in metal engineering (JA) and a cartel of unions (CO-Metal) led by the skilled metalworkers' union concluded an unusual four-year contract with a provision for adjustment after two years. This settlement "was virtually 'carbon-copied' by the other bargaining units" (Scheuer 1997b, p. 163); it meant a change in wage leadership (Boje and Kongshoj Madsen, 1994, p. 100) from SiD (unskilled workers) in 1985 to Metal in

1987, with an increased role of the salaried employees within the CO-Metal coalition in 1987, 1989 and 1991. In 1989 a group of unions led by HK (white-collar employees) was the first to settle, and in that same year the public sector introduced new pension schemes for lower-level employees and unskilled workers, which were subsequently copied by the private sector. In 1991 the public sector was the first to reach agreement over wages, followed by the private sector.

In addition to these changes in wage leadership, there was decentralization in a further sense: a shift from standard job-related wages to person-related pay by means of the gradual replacement of what in Denmark is called the "normal wage" by the "minimum wage" system. Under the normal wage system the standard rates, negotiated at the sectoral or national level, cannot be improved through local bargaining. This system is (still) prevalent in the financial sector, transport (for manual workers), and in the public sector. Under the "normal wage" system, the role of the local union representatives is mainly to monitor compliance, not to renegotiate wages. Under the minimum wage system, only minimum pay levels are regulated through sectoral bargaining; this was originally the domain of craftworkers, who could negotiate piece rates locally. Actual levels are determined through additional local pay bargaining.

In Denmark local bargaining occurs more or less on an annual basis, but under a peace obligation, and takes the form of pay sum bargaining over the "aggregate size of the pay rise for the group of workers represented by the shop steward" (Scheuer, 1997b, p. 167), leaving it to the management to allocate the award to individual workers. Hence, it remains possible for management to link pay to performance or ability, and for stewards to assert their role despite the fact that the main bargaining process takes place outside the plant. In the collective agreement for 1991 the wage system for unskilled workers was changed. Previously their "normal" wages had been negotiated by the external unions and fixed for the whole agreement period; the new collective agreement fixed a minimum wage level, and a significant add-on was negotiated at establishment level in a performance-linked system. Furthermore, the 1991 agreement introduced different forms of flexible working time. All this adds up to considerable decentralization. In the LO-DA area (applying to 25 per cent of all unionized workers), only 16 per cent of all employees in 1997 were covered by the "normal wage" system compared with 34 per cent in 1989 (DA figures, reported by Scheuer (1997b, p. 165), who comments that "this indicates that decisions about actual pay are being moved from the sectoral to the workplace level and sometimes to the level of the individual"). Minimum pay systems have increased from 62 per cent in 1985 to 67 per cent in 1995; the remainder (17 per cent) have no pay clause in collective agreements.

An interesting aspect of the 1995 bargaining round in Denmark was the insertion of so-called "social chapters" in addition to issues like training, maternity pay, leave systems, and flexible working time. Following a proposal by the Public Conciliator, wage negotiations are encouraged "to consider appropriate suggestions to further the employment of persons who due to health problems, reduced working ability or long-term absence from the labour market, cannot be employed in a full-time, normal job. The intention must be to reach local agreements ... which must be approved by the parties to the collective agreement and might include deviations from the normal regulations on wages, working time, etc." (cited in Lind, 1997, p. 151). According to Lind, the intention of the LO, when asking for such social chapters, was to negotiate rules on how to deal with people who, for one reason or another (physical disability or long-term unemployment), are considered to be less productive than other workers. The LO wants to set minimum standards of pay in order to prevent "normal labour" being priced out of their jobs. In particular, the public sector unions have experienced strong downward pressure on wages, which they attribute to the creation of spiralling number of subsidized or low-paid jobs. Social chapters are "typically not very detailed" and are mainly declarations of "good will" in order "to ensure that persons who cannot meet the normal standards of collective agreements can find a place in the labour market" (Lind, 1997, p. 150).

Ireland: National recovery through centralized and concerted policies

The voluntarist nature of Irish industrial relations has put collective bargaining at the centre of all union activity, and it has been long-term public policy to support this. But support is not unqualified: in recent decades the belief has become widespread that the inflationary effects of collective bargaining must be reined in and that this task becomes easier in the context of centrally determined pay norms. How these pay norms are to be set is another matter, however. Historically, collective bargaining in Ireland has proceeded on several levels. General pay increases have tended to be determined at the most centralized level available; so-called "special" increases – meaning all those pay increases justified by something other than inflation, such as productivity, changes in working practices, relative pay, and so forth – have tended to be negotiated at the level of the firm or, sometimes, the plant; other terms and conditions of employment, and matters of local procedure, have also been the subject of lower-level bargaining. Industry-wide bargaining, common in other countries, has become rare in Ireland, although it does exist in certain sectors, such as some domestic services and construction.

Following widespread industrial unrest in the 1960s, the Government published a Prices and Incomes Bill in 1970 (table 5.10), in which it threatened to exercise statutory control over wage and price increases (McCarthy, 1973). Employers and unions were sufficiently jolted to set up the Employer-Labour Conference, where they negotiated a National Wage Agreement (NWA) for 1971, followed by similar agreements in 1972, 1974, 1975, 1976 and 1978 (O'Brien, 1981). These agreements, which set the agreed rate of pay increases for the entire national workforce, were initially deemed a success: they contributed to industrial peace, adopted recognizable principles of equity (including special provisions for women and the lower paid), were generally non-inflationary, and stabilized what had previously been a chaotic picture. According to some observers, however, "in the period 1970–81 there was extensive evasion of national wage norms" (Roche and Larregy, 1990, p. 65). In any case, after the oil shock of 1973–74, the Irish Government was no longer prepared to leave the matter entirely in the hands of employers and unions; it began to seek tripartite agreements (table 5.10). The significance of this development was that a precedent was set for an annual or pluri-annual bargaining round with unions and employers, in which the subject matter for negotiation included aspects of government policy and parliamentary initiatives. Economic recession had pushed Ireland further down the road towards corporatism, and established a tendency which has persisted since.

In 1979 the Government was determined to secure non-inflationary growth through centralized collective bargaining, and when the proposal for another National Wage Agreement was rejected by the unions, it offered the social partners a new concept, described as a "National Understanding" (table 5.10). Voluntary pay restraint was to be combined with a social contract style agreement on economic and social policy. But the concept remained a mere proposal, partly because the employers were now determined to have local pay bargaining, and partly because the Government had been unable – or in some cases unwilling – to deliver on the commitments it had given in the areas of economic and social policy; job creation targets, in particular, were not met. From 1981 until 1987 there was no central agreement, and collective bargaining was mostly conducted on a company-by-company or group-by-group basis. With little apparent success, the Government tried to use its position as the country's largest employer (around half of all union members in Ireland work in the public sector, which absorbs about one-third of employment outside agriculture) to set the trend. In the mid-1980s the Government attempted to impose a norm through pay guidelines, but these guidelines were largely ignored in the private sector, and should more realistically be seen as opening shots in the public service pay negotiations (van Prondszynski, 1997).

The central agreement of 1987 marked a major change. The incoming Fianna Fáil minority administration embarked on a new attempt to enter into a national agreement, at the prompting of the Irish Congress of Trade Unions (ICTU). Later that year the Government, unions, employers, and a small number of other interest groups (including a farmers' organization) entered into a national agreement entitled the Programme for National Recovery, PNR (table 5.11). Covering the period to the end of 1990, the Programme expressed the parties' commitment to providing an economic climate conducive to growth, constructing a more equitable tax system, reducing social inequalities, and creating employment. Pay rises were not to

Table 5.11 Wage increases under centralized bargaining in Ireland, 1987–2000

Programme	Period	Year	Terms
PNR: Programme for National Recovery	1987–91		Average 2.5% per annum wage increase
PESP: Programme for Economic and Social Progress	1991–94	1	4% wage increase
		2	3% wage increase (plus 3% contingent local increase)
		3	3.75% wage increase
PCW: Programme for Competitiveness and Work	1994–97	1	2.5% wage increase
		2	2.5% wage increase
		3	2.5% wage increase
Partnership 2000 for Inclusion, Employment and Competitiveness	1997–2000	1	2.5% wage increase
		2	2.25% wage increase (plus 2% contingent local increase)
		3	1.5% wage increase first half 1% wage increase second half

Source: Adapted from Turner and D'Art, 1997.

exceed 2.5 per cent a year, and a special provision was made for the low paid: there was a higher percentage increase for the first £120 of weekly pay, and a flat-rate minimum increase. The basic similarities between the PNR and the National Understandings of 1979 and 1980 are that both deal with wage moderation, on the one hand, and issues of social and economic policy, on the other. There, however, the similarity ends. The PNR was an agreement covering three years; the pay terms of the PNR were not fixed norms, but guidelines which had, in the private sector at least, to be converted into agreed rates through local bargaining (thus meeting a major employer demand); and the references to economic and social policy were to a much lesser extent government commitments, but rather targets for all relevant parties participating in an ongoing concertation process. The job-creation targets were for the private sector, rather than based on the more traditional approach of boosting public sector employment. As it turned out, the PNR was to run side by side with a government programme of massive cost cutting in the public sector, as well as a number of other measures to reduce inflation and the public deficit.

On the surface, at least, the PNR was remarkably successful. Pay bargaining at the local level, which was to continue under the Programme, produced results which were almost invariably those suggested by the PNR; over the three-year period, these rates in turn were more or less in line with inflation, which fell steadily to under 3 per cent in early 1991. With strong manufacturing and export performance, job-creation targets were also generally met in the private sector. Economic growth averaging more than 4 per cent a year between 1987 and 1990 helped reduce the gap between Ireland and the stronger European economies: GDP per head rose from 64 per cent of the EU average in

1987 to 68 per cent in 1990. There was a clear fall in unit labour costs and a significant improvement in the competitiveness of the Irish economy after 1987.

Was this the effect of the PNR agreement of 1987? Walsh (1993) doubts it and attributes the success to the international economic boom of the late 1980s. Teague (1995) is more generous and points out that skilled workers might have obtained a better deal without the central agreement (as had been the case in earlier years), whereas unskilled workers would not. One of the effects of the PNR agreement was that it constrained wage rises in the sheltered sector. The PNR also induced employers to sign a framework agreement on working-time reduction, and local negotiations did result in the shortening of the working week for most workers by one hour to 39 hours. However, while the employers' federation described the PNR as an "unprecedented success", the agreement did not meet with the same degree of enthusiasm on the union side (van Prondszynski, 1997). For the duration of the PNR, the ICTU was engaged in soul-searching over its role in the agreement, and whether it should continue to operate it. In the end the PNR held together, and was followed by a similar arrangement, the Programme for Economic and Social Progress (PESP), 1991–94.

The PESP agreement described as its core objective the development of "a modern, efficient market economy with innate capacity for satisfactory and sustainable growth and discharge of the obligations of a developed social conscience". This agreement was described by a senior trade union official as one which demonstrated that "issues like taxation, inflation and economic growth are a legitimate and necessary part of the trade union agenda, since they all have bearings on the standard of living". As with the PNR, the PESP set targets for job creation: 20,000 new jobs each year in manufacturing and a similar number in the international services sector. It also acknowledged the need for special measures to help long-term unemployed persons, and the Government committed itself to enact legislation to protect part-time workers, to amend equal opportunities and unfair dismissals law, and to review other aspects such as conditions of employment, holidays and the rules governing employment agencies. As also was the case with the PNR, the PESP contained a pay policy set out in the form of a separate agreement between the unions and the employers' federation. Another aspect was employee participation. A joint declaration welcomed the development of "employee involvement" in firms, in the form of communication and consultation arrangements, financial participation schemes, quality-of-working-life programmes and quality circles.

According to one observer, the PNR and PESP agreements helped in segmenting sectors and forestalled spill-overs and "have been broadly consistent with government attempts to improve competitiveness through pursuing a 'hard ERM' monetary policy" (Teague, 1995, p. 262). He adds that in 1992 the Irish unions were among the fiercest opponents of a devaluation of the Irish pound, and takes this as an indicator of the unbalanced nature of Irish corporatism, with unions unable to decide their preferred course of economic policy.

Of perhaps greater interest for the unions and their constituency is the fact that wage dispersion in Ireland, which had risen sharply under decentralized bargaining, did stabilize after 1987 (according to data in Nolan, 1993). Under the PESP agreement the rise in wage inequality was halted, with a decrease in the private and an increase in the public sector, the latter based on performance indicators and market scarcities. The low-paid sector (especially at 50 per cent of the median) is larger in Ireland than in the other countries, comparable with Spain and Italy, but double the rates in, for instance, the Netherlands, Germany or Denmark. At 60 per cent of the median, the sector is still larger in Ireland, and roughly similar to that in the United Kingdom (Nolan, 1993).

During the final months of the PESP agreement, the trade unions and employers went through what had by now become a standard ritual, expressing serious reservations both with the national bargaining process and with the idea of another centralized agreement. In the end, however, they decided to enter into a new agreement, the Programme for Competitiveness and Work (PCW) of February 1994. This was another three-year agreement, the provisions of which, for the first time, differentiated between public service employees and other workers. The rate of increase over three years was to be 8 per cent for all groups, with some difference in timing for the public services. As with previous agreements, there were special provisions for low-paid workers. The period preceding the expiry of the PCW was characterized by the usual uncertainties and posturing on the part of all the parties. Nevertheless, early in 1996, the main trigger for another set of negotiations – the decision by the ICTU to enter into discussions on a new agreement – was followed by a period of bargaining and analysis. This time there was a larger role for bodies representing socially disadvantaged groups, such as the Irish National Organisation of the Unemployed (INOU) and the Community Platform (representing a number of voluntary organizations). In opening the negotiations between the parties, the Taoiseach (Prime Minister) listed "the fostering of increased social inclusion" as the second of six objectives of the new programme (Government press release, 23 October 1996).

A new three-year programme was agreed in mid-December 1996: Partnership 2000 for Inclusion, Employment and Competitiveness. Despite strong opposition from some trade unions (especially from its public sector affiliate, MANDATE), the ICTU ratified the agreement early in 1997. Partnership 2000 represents something of a change of direction compared with its predecessors. Unlike the previous programmes, its emphasis is not as single-mindedly focused on economic competitiveness. In its introduction, the programme lists three challenges to which it intends to give a strategic response: (a) "maintaining an effective and consistent policy approach in a period of high economic growth"; (b) "significantly reducing social disparities and exclusion, especially by reducing long-term unemployment"; and (c) "responding effectively ... to global competition and the information society". It presents a detailed programme of social, economic and fiscal policies accompanied, as has become the custom, by a separate pay agreement between the IBEC and the ICTU. This is to last for three years, with phased increases in pay during that period; as before, low-paid workers are given special protection through minimum amounts of increases for each phase. Public service pay is dealt with in an additional annex to this pay agreement, and involves the same basic phased increases, but subject to a later implementation of the first full phase.

The Netherlands: Self-regulation under a shadow of hierarchy

There are parallels between the Danish and Dutch histories of state intervention and inflationary pressures in the 1970s, despite the differences that otherwise exist between the industrial relations systems of these two countries. In the Netherlands, the tradition of state intervention in wage setting began in the Second World War, during the German occupation. Between 1945 and 1963, formally even until 1970, and thus longer than any other Western democracy, the Netherlands ran a statutory wage policy (Windmuller, 1969). Collective agreements needed prior approval from a Board of State Mediators who were bound by wage guidelines issued by the Minister of Social Affairs. These annual guidelines were subject to central negotiations and intense consultation with the central organizations of unions and employers, which kept tight control over their affiliates. Statutory wage policy disintegrated in the 1960s under the pressure of tight labour markets (official unemployment rates were in some years under 1 per cent) and considerable wage drift.

After some failed experiments with self-regulation and intermittent state intervention in the 1960s, the new Wage Act of 1970 handed responsibility for wage setting back to unions and employers. The Government retained the power to order a temporary wage stop or impose a ceiling on wages if, in its view, the economic situation justified such a step. Despite the new "freedom" of collective bargaining, the Government intervened repeatedly (in 1971, 1974, 1976, 1979, 1980, 1981, and 1982; see table 5.10). Negotiations remained centralized and were conducted annually between the peak federations but, only once, in 1972, did they reach a central agreement. In the other years, sectoral and (large) company agreements in industry set the pattern for all others. Where the Government set wage standards, all contractual arrangements that deviated from the measure were null and void, and employers were subject to penalties. As in Denmark, frequent intervention suggested to employers that the system was not working. However, radical decentralization was an option that would have penalized SMEs (a sizeable part of the membership of the main employers' federations) and was not feasible before the labour market had slackened and union bargaining power weakened. Here, too, decentralization was not implemented until the 1980s. Unions also resented government intervention (which made them seem superfluous), but they remained strongly in favour of central bargaining.

In the central agreement of November 1982 (the famous Wassenaar agreement) the central employer and union organizations secured a deal which staved off further government intervention and agreed on a set of guidelines for decentralized (sectoral and large-company) bargaining (table 5.9). The content of these guidelines was: wage moderation, non-payment of the indexation due in 1983 and 1984, with some of the money used for a cost-neutral introduction of shorter working hours (38 hours). Unlike previous agreements, this and subsequent agreements did not mention a concrete figure concerning wage growth. The Wassenaar agreement suggested that wages should stay below productivity increases and that unions should not claim compensation for price increases (in spite of the guaranteed cost-of-living adjustment or indexation clauses written into most collective contracts); this was then to become the basis for a reduction in working hours and a job-sharing policy which is cost neutral to firms. Although it was only a set of recommendations, the central organization commanded sufficient authority to make the agreement work, and in 1983 and 1984 the recommendations were largely followed (Hemerijck and Visser, 1995). Wassenaar has become the basis for a de facto system of free collective bargaining or "*Tarifautonomie*". Since 1982 there have been no more government-imposed wage measures; the Wage Act was amended in 1987, and the possibility of intervention has been restricted to a major external shock affecting the nation.

Another important change was that wage trends and wage bargaining in the public sector were no longer tied to developments in the private sector. In a system that evolved in the 1980s and was formalized in the 1990s, the public sector unions now negotiate in eight sectoral jurisdictions on behalf of approximately 850,000 civil servants, whose rights and conditions of employment (right to strike, dismissal protection, pensions, unemployment insurance) have steadily approached those in the private sector, while they have exerted greater wage restraint.

Continuing a policy of wage restraint, the central collective organizations concluded another major agreement in December 1993 (Visser, 1998a). This agreement took effect for the next four years and was more or less prolonged in 1997. It paved the way for "responsible wage growth", although, like Wassenaar, and unlike the Irish agreements discussed earlier, it did not mention any specific figure. The decisive move towards this agreement may have been the Government's threat to use its legal power and impose a wage freeze (rendering all wage increases in collective and individual contracts illegal). The central organizations set their differences aside and rescued their bilateral "autonomy". In fact, the "New Course" agreement of 1993 – besides continuing a policy of wage moderation (wage increases stayed below productivity and price increases for the next few years) and cautiously opening the way to a 36-hour working week, as demanded by the unions – became the basis for further decentralization. Whereas 15 years ago it was possible to evaluate the content of collective agreements in the Netherlands on the basis of a few leading ones (e.g. metal manufacturing, Philips, construction), this is no longer the case. Moreover, many agreements are now concluded for two, three, sometimes even four years, upsetting any common timing in the negotiations. Furthermore, whereas the scope of collective agreements has increased and more issues are included, to a greater extent the actual implementation takes place at the level of firms and company units, leaving increased space for negotiation or consultation by works councils and representatives.

Research has shown that various horizontal and vertical ties remain between the 5,000 or so negotiators who bargain the little less than 1,000 collective agreements that exist in the country (van den Toren, 1996). Before any actual bargaining there is what Walton and McKersie (1965) call a great deal of "attitudinal structuring" within and between the main organizations of employers and the unions, to some extent shaped through concertation with members and representatives of the Government. Coordination mechanisms within the main union organization, the FNV in particular, and within the employers' organization VNO-NCW have remained in place. This is why it is possible to speak of "controlled decentralization" in the Netherlands; local bargainers are on a longer lease, but on a lease nevertheless (Visser, 1998b). Under recent central agreements (in particular the "New Course", reached in 1993 and prolonged since), both employers and unions have agreed to increase, where possible, the role of works councils, union representatives or individual employees in the implementation of collective agreements, as a further tribute to the "individualization" of collective bargaining and the creation of more "choice" in what they call "mature" labour relations. It should be noted that – similar to Denmark – most collective agreements outside the public sector define minimum rates of pay and that all local bargaining takes place under the presumption of a peace obligation. However, employers report that they are reluctant to involve works councils or local union representatives in collective bargaining over pay (Teulings, 1996; Teulings and Hartog, 1998). The effective function of works councils is probably facilitated by sectoral or company bargaining away from the plant, which removes distributive conflicts from the negotiating table of works councils and enhances their capacity to reach cooperative solutions. Works councils rarely take over the role of unions; more frequently they seek union support when their bargaining task becomes more demanding. Decentralization and extension of the union role to the company and plant level is still a major task ahead for Dutch unions.

Finally, the Government casts another, more subtle "shadow of hierarchy" (Scharpf, 1993) over the bargaining table. Until fairly recently the practice of extending collective agreements – although on paper limited to specific employees – to wider groups of workers used to be a routine affair. In the early 1990s there was some pressure to remove this instrument from the statute book. In 1993 the debate over the extension of collective agreements was revived when the Government tried to lower coverage and the level of sickness and disability benefits. In a number of cases, unions were successful in repairing some of the damage through collective agreements negotiated with organized employers that were then presented for extension to non-organized employers. The Government found itself in a dilemma (Visser and Hemerijck, 1997). The proposal to abolish the 1937 Extension Law was, however, withdrawn after the change of government in 1994. From about this time the Ministry of Social Affairs and Employment tied its willingness to extend collective agreements to a show of "good will" on the part of the bargaining parties: they must allow new firms and firms in obvious economic difficulties the possibility to deviate from the sectoral agreement through "dispensation clauses", and create "low wage scales" for entrants and people with long spells of unemployment, lack of job experience or other difficulties in the labour market. This particular "shadow of hierarchy" has apparently worked. Dispensation clauses have become fairly widespread, allowing greater flexibility and variation across firms, and the number of agreements with special wage scales for new entrants and people with labour market difficulties, or low skill and experience profiles, has rapidly increased. The gap between the statutory minimum wage and the actual minimum wage level in collective agreements fell from 12 per cent of the former in 1994 to 7 per cent in 1997.

5.5 BIPARTITE AND TRIPARTITE NATIONAL INSTITUTIONS AND CORPORATISM

Joint institutions can be very helpful in preparing the ground for concertation and bargaining. Their main function is the creation of a forum for the "joint observation of facts" (Streeck, 1998) and the concatenation of various bargaining issues and tables, referred to in section 5.1.

In Austria the central institution of social dialogue and concertation is the Bipartite Commission on Wages and Prices (Paritätische Kommission für Lohn- und Preisfragen). This was established in 1957 by mutual agreement of the Government and the social partners as a provisional body, without any legislative basis, for the purpose of wage and price regulation. In addition to government representatives, the Austrian Economic Chamber (WKÖ), the Conference of Presidents of the Agricultural Chamber, the Austrian Federation of Trade Unions (ÖGB) and the Federal Chamber of Labour (BAK) are all equally represented on the Commission; the Association of Austrian Industrialists (VÖI), by contrast, has no representative on the Commission. Formal decisions are taken in plenary sessions, in which the Government members do not vote; informally, however, decisions are made in the preparatory meetings of the presidents of the four organizations and in the meetings of advisory bodies and subcommittees (Traxler, 1997). Of these, the most important are the Subcommittee on Prices (in 1992, in view of membership of the EU, its title was changed to Subcommittee on Competition Issues), the Subcommittee on Wages, and the Advisory Committee on Economic and Social Issues (Beirat für Wirtschafts- und Sozialfragen, established in 1963). The latter committee conducts scientific studies with the objective of drafting joint proposals by the social partners for the Government and for Parliament. As a rule, the Government and the parliamentary majority seek to reach agreement with the social partners, in particular where economic and social policy is concerned. The objective is to facilitate the implementation of political decisions and to underline their legitimacy vis-à-vis the public. The fact that Austria's social partners are willing to support decisions which may be painful for their members in the short run, if this is necessary to safeguard national interests, was exemplified by their participation in the decisions on the federal budgets for 1996 and 1997 which resulted in fiscal consolidation policies. Most of the expenditure cuts and tax increases foreseen in the budget plans had in fact been proposed by the Advisory Committee on Economic and Social Issues in mid-1995, and the leaders of the social partnership organizations participated in all stages of the concrete negotiations.

The Government members on the commission include the Federal Chancellor and representatives of the ministries of finance, social affairs, trade, manufacturing, industry, and agriculture and forestry. This presence may be more form than substance, however, since the Government typically abstains on wage and price decisions. In the absence of a legal basis for the institution, participation is voluntary and, as in the chambers, decisions must be unanimous, a feature that may have been significant in reducing the incentives of any one party to drop out of the institution.

In recent years, the Bipartite Commission appears to have lost much of its importance as the central forum of social partnership; the last time it was convened was in November 1995. But what used to be called the "preparatory meeting of the presidents" has survived as a "summit of the social partners", and, on a lower level, the meeting of the organizations' general secretaries have also gained importance. The subcommittees of the commission continue to function smoothly – perhaps the reason why no need is felt to convene the commission as such (Traxler, 1997). The Subcommittee on Wages consists of two representatives each from the WKÖ and the ÖGB, and one representative each from the chambers of labour and agriculture. There is no wage guideline or rule that it enforces, and it has no ultimate authority to influence the size of the wage increase or any other benefits. Instead, the principal role of the subcommittee is in deciding when to start new wage negotiations, thus influencing the period of validity of collective agreements and helping to ensure a degree of coordination through synchronization (Chaloupek, 1995).

In Denmark, as in Austria, unions and employers, mainly through their peak associations, are involved in drafting legislation and in implementing the provisions subsequently passed in Parliament. A consensus has developed that, particularly in the arena of labour relations and labour market regulation, prior agreement with the social partners (initially peak associations but now wider) is required before legislation is passed. On economic policy their influence is also channelled informally, although since 1963 there is an Economic Advisory Council (Det Økonomisk Råt), with representatives from the social partners under the chair of three professional economists (a total of 29 members, from government agencies, social partners, plus the president of the central bank, and leading economists). Representation on councils and advisory bodies, once dominated by the LO and the DA, has become broader (Due, Madsen and Jensen, 1997, p. 129).

For the purpose of concertation of social economic policies and wage bargaining the two most important bodies in the Netherlands are the Foundation of Labour (Stichting van de Arbeid, STAR) and the Social-Economic Council (Sociaal-Economische Raad, SER). STAR is co-chaired by the presidents of the FNV and VNO-NCW, and is the forum in which the various central accords of recent years were negotiated. It also issues various guidelines, studies, recommendations or advice on numerous issues. Smaller, but basically with the same union and employer representatives (eight on either side), STAR is housed in the building of the SER. In addition to 11 union and 11 employer representatives, the SER also includes 11 government-appointed experts, including the president of the Netherlands Central Bank and the director of the Central Planning Bureau, the Government's economic forecasting institute. Once the "apex" of corporatism and elite cooperation (Lijphart, 1968), the SER saw its capacity to offer unanimous advice and influence government policy decline during the 1970s and 1980s. In 1995 Parliament abolished the council's prerogative to be consulted over every piece of social and economic legislation, but it appears that this has shocked the council into new activity. In recent years the SER has produced more unanimous advice than in preceding decades. Twice each year, at the time of the budget and the next round of wage negotiations, there is intense consultation between the social partners and a delegation of the Cabinet, led by the Prime Minister. This takes place mainly within the STAR.

In Ireland an Employer-Labour Conference was set up in 1970. It is an ad hoc body, with no statutory basis. Its original purpose was to rationalize pay bargaining after a period of turbulence in the late 1960s, and to avert the Government's threat to introduce a statutory incomes policy (McCarthy, 1973). The conference is bipartite or tripartite in nature: members are nominated in equal numbers by the ICTU and various employer bodies, but the employer nominees include government representatives; in any case, its conduct since the mid-1970s has been tripartite, with the Government taking a distinct line in its deliberations. During the 1970s the Conference was responsible for negotiating the succession of National Wages Agreements (table 5.10), but since around 1980 it has merely been a forum for union-employer discussions: recent national bargaining has taken place elsewhere. The first multi-annual Recovery Pact (1987–91) was prepared in the tripartite National Economic and Social

Council (NESC), created at the time of Ireland's entry into the European Community, in 1973. A joint strategy report of the NESC uncovered the deplorable state of the Irish economy in the mid-1980s and convinced union leaders and employers' representatives to take a joint initiative and approach the Government with a rescue plan. As part of this first pact, and for the purpose of monitoring its results, the social partners created a Central Review Committee, whose members also include representatives from government departments. In 1993, as part of the third pact and in an attempt to widen the societal basis of concertation, the National Economic and Social Forum (NESF) was founded. The NESF includes members of social community groups, associations of the unemployed and voluntary organizations. These groups were included in the negotiations on the most recent pact. More than in the three previous pacts, the 1997–2000 pact stresses the need to articulate the partnership approach at the local level, not unlike the approach of the Dutch central agreement of 1993. ICTU (1993) recognizes that building a "supply-side" dimension to Ireland's corporatist approach is needed and argues in favour of cooperation with employers in diffusion of policies and a participation approach at the local level.

5.6 THE ROLE OF SOCIAL DIALOGUE AND SOCIAL LEARNING: AN EVALUATION

The role of social dialogue or concertation – recalling our earlier definition – is to improve the quality of information across actors and policy domains, so as to speed up the response time to external shocks, and the "goodness of fit" between policies. Concertation often begins with a shared awareness of vulnerability. A sense of national crisis was important in the re-invigoration of concertation, in the case of the Netherlands and Ireland. The argument that "a limit was reached and a change in policy and mentality was needed" (Visser and Hemerijck, 1997, p. 13) played an important role in the turnaround in Dutch politics in 1982. According to one Irish union leader involved in the construction of the first of the social pacts in Ireland, he and his colleagues had sat together and had convinced the incoming Government that a new approach was needed in order to avoid the country "going down the drain" (personal communication to the author). In 1987 the Irish economy "was almost universally seen to have reached its nadir"; the agreement was negotiated, as it were, "out of the last ditch'" (Roche, 1992, p. 325).

Concertation begins with, and deepens, a sense of interdependence between actors; parties realize that they depend on each other for achieving certain policy objectives or avoiding negative trends (Chaloupek et al., 1997). This is not the same as consensus over these objectives, nor does it presuppose the absence of conflict. Each of the two cases mentioned above began with conflicting views on the nature of the crisis, who was to blame and how it was to be solved. Yet what does not start as a consensus – other than the joint awareness that "things cannot go on" and that "something needs to be done" – may nevertheless produce one (a feeling of "having done the right thing"). In the Netherlands, for instance, concertation – and its core policies of wage restraint, redistribution of work and flexibility – earned a consensus; in the end, it produced new jobs and less dependence on benefits, employers saw profits soar, the Government was able, thanks to a more robust economy, to reform the welfare State, and the unions gained members and prestige. Nothing succeeds like success; these outcomes reinforced the participants in their belief that they were on the right track and should stick to it.

Roche (1992, pp. 323–324) reports that the Irish unions were critical of the first agreement (PNR, 1987–91), especially since little had been achieved with regard to tackling unemployment. Many held the view that the notable improvement of the Irish economy towards the end of the decade was caused by the international recovery. "Yet in a manner unprecedented in the history of tripartism in Ireland, all parties to the agreement pointed to areas or issues with respect to which they considered themselves 'winners'" (Roche, 1992, p. 324). This was the basis for the negotiation of a new pact and led to a gradual institutionalization, through trust-building and social learning, of central bargaining and concertation.

In addition to the principal orientation towards consensus in decision-making processes, the main advantages of the social partnership model in Austria are seen as the integration of particular interests within the larger context of national economic interests; the enhancement of informality and confidentiality, and voluntary cooperation of elites and experts; together with the way that it ensures the binding character of agreements and commitments, both vis-à-vis external interests, and within one's own organization (Traxler, 1997). The practice of mediation and reconciliation of interests in the social partnership system was and is firmly based on a fundamental consensus on the following objectives: joint control of economic and social policy, with particular attention to policies affecting the labour market, wages, external trade and competition; promotion of economic growth and economic competitiveness; securing stability for the national economy; maintaining and raising social standards and developing the welfare State, while maintaining an unchanged functional income distribution; and the maintenance of social peace. Because the social partnership organizations are not subject to the electoral competition of the kind which political parties face, social partnership can be regarded as a stabilizing element in the political system. This may explain the simultaneous praise and criticism expressed in the public debate and the press (see Gerlich, Grande and Müller, 1988; Karlhofer and Tálos, 1996). Seen positively, it means that the social partners are able to design policies with a view to the long term – which is often impossible for parties in power because the latter are subject to short-term electoral and media pressure; the reverse side of the coin is that the social partners and their policies lag behind when it comes to adjusting to changes in the economic and social policy framework.

It is not hard to identify the main challenges facing the Austrian model. Changes in the social structures tend to narrow the traditional organizational foundations of the social partnership associations; other conflicts, centring around gender and ecology, tend to be left out; the electoral decline of the traditional parties of Social and Christian Democracy, and their lesser hold within the social partnership organizations, create space for attacks from the political Right; the decline in unionization is bound to lead to questions about the monopoly of representation of the ÖGB; the compulsory membership basis of the chambers raises doubts about the basis of their representation and the legitimacy of their influence; and within Europe the Austrian system of interest representation is unique and isolated. In the early 1990s, in the run-up to EU membership and in response to domestic criticism, the economic and labour chambers felt obliged to poll their members. These elections turned out to be quite successful; 82 per cent (WKÖ members) and 85 per cent (BAK members) of the valid votes cast were in favour of their continued existence, with a turnout of 36 per cent of the eligible members in the case of the WKÖ and 58 per cent in the BAK.

In its most recent "Room for Manoeuvre in Economic Policy" study, the Beirat für Wirtschafts- und Sozialfragen (BWS, 1998) recommends further changes towards a leaner welfare State. In the area of wage and income policy the message is: more of the same, with some decentralization and somewhat greater flexibility in pay structures and working hours. The social partners and their advisers remain convinced of the benefits of the small-step approach towards adjustment, of change through careful negotiations, involving all major interest groups. The way in which the Sparpaket 1995 (austerity package) was first rejected and then, on the basis of proposals by the social partners, was made tougher but more balanced, and was accepted, would seem a good illustration of the merits of negotiated change involving the social partners. The politics of consistent and coherent changes, in small steps but over many years, is also characteristic of the approach which became the basis for the "Dutch miracle" (Visser and Hemerijck, 1997).

In its recent evaluation, the NESF attributes five main effects to social dialogue – or partnership, as it is called in Ireland: a shared understanding of the key mechanisms and relationships in the formulation and implementation of policy; a better understanding of the interdependence between the organized actors; a greater sense of fairness and sharing of benefits; a problem-solving approach in which various interest groups address joint problems; and a deepening of participation at all levels (NESF, 1997, p. 33). Probably the most interesting property of concertation lies in the possibility that interest-representation organizations, like trade unions and employers' associations, redefine the content of their self-interested strategies in a "public regarding" way. The Irish study, for instance, highlights the fact that "participation and inclusion" have become goals in themselves; the Dutch accord of 1993 explicitly places the policies of employers and unions in the context of an "activating labour market policy". It is not that interest groups give up their own objectives or mission, but that they add something to them and draw a new balance between public and private interests. The Irish study, for instance, rejects what it calls the hard-headed view that concertation is exclusively driven by the self-interests of the actors (NESF, 1997, p. 31). According to Dore (1994, p. 8), responsible wage policies were in the past always motivated by a mixture of three types of arguments: patriotism, social solidarity and self-interest. In addition, what mattered was the development of levels of mutual trust which assured those who were swayed by these arguments that others would not take advantage of them or, where trust was weak, a possibility to back such arguments up with statutory instruments and legal sanctions.

A concerted approach to problems and policy failures is founded, in the typology of Hirschmann (1970), on the deployment of "voice" rather than "exit". Participants are obliged to explain, give reasons and take responsibility for their decisions and strategies to each other, to their rank and file, and to the general public. They are involved in a wider range of policy issues and take account of more alternative policy options. This creates a pressure to compromise, which over time may produce a sense of mutual debt and become an element of "loyalty". The interest groups become aware of each other's capacities and may learn to trust (Schmitter, 1983).

Game theory explanations have exploited the idea of a "shadow of the future" in seeking to understand the emergence of trust (Axelrod, 1984). Institutionalized concertation tends to stabilize participation and give negotiators a wider time horizon. Continued participation helps to increase compliance, since promises not kept amount to loss of bargaining credibility in the next round. This is particularly important with regard to policies which are difficult to monitor and take a long time to implement or show effect. Institutionalized concertation is based on commitment. Italian union leader Cofferati (1997, p. 51) cites his predecessor, Trentin, who observed that concertation "is not a streetcar which you board or leave just when it suits you". You have to forgo flexibility in the choice of your partners or the method of decision-making in order to gain flexibility in actual conditions of pay, working hours or job assignments. This is what "negotiated flexibility" is all about. It was long ago noted by Deutsch (1966) that commitment is associated with a loss of flexibility. To avoid all commitments is to behave like "the investor who keeps his money under the mattress" which, according to Deutsch (1966, pp. 231–232), is not only a manifestation of self-centredness, but also associated with poor learning.

According to Schmitter (1983, p. 8), concertation lies in the fuzzy zone between bargaining and problem-solving or, as he calls it, between the "accommodation of interests", in which contracting parties "agree to some specific distribution of initial contributions and subsequent outcomes", and the "reconciliation of purposes" in which they "learn to interpret reality in broadly the same way and to value generally the same thing". In the Irish study cited above, the same idea is expressed: "partnership involves the players in a process of deliberation which has the potential to shape and reshape their understanding, identity and preferences" (NESF, 1997, p. 33). Concertation encourages a "problem-solving" style of decision-making; indeed, it works rather badly, and can produce prolonged stalemates, if any of the two other decision-making styles distinguished by Scharpf (1989), "confrontation" or "bargaining", are adopted. This is because, if "exit" is constrained, each party tends to acquire a right of veto. In a confrontational style of decision-making, each party keeps its own preferences and identity, and is not interested in a joint solution; in a bargaining context each party comes with predefined preferences and seeks solutions which maximize its gains. In a problem-solving context the participants develop a "joint utility function" (see table 5.1 concerning the ideal types of industrial relations systems in Europe). Concertation does not work at all well in combination with "confrontation" or "bargaining", since the "unanimity rule" implicit in concertation gives any participant the power to hold out for more, and frustrate decision-making. Dutch corporatism, it is important to note, has not always worked well; in the 1970s it went through a particularly difficult phase in which the lack of consensus produced a lasting stalemate (Hemerijck, 1995). In his classic study of Dutch labour relations, Windmuller (1969) pointed out that organized consultation was an asset most of the time. But it was not an unmixed blessing. If the will to shoulder common problems is lacking, it can cause delays in adapting to changing circumstances, and thus hand out veto power to minority groups. He commented that the implicit commitment to go to extraordinary lengths to find compromise solutions through institutionalized consultation might also result in an excessive tendency to allow mediocrity and safety to prevail where calculated risk-taking might reap a harvest of excellence.

The problem is that one never knows; there might be a harvest of excellence but also one of misery. In the cases discussed here, most actors have been prepared to take those "calculated risks" under stress, but within the safety of strong organizational networks and institutions. It seems that the lesson to learn from these four small countries is that systems of organized consultation have much to recommend them, they are not incapable of change and learning, and they can promote the creation of more employment opportunities, while maintaining the basic social and industrial rights established by the post-war welfare State.

Bibliography

Albert, M. 1991. *Capitalisme contre capitalisme* (Paris, Seuil).

Amin, A.: Thomas, D. 1996. "The negotiated economy: State and civic institutions in Denmark", in *Economy and Society*, Vol. 25, No. 2, pp. 255–281.

Armingeon, K. 1994. *Staat und Arbeitsbeziehungen. Ein internationaler Vergleich* (Opladen, Westdeutscher Verlag).

Auer, M.; Welte, H. 1994. "Öffnungsklauseln in der tariflichen Lohnpolitik Österreichs", in *Industrielle Beziehungen*, Vol. 1, pp. 297–314.

Axelrod, R. 1984. *The evolution of cooperation* (New York, Basic Books).

Baglioni, G.; Crouch, C. (eds.). 1990. *European industrial relations: The challenge of flexibility* (London, Sage).

Bispinck, R.; Lecher, W. (eds.). 1993. *Tarifpolitik und Tarifsysteme in Europa* (Cologne, Bund Verlag).

Blanchflower, D.; Freeman, R.B. 1990. *Going different ways: Unionism in the US and other advanced OECD countries*, Discussion Paper No. 5 (London, LSE, Centre for Economic Performance).

Blyth, C.A. 1979. "The interaction between collective bargaining and government policies in selected member countries", in OECD: *Collective bargaining and government policies* (Paris).

Boje, T.P.; Kongshoj Madsen, P. 1994. "Wage formation and incomes policy in Denmark in the 1980s", in Dore, Boyer and Mars (eds.), 1994, pp. 94–117.

Braun, A.R. 1976. "Indexation of wages and salaries in developed economies", in *IMF Staff Papers*, Vol. 23, No. 1, pp. 226–271.

Bruno, M.; Sachs, J. 1985. *The politics of worldwide stagflation* (Cambridge, MA, Harvard University Press).

Brown, W. 1993. "The contraction of collective bargaining in Britain", in *British Journal of Industrial Relations,* Vol. 31, No. 2, pp. 189–200.

BWS (Beirat für Wirtschafts- und Sozialfragen). 1998. *Wirtschaftspolitische Handlungsspielräume* (Vienna).

Calmfors, L. 1993. "Centralisation of wage bargaining and economic performance: A survey", in *OECD Economic Studies*, Vol. 21, Winter, pp. 159–191.

——.; Driffill, J. 1988. "Bargaining structure, corporatism and macroeconomic performance", in *Economic Policy*, Apr., pp. 15–61.

Cameron, D.R. 1984. "Social democracy, corporatism, labour acquiescence, and the representation of economic interests in advanced capitalist society", in J.H. Goldthorpe (ed.): *Order and conflict in contemporary capitalism* (Oxford, Clarendon Press), pp. 143–178.

Cassells, P. 1989. "The organisation of trade unions", in Murphy, Hillary and Kelly (eds.), 1989, pp. 13–20.

Chaloupek, G. 1995. "Entwicklung und Zukunft der österreichischen Sozialpartnerschaft", in *Materialien zu Wirtschaft und Gesellschaft*, No. 59 (Vienna, Kammer für Arbeiter und Gesellschaft für Wien).

——.; et al. 1997. "Beschäftigungs- und Budgetpolitik: Erfahrungen in Irland, den Niederlanden, Dänemark – und was daraus zu lernen ist", in *Materialien zu Wirtschaft und Gesellschaft*, No. 66 (Vienna, Kammer für Arbeiter und Gesellschaft für Wien).

Clark, A. 1997. "Economic performance and the structure of collective bargaining", in *Employment Outlook 1997* (Paris, OECD), pp. 63–92.

Cofferati, S. 1997. *A ciascuno il suo mestiere. Lavore, sindacato e politica nell'Italia che cambia* (Milan, Mondadori).

Crouch, C. 1985. "The conditions for wage restraint", in L. Lindberg and C. Maier (eds.): *The politics of inflation and economic stagflations* (Washington, DC, The Brookings Institution), pp. 105–148.

——. 1986. "Sharing public space: States and organized interests in Western Europe", in J. Hall (ed.): *States in societies* (Oxford, Blackwell), pp. 179–180.

——. 1993. *Industrial relations and European state traditions* (Oxford, Clarendon).

——. 1995. "Reconstructing corporatism: Organized decentralization and other paradoxes", in Crouch and Traxler (eds.), 1995, pp. 311–330.

——. 1996. "Revised diversity: From the neo-liberal decade to beyond Maastricht", in van Ruysseveldt and Visser (eds.), 1996, pp. 358–375.

——.; Traxler, F. (eds.) 1995. *Organized industrial relations in Europe. What future?* (Aldershot, Avebury).

CPB (Centraal Planbureau). 1998. *Macro-economische verkenning 1999* (The Hague).

DA (Danish Employers' Confederation). 1998. *Current challenges in the Danish labour market* (Copenhagen; summer; mimeo.).

Deutsch, K. 1966. *The nerves of government: Models of political communication and control* (New York, The Free Press).

Dolado, J. et al. 1996. "Minimum wages: The European experience", in *Economic Policy*, Vol. 23, pp. 319–372.

Dore, R. 1994. "Incomes policies: Why now?", in Dore, Boyer and Mars (eds.), 1994, pp. 1–30.

——.; Boyer, R.; Mars, Z. (eds.). 1994. *The return to incomes policy* (London, Pinter).

Due, J.; Madsen, J.S.; Jensen, C.S. 1997. "Major developments in Danish industrial relations since 1980", in Mesch (ed.), 1997, pp. 127–159.

——.; et al. 1994. *The survival of the Danish model: A historical sociological analysis of the Danish system of collective bargaining* (Copenhagen, DJØF Publishing).

——.; et al. 1995. "Adjusting the Danish model: Towards centralized decentralization", in Crouch and Traxler (eds.), 1995, pp. 121–150.

Ebbinghaus, B.; Visser, J. 1997. "Der Wandel der Arbeitsbeziehungen im westeuropäischen Vergleich", in S. Hradil and S. Immerfall (eds.): *Die westeuropäischen Gesellschaften im Vergleich* (Oplanden, Leske and Budrich), pp. 333–376.

——.; ——. 1999. "When institutions matter: Union growth and decline in Western Europe, 1950–95", in *European Sociological Review*, Vol. 15, No. 2, pp. 135–58.

——.; ——. 2000. "Trade unions in Western Europe since 1945" in *Societies of Europe*, series of historical data handbooks (London, Macmillan).

Elvander, N. 1990. "Incomes policies in the Nordic countries", in *International Labour Review*, Vol. 29, No. 1, pp. 1–21.

Esping-Andersen, G. 1990. *The three worlds of capitalism* (Princeton, NJ, Princeton University Press).

Fajertag, G.; Pochet, P. (eds.). 1997. *Social pacts in Europe* (Brussels, European Trade Union Institute with Observatoire Social Europeén).

Ferner, A.; Hyman, R. (eds.). 1992. *Industrial relations in the New Europe* (Oxford, Blackwell Publishers).

——.; ——.1997. *Changing industrial relations in Europe* (Oxford, Blackwell Publishers).

Flanagan, R.J.; Hartog, J.; Theeuwes, J. 1993. "Institutions and the labour market: Many questions, some answers", in Hartog and Theeuwes (eds.), 1993, pp. 415–446.

——.; Soskice, D.W.; Ulman, L. 1983. *Unions, economic stabilisation and incomes policies: European experience* (Washington, DC, The Brookings Institution).

Flanders, A. 1975. *Management and unions. The theory and reform of industrial relations,* (London, Faber and Faber, 2nd ed.).

Freeman, R.B. 1993. "How labor fares in advanced economies", in idem (ed.): *Working under different rules* (New York, Russell Sage Foundation), pp. 1–28.

——.; Pelletier, J. 1990. "The impact of industrial relations legislation on British union density", in *British Journal of Industrial Relations*, Vol. 28, No. 2, pp. 141–164.

Gerlich, P.; Grande, E.; Müller, W.C. 1988. "Corporatism in crisis: Stability and change of social partnership in Austria", in *Political Studies*, No. 36, pp. 209–223.

Goldthorpe, J.H. (ed.) 1984. *Order and conflict in contemporary capitalism* (Oxford, Clarendon Press).

——.; Whelan, C.T. (eds.). 1992. *The development of industrial society in Ireland* (Oxford, Oxford University Press).

Guger, A. 1993. "Lohnpolitik und Sozialpartnerschaft", in Tálos (ed.), 1993, pp. 227–241.

——.; Polt, W. 1994. "Corporatism and incomes policy in Austria", in Dore, Boyer and Mars, (eds.), 1994, pp. 141–60.

Gunnigle, P.; Roche, W.K. 1995. *New challenges to Irish industrial relations* (Dublin, Oak Tree Press and Industrial Relations Commission).

——.; et al. 1997. *Human resource management in Irish organizations. Practice in perspective* (Dublin, Oak Tree Press).

Hardiman, N. 1988. *Pay, politics and economic performance in Ireland* (Oxford, Oxford University Press).

——. 1992. "The state and economic interests", in Goldthorpe and Whelan (eds.), 1992, pp. 329–358.

Hartog, J.; Theeuwes, J. (eds.) 1993. *Labour market contracts and institutions: A cross-national comparison* (Amsterdam, North-Holland).

Headey, B.W. 1970. "Trade unions and national wage policies", in *Journal of Politics*, No. 32, pp. 407–438.

Hemerijck, A.C. 1995. "Corporatist immobility in the Netherlands", in Crouch and Traxler. (eds.), 1995, pp. 183–224.

Hirschmann, A.O. 1970. *Exit, voice and loyalty: Responses to decline in firms, organizations and States* (Cambridge, MA, Harvard University Press).

Hofstede, G. 1989. *Culture's consequences* (London, Sage).

Hyman, R.; Ferner, A. (eds.). 1994. *New frontiers in European industrial relations* (Oxford, Blackwell Publishers).

ICTU (Irish Congress of Trade Unions). 1993. *New forms of work organization* (Dublin).

IVA. 1997. *De naleving van de wet op de ondernemingsraden* (The Hague, Department of Social Affairs and Employment).

Iversen, T. 1996. "Power, flexibility and the breakdown of centralized wage bargaining in Denmark and Sweden in comparative perspective", in *Comparative Politics*, July, pp. 399–436.

Jessop, B.; Nielsen, K.; Pedersen, O. 1993. "Structural competitiveness and strategic capacities. Rethinking the State and international capital", in S.E. Sjöstrand (ed.): *Institutional change: Theory and empirical findings* (New York, M.E. Sharpe).

Karlhofer, F.; Ladurner, U. 1993. "The Austrian labour market: Description and analysis of structures and institutions", in Hartog and Theeuwes (eds.), 1993, pp. 185–208.

——.; Tálos, E. 1996. *Sozialpartnerschaft und EU* (Vienna, Schriftenreihe des Zentrums für angewandte Politikforschung).

Klandermans, P.G.; Visser, J. (eds.). 1995. *De vakbeweging na de welvaartsstaat* (Assen, van Gorcum).

Kerr, T. 1989. "Trade unions and the law", in Murphy, Hillary and Kelly (eds.), 1989, pp. 217–234.

Knudsen, H. 1998. "Danish industrial relations and EMU: A silent issue", in T. Kauppinen (eds.): *The impact of EMU on industrial relations in the European Union* (Helsinki, Finnish Industrial Relations Association), pp. 40–49.

Kristensen, P.H.; Sabel, C. 1993. "The small-holder economy in Denmark: The exception as variation", in C. Sabel and J. Zeitlin (eds.): *Worlds of possibility: Flexibility and mass production in western industrialization* (New York, Doubleday).

Landes, D. 1997. *The wealth and poverty of nations: Why some are so rich and some so poor* (New York, Norton).

Lane, C.1989. *Management and labour in Europe* (Aldershot, Edward Elgar).

Layard, R. 1997. "Sweden's road back to full employment", in *Economic and Industrial Democracy*, Vol. 18, No. 1, pp. 99–118.

——.; Nickel, S.; Jackman, R. 1991. *Unemployment, macroeconomic performance and the labour market* (Oxford, Oxford University Press).

Lehmbruch, G. 1982. "Introduction: Neo-corporatism in comparative perspective", in G. Lehmbruch and P.C. Schmitter (eds.): *Patterns of corporatist policy-making* (Beverly Hills, CA, London, Sage), pp. 1–27.

——. 1984. "Concertation and the structure of corporatist networks", in Golthorpe (ed.), 1984, pp. 60–80.

Lijphart, A. 1968. *The politics of accommodation. Politics and democracy in the Netherlands* (Berkeley, CA, University of California Press).

——.; Crepaz, M. 1991. "Corporatism and consensus democracy in eighteen countries: Conceptual and empirical linkages", in *British Journal of Political Science*, Vol. 21, pp. 235–256.

Lind, J. 1997. "EMU and collective bargaining in Denmark", in Fajertag and Pochet (eds.), 1997, pp. 145–155.

Locke, R.; Kochan, T.; Piore, M. 1995. "Reconceptualising comparative industrial relations: Lessons from international research", in *International Labour Review*, Vol. 134, No. 2, pp. 38–161.

McCarthy, C. 1973. *The decade of upheaval: Irish trade unions in the 1960s* (Dublin, Institute of Public Administration).

——. 1997. *Trade unions in Ireland: 1890–1960* (Dublin, Institute of Public Administration).

Meinertz, I. 1993. "Dänemark", in Bispinck and Lecher (eds.), 1993, pp. 80–104.

Mesch, M., 1995. *Sozialpartnerschaft und Arbeitsbeziehungen in Westeuropa* (Vienna, Verlag der Gesellschaftskritik).

——. (ed.). 1997. *Social partnership and labour relations in Western Europe* (Aldershot, Edward Elgar.)

Murphy, T.; Hillary, B.; Kelly, A. (eds.). 1989. *Industrial relations in Ireland. Contemporary issues and developments* (Dublin, University College Dublin).

Nevin, D. 1997. "Ireland", in *Handbook of trade unions in Europe* (Brussels, European Trade Union Institute), pp. 3–29.

Nolan, B. 1993. *Low pay in Ireland,* General Research Series, Paper No. 159 (Dublin, Economic and Social Research Institute).

NESF (National Economic and Social Forum). 1997. *A framework for partnership – Enriching strategic consensus through participation*, Report No. 16 (Dublin, Dec.).

Nickell, S.; Layard, R. 1997. *Labour market institutions and economic performance* (Oxford, Institute of Economics and Statistics; unpublished paper).

Nielsen, K. 1991. "Learning to manage the demand-side. Flexibility and stability in Denmark", in B. Jessop, H. Kastendiek and O. Pedersen (eds.): *The politics of flexibility* (Aldershot, Edward Elgar), pp. 282–313.

——. Pedersen, O. 1991. "From the mixed economy to the negotiated economy: The Scandinavian countries", in R. Coughlin (ed.): *Morality, rationality and efficiency: New perspectives on socio-economics* (New York, M.E. Scharpe).

O'Brien, J.F. 1981. *A study of national wage agreements in Ireland* (Dublin, Economic and Social Research Institute).

——. 1989. "The role of employer organizations in Ireland", in Murphy, Hillary and Kelly (eds.), 1989, pp. 73–82.

O'Donnell, R.; O'Reardon, C. 1997. "Ireland", in Fajertag and Pochet (eds.), 1997, pp. 79–95.

OECD (Organisation for Economic Co-operation and Development). 1983. *Collective bargaining and economic policies: Dialogue and consensus* (Paris).

——. 1985. "Employment in large and small firms", in OECD: *Employment Outlook,* (Paris), July, pp. 64–82.

——. 1994a. *The OECD Jobs Study* (Paris).

——. 1994b. *The OECD Jobs Study,* Part II: *The adjustment potential of the labour market* (Paris).

——. 1997. *Implementing the OECD Jobs Strategy: Lessons from member countries' experience* (Paris).

O'Kelly, K.P. 1993. "Irland", in Bispinck and Lecher (eds.), 1993, pp. 181–202 (in German).

Olson, M. 1982. *The rise and decline of nations: Economic growth, stagflation, and social rigidities* (New Haven, CT, Yale University Press).

Pedersen, D.; Pedersen, O.; Ronit, K. 1994. *The organization of employers in Denmark,* COS Research Report No. 2 (Copenhagen, Centre for Public Organization and Management, Copenhagen Business School).

Prondszynski, F. van. 1992. "Ireland; Between centralism and the market", in Ferner and Hyman (eds.), 1997, pp. 69–87.

——. 1997. "Ireland; Corporatism revived", in Ferner and Hyman (eds.), 1997, pp. 55–73.

——.; McCarthy, C. 1989. *Employment law in Ireland* (London, Sweet and Maxwell).

Roche, W.K.1983. "Social partnership and political control: State strategy and industrial relations in Ireland", in M. Kelly, L. O'Dowd and J. Wickham (eds.): *Power, conflict and equality* (Dublin, Turoe Press), pp. 44–67.

——. 1989. "State strategies and the politics of industrial relations in Ireland", in Murphy, Hillary and Kelly (eds.), 1989, pp. 115–31.

——. 1992. "The liberal theory of industrialism and the development of industrial relations in Ireland", in Goldthorpe and Whelan (eds.), 1992, pp. 291–327.

——.; Geary, J. 1996. "Multinational companies in Ireland: Adapting to or diverging from national industrial relations practices and traditions", in *Journal of Irish Business and Administration Research,* No. 17, pp. 14–31.

——.; Larregy, J. 1990. "Cyclical and institutional determinants of annual trade union growth in Ireland: Evidence from the DUES data series", in *European Sociological Review,* Vol. 6, No. 1, pp. 49–72.

Rogers, J.; Streeck, W. (eds.). 1995. *Works councils: Consultation, representation, coordination* (Chicago, IL, University of Chicago Press).

Roorda, W.B.; Vogels, E.H.W.M. 1997. *Concurrerende arbeidsverhoudingen,* Werkdocument No. 33 (The Hague, Ministry of Social Affairs and Employment).

Rothstein, B. 1992. "Labour market institutions and working-class strength", in S. Steinmo, K. Thelen, and F. Longstreth (eds.): *Structuring politics* (Cambridge, Cambridge University Press), pp. 33–56.

Rowthorn, R.E. 1992. "Centralisation, employment, and wage dispersion", in *Economic Journal,* No. 102, pp. 506–523.

Ruysseveldt, J. van; Visser, J. (eds.). 1996. *Industrial relations in Europe. Traditions and transitions* (London, Sage).

Scharpf, F.W. 1989. "Decision rules, decision styles, and policy choices", in *Journal of Theoretical Politics*, No. 1, pp. 149–176.

——.; 1993. "Co-ordination in hierarchies and networks", in F.W. Scharpf (ed.): *Games in hierarchies and networks: Analytical and empirical approaches to the study of governance institutions* (Frankfurt am Main, Boulder, CO, Campus and Westview).

——. 1997. *Games real actors play: Actor-centered institutionalism in policy research* (Boulder, CO, Westview).

Scheuer, S. 1992. "Denmark: Return to decentralisation", in Ferner and Hyman (eds.), 1997, pp. 168–197.

——. 1997a. "Collective bargaining coverage under trade unionism: A sociological investigation", in *British Journal of Industrial Relations*, Vol. 35, No. 1, pp. 65–86.

——. 1997b. "Denmark: A less regulated model", in Ferner and Hyman (eds.), 1997, pp. 146–170.

Schmitter, P.C. 1981, "Interest intermediation and regime governability in contemporary Western Europe and North America", in S. Berger (ed.): *Organizing interests in Western Europe* (Cambridge, Cambridge University Press).

——. 1983. *Neo-corporatism, consensus, governability, and democracy in the management of crisis in contemporary advanced industrial-capitalist societies* (Florence, European University Institute; unpublished paper).

Sexton, J.J.; O'Connell, P. 1996. *Labour market studies: Ireland* (Luxembourg, European Commission).

Siebert, W. S. 1997. "Overview of European labour markets", in J.T. Addison and W.S. Siebert (eds.): *Labour markets in Europe. Issues of harmonisation and regulation* (London, Dryden Press), pp. 230–237.

Sisson, K. 1987. *The management of collective bargaining* (Oxford, Blackwell Publishers).

Soskice, D. 1990. "Wage determination: The changing role of institutions in advanced industrialised countries", in *Oxford Review of Economic Policy*, Vol. 6, No. 4, pp. 36–61.

Streeck, W. 1992. *Social institutions and economic performance: Studies of industrial relations in advanced capitalist economies* (London, Sage).

——. 1996. "Anmerkungen zum Flächentarif und seiner Krise", in *Gewerkschaftliche Monatschefte*, Vol. 46, No. 2, pp. 86–97.

——. 1998. *Bündnis für Arbeit: Bedingungen und Ziele*, lecture given at SPD-Forum, Klartext: Moderne Arbeidsgesellschaft, moderner Sozialstaat (Hanover, 3 June).

——.; Visser, J. 1998. *An evolutionary dynamic of trade union systems*, Discussion Paper No. 98/4 (Cologne, Max Planck Institute for the Study of Societies).

Svensen, P. 1989. *Fair shares: Unions, pay, and politics in Sweden and West Germany* (Ithaca, NY, Cornell University Press).

Tarantelli, E. 1986. *Economia politica del lavoro* (Turin, UTET).

Tálos, E. (ed.). 1993. *Sozialpartnerschaft* (Vienna, Verlag für Gesellschaftskritik).

Teague, P. 1995. "Pay determination in the Republic of Ireland: Towards social corporatism?", in *British Journal of Industrial Relations*, Vol. 33, No. 2, pp. 253–273.

Teulings, C.N. 1996. *De plaats van de vakbeweging in de toekomst* (Amsterdam, Welboom).

——.; Hartog, J. 1998. *Corporatism or competition: Labour contracts, institutions and wage structures in international comparison* (Cambridge, Cambridge University Press).

Toren, J.P. van den. 1996. *Achter gesloten deuren? CAO-overleg in de jaren negentig* (Amsterdam, Welboom).

Traxler, F. 1993. "Business associations and labour unions in comparison: Theoretical perspectives and empirical findings on social class, collective action and associational organizability", in *British Journal of Sociology*, No. 44, pp. 673–691.

——. 1994. "Collective bargaining: Levels and coverage", in OECD: *Employment Outlook 1994* (Paris), pp. 167–194.

——. 1996. "Collective bargaining and industrial change: A case of disorganisation? A comparative analysis of eighteen OECD countries", in *European Sociological Review*, Vol. 12, No. 3, pp. 271–287.

——. 1997. "Austria: Still the country of corporatism", in Ferner and Hyman (eds.), 1997, pp. 239–261.

——.; Kittel, B.; Lengauer, S. 1996. *Globalisation, collective bargaining and performance*, paper presented at the Eighth Conference of Socio-Economics, Geneva, 12–14 July.

Turner, T.; D'Art, D. 1997. *A review of centralised wage agreements in Ireland, 1987–1997,* paper presented at the Fifth European Congress of the International Industrial Relations Association, Dublin, 25 Aug.

Venema, P.M.; Faas, A.; Samadhan, J.A. 1996. *Arbeidsvoorwaardenontwikkeling in 1995* (The Hague, Department of Social Affairs and Employment, Labour Inspectorate).

Visser, J. 1984. *The position of central confederations in the national union movement: A ten country study*, Working Paper No. 102 (Florence, European University Institute).

——. 1990. *In search of inclusive unionism* (Deventer and Boston, MA, Kluwer).

——. 1991. "Trends in union membership", in OECD: *Employment Outlook 1991* (Paris), pp. 97–134.

——. 1995. "The Netherlands: From paternalism to representation", in J. Rogers and W. Streeck (eds.): *Works councils. Consultation, representation, and cooperation in industrial relations* (Chicago, IL, Chicago University Press), pp. 79–114.

——. 1997. "The Netherlands: The return of responsive corporatism", in Ferner and Hyman (eds.), 1997, pp. 283–314.

——. 1998a. "The art of making social pacts", in J. Delors et al. (eds.): *National social pacts: Assessment and future prospects* (Paris, Brussels, Notre Europe and European Trade Union Institute), pp. 42–54.

——. 1998b. "Two cheers for corporatism, one for the market", in *British Journal of Industrial Relations*, Vol. 36, No. 2, pp. 269–292.

——. 1998c. *Organizational conditions for social dialogue in Europe. The state of the unions and employers' associations in the 1990s,* CESAR Working Paper (Amsterdam, Centre for the Study of European Societies and Labour Relations).

——.; Hemerijck, A.C. 1997. "*A Dutch miracle." Job growth, welfare reform and corporatism in the Netherlands* (Amsterdam, Amsterdam University Press).

——.; Meer, M. van der. 1998. "Interest organisations and collective bargaining in the Dutch consultation economy", in *National Report prepared for the European Commission,* Part 2 (Amsterdam, Amsterdam University Press).

Waarden, F. van 1995. "The organisational power of employers' associations: Cohesion, comprehensiveness and organisational development", in Crouch and Traxler (eds.): *Organised industrial relations in Europe: What future?* (Aldershot, Avebury), pp. 45–97.

Wallace, J.; Clifford, N. 1998. *Collective bargaining and flexibility in Ireland,* Labour Law and Labour Relations Programme, Working Paper No. 1 (Geneva, ILO).

Wallerstein, M.; Golden, M. 1997. "The fragmentation of bargaining society: Wage setting in the Nordic countries, 1950–1992", in *Contemporary Political Studies,* Vol. 30, No. 6, pp. 699–732.

Walsh, B. 1993. "Credibility, debt and the ERM: The Irish experience", in *Oxford Bulletin of Economics and Statistics,* No. 55, pp. 402–418.

Walther, H. 1997. "Lohnpolitik und Beschäftigung", in *Materialien zu Wirtschaft und Gesellschaft* (Vienna, Arbeiterkammer Wien), May, pp. 23–46.

Walton, R.E.; McKersie, R.B. 1965. *A behavioral theory of labor negotiations* (Maidenhead, McGraw Hill).

Wilensky, H. 1976. *The new corporatism, centralization and the welfare State* (Beverly Hills, CA, London, Sage).

Windmuller, J.P. 1969. *Labor relations in the Netherlands* (Ithaca, NY, Cornell University Press).

INDEX

Note: Tables, figures and boxes are indicated by *italic* page numbers; major treatment of subjects by **bold** numbers.